The Man Who Could Fly

The Man Who Could Fly

St. Joseph of Copertino and the Mystery of Levitation

Michael Grosso

ROWMAN & LITTLEFIELD
Lanham • Boulder • New York • London

Published by Rowman & Littlefield
A wholly owned subsidiary of The Rowman & Littlefield Publishing Group, Inc.
4501 Forbes Boulevard, Suite 200, Lanham, Maryland 20706
www.rowman.com

Unit A, Whitacre Mews, 26-34 Stannary Street, London SE11 4AB

Copyright © 2016 by Rowman & Littlefield

All rights reserved. No part of this book may be reproduced in any form or by any electronic or mechanical means, including information storage and retrieval systems, without written permission from the publisher, except by a reviewer who may quote passages in a review.

British Library Cataloguing in Publication Information Available

Library of Congress Cataloging-in-Publication Data Available
ISBN: 978-1-4422-5672-9 (cloth : alk. paper)
ISBN: 978-1-4422-5673-6 (electronic)

∞™ The paper used in this publication meets the minimum requirements of American National Standard for Information Sciences—Permanence of Paper for Printed Library Materials, ANSI/NISO Z39.48-1992.

Printed in the United States of America

To Pope Francis
A man for all humanity

Contents

Acknowledgments ix

Chronology xi

Introduction 1

PART I: THE MAN AND HIS MARVELS 13

  1 Life and Times 15

  2 A New Force 37

  3 The Case for Joseph's Levitations 69

  4 A Complement of Talents 91

  5 The Mystic 111

PART II: STEPS TOWARD UNDERSTANDING 129

  6 Reconnoitering Explanations 131

  7 Joseph as Performance Artist 153

  8 Speculations on the Physics of Levitation 171

PART III: CONCLUDING REFLECTIONS 189

  9 The Parapsychology of Religion: A New Science of Spirit? 191

Appendix	219
References	223
Index	239
About the Author	251

Acknowledgments

The seeds of this book were sown on a trip to Italy when by luck I obtained a copy of Domenico Bernini's 1722 biography of St. Joseph of Copertino. I read parts of it with interest, noting the frequency of words like *estasi* (ecstasies) and *ratti* (raptures); colleagues Ed Kelly and Mike Murphy suggested we find a translator and make the text available to interested readers. This was the starting point for writing about the extraordinary friar. It grew out of an ongoing yearly seminar with scholars and thinkers from many disciplines. Two things bound us together: discontent with the intellectual status quo and enthusiasm in the quest for a greater vision.

So first thanks go to Cedar Creek Institute and the Esalen Center for Research and Theory for providing funds (and the all-important intangible, enthusiasm) to get a key document translated. The translation gave eyewitness accounts of phenomena germane to our ongoing seminar at Esalen, hosted by Michael Murphy.

In deciding to write a book about Joseph, apart from the translation of his biography, I received various kinds of backing, helpful suggestions, and useful criticism. Special thanks are due to Michael Murphy, Ed Kelly, Bob Rosenberg, and Jeff Kripal, each in more than one way. Kripal read and commented on the entire manuscript, with many enlightening effects. I'm warmly indebted to Cynthia Clough for her excellent translation of Bernini's biography of St. Joseph and for her unfailing high spirits, without which the entire project would not have gotten off the ground. Thanks to various friends and colleagues who read parts of a slowly evolving manuscript and from whom I gained various helpful comments: Carlos Alvarado, Frank Applin, Harald Atmanspacher, Bernie Beitman, Loriliai Biernacki, Bernard Carr, Adam Crabtree, Frank DeMarco, Ross Dunseath, Bruce Greyson, Anne Grosso de Leon, Patrick Huyghe, David Hufford, Rafael Locke, Paul Marshall, Frank Pasciuti, Frank Poletti, David Presti, Cynthia Read, Gregory Shaw, Henry Stapp, Shannon Taggart, Troy Tice, Jim Tucker, and Robert Van der Castle. Last but not least, a large thanks to Lori Derr at the University of Virginia for tracking down source materials that were essential to the project.

Chronology

1603, Joseph born in the village of Copertino to Felix Desa, a local carpenter, and Franchescina Panaca.
1614–1619, sick and bedridden.
1625, entered Order of Conventuals in Grottella and began novitiate for priesthood.
1628, ordained as priest; extraordinary phenomena become matters of public interest.
1630, phenomena increase and become more pronounced.
1634, travels through Puglia with Provincial, Master Antonio of San Mauro for about a year. Questions arise about Joseph's motivations and extravagant behavior.
1638, trials with inquisition at Naples.
1639, sent to Rome by Holy Office for further inquisitions, then to Assisi, by order of Pope Urban VIII.
1644, sent to Rome for advice at the request of John Waza, Polish prince, who later became king of Poland; then back to Assisi.
1653, Inquisitor of Perugia removes Joseph from Assisi to Pietrarubbia for three months, followed by further removal to Fossombrone for three years.
1657, Alexander VII removes Joseph to Franciscan monastery in Osimo.
1663, death of Joseph.
1753, Joseph beatified.
1767, Joseph canonized.

Introduction

The lamps are different, but the Light is the same; it comes from Beyond.

—Jalal al-din Rumi

What counts in a democracy is the experience of the citizens, i.e., their subjectivity and not what small gangs of autistic intellectuals declare to be real.

—Paul Feyerabend

In considering religion, we should not be obsessed by the idea of its necessary goodness. This is a dangerous delusion. The point to notice is its transcendent importance; and the fact of this importance is abundantly made evident by the appeal to history.

—Alfred North Whitehead

This book is about the possibility of transcendence, with a focus on the mystical and extraordinary phenomena of one case history, St. Joseph of Copertino.[1] According to the prevailing academic outlook, some of the phenomena we will discuss are controversial, if not impossible; nevertheless, if one takes the trouble to look, it appears that quite a bit of testimony attests to the reality of what many may think is "impossible." This, then, is the story of a man whose life calls into question certain mainstream assumptions about the scope of human capacity and the range of human experience. Joseph's story has implications for the mind-body problem, for the study of extraordinary mental and physical phenomena, for possible links to the new physics, and for new ways of approaching the old debate between science and religion.

This is a book about the mysteries of consciousness. Joseph was famous for physical anomalies, which were based on a rare gift he had for ecstatic dissociation, a unique state of consciousness. Most of us occasionally lose touch with our normal selves in moments of reverie or deep thought, but Joseph drove himself, systematically, beyond the boundaries of his everyday self. And in these extraordinary states extraordinary things happened, phenomena that raise questions about the enigma of mind and body.

CONSCIOUSNESS IN REVOLT

The life of Joseph of Copertino exemplifies Whitehead's *transcendent* side of religion—the side most viewed with suspicion by scholars wed to the materialist outlook. *Transcendent* in Whitehead's philosophy refers to "creative advance." In this book, I will use the term to refer to phenomena in the family of mysticism and parapsychology. These in turn enlarge our idea of nature. The transcendent factor is what Richard Rorty and Gianni Vattimo leave out in their important book on the future of religion.[2] They envisage a future religion molded by the virtues of irony, charity, and solidarity—but not of transcendence.

Joseph was a Franciscan friar, and brazenly transcendent. The Church viewed the friar's strange behaviors with consternation. His strangeness was ambiguous and therefore problematic; clearly, he possessed strange powers. But where were they coming from? Called before the Inquisition several times, he was placed under surveillance and gradually under house arrest. The Church tried as hard as it could to exclude him from participating in public life. There were some good reasons for this and some based on fear, paranoia, and spiritual envy. Ironically, the Church had to conceal one of its own who displayed gifts that rivaled those recounted of Jesus in the Gospels.

Meanwhile, in another part of Italy, Galileo (1564–1642) was laying the foundations of experimental physics and modern cosmology; both saint and scientist ended up under house arrest by decree of the Holy Office. In retrospect, we think of Galileo as vindicated by history. Once under way, the scientific revolution advanced with brilliant and sometimes devastating success. Science gave rise to a Promethean power over nature and created all the new and indisputable miracles of modern technology.

The old miracles and phenomena of Joseph went out of fashion, eclipsed by the more reproducible marvels of science. The mechanistic worldview invalidated Joseph's brand of mystical spirituality, especially when accompanied by something as shocking as levitation. The educated public learned to deride the old miracles (on any account, rare and elusive), which it sent packing to the quaint cubbyholes of folklore and mythology. Ancient materialism was reborn with a new scientific imprimatur, and it would settle in the mind of academe; all things in nature were now to be best explained by and reduced to material science.

Today, in light of the enigma of quantum mechanics and the rise of postmodern critics of science like Paul Feyerabend, the notion of privileged, all-encompassing accounts of reality has lost much of its cachet. The reductive scientific stance based on classical Newtonian physics has been displaced by a new physics in which the power of mind reasserts itself as central to the scheme of nature (see chapter 8); more than a few official scientific dogmas are currently under critical fire.[3] One can find symptoms of paradigm malaise in medicine, in psychology and neuroscience, in anthropology, among scholars of religion, among theoretical physicists, and in other academic enclaves.

The problem revolves around the status of mind and consciousness in nature—there are different ways of seeing and defining ourselves. There is a difference between being an independent reality—a personality or a soul—and being a complex, evanescent pattern of neurochemistry. The story of Joseph is to my mind compelling as a weighty counterexample to the popular scientific creed of materialism, which minimizes the significance of mind and subjectivity, and of any real creative power lurking behind terms like "soul" and "spirit."

MATERIALISM AS IDEOLOGY

About the term *materialism*, there are two senses that concern us. In one, we might call a person *materialistic* who values and covets material goods excessively or exclusively; this sense of the term is tinged with a note of moral disapproval.

But materialism is also a metaphysical doctrine, grown fat and triumphant on the back of modern science. In this sense, materialism is not a fact but an interpretation of facts. It insists that anything that is really real must be material; in short, *all* facts are material or physical facts. *All* reality is reducible to the material, more broadly, the physical—and that presumably includes our doubts, dreams, feelings, sensings, willings, reasonings, memories, intuitions, and imaginings. According to most forms of materialism, the inner shows of our experience are "epiphenomena," qualities ranked as secondary and derivative. We may of course fully cherish modern science but *not* be materialists in the philosophical sense.

Talking about the metaphysics of materialism is a harmless pastime, and a good problem to discuss in Philosophy 101. In itself, strictly speaking, it's a morally neutral concept. Problems arise when materialism becomes part of an *ideology*, as in the fourth sense of the word in the Oxford English Dictionary

(OED): "A systematic scheme of ideas, usu. relating to politics or society, or to the conduct of a class or group, and regarded as justifying actions, especially one that is held implicitly or adopted as a whole and maintained regardless of the course of events."

Raymond Geuss's analysis of ideology from the standpoint of Habermas and the Frankfort School is helpful, in particular what he says about "ideology in the programmatic sense." This type of ideology is *total*: it aims to transform the whole of society in its image. It is "held with more confidence than the evidence for the theory or model warrants."[4]

Suppose a group of philosophers or neuroscientists decided that "free will" is an illusion and explained their reasons to the public on National Public Radio. What effect on the practical life of America would it likely have? Probably very little, although the conversation would go on among professional philosophers. The ideology of materialism is more worrisome. Militarism, capitalism, consumerism, pharmaceuticalism, and the mighty sway they exert upon our lives—to give a few examples—suggest a more sinister influence. In each, the default deity is material: bombs not persuasion, money not humanity, appetite not insight, Big Pharma not reason and compassion. Ideological materialism is prepared to justify its actions and, as the OED puts it, be "maintained regardless of the course of events." The ideology of materialism in these guises spins, ignores, deflects, or, if need be, tramples anything that opposes it.

Materialism (as metaphysics) is not a morally repulsive doctrine as such nor do idealistic philosophers monopolize humane values. Lofty ideals are regularly used to justify terrible crimes against humanity. Philosophical materialists aligned themselves with progressive causes during the European Enlightenment. Thomas Paine and Clarence Darrow—the purest of spirits—were materialists. Materialism becomes an ideology when it's joined at the hip with practices that restrict, dominate, or destroy human experience.

At its invasive worst, materialism can become an ideological howitzer for wrecking the myths, customs, beliefs, and life-ways of colonized societies. Superior military technology, vast wealth, and organized rationality enable the ruin and subjugation of native cultural habitats. Western colonialists used the new scientific materialism to bully the native peoples they subjugated into renouncing their life-ways and belief-systems, herding them into various ghettoes, "reservations," and unspecified zones of oppression.

The destruction of entire modes of thought and modes of being—symbols, stories, languages, arts, crafts—are all part of the debacle of ideological materialism.[5] About these concerns, one should consult Edward Said's *Orientalism* (1979) and *Culture and Imperialism* (1991), and in the spirit of Joseph, liberation theologian Leonardo Boff's *Saint Francis* (1984).

Materialism, as an implicit creed, throws a shadow of suspicion on whole classes of experience; the mystical, visionary, inspired, intuitive, esthetic, contemplative, magical, and so on. The interior life of human beings becomes a casualty, the soul an endangered species. The insidious loss of privacy and cryptic shift toward surveillance are indicators of materialism inveigling its way into the entrails of our most intimate selves. Scientific materialism's powerful and successful alliance with global capitalism illustrates this trend. About this large but ignored question of dehumanizing ideology, Paul Feyerabend wrote in *Farewell to Reason*:

> I say that Auschwitz is an extreme manifestation of an attitude that still thrives in our midst. It shows itself in the treatment of minorities in industrial democracies; in education, which most of the time consists in turning wonderful young people into colorless and self-righteous copies of their teachers; it becomes manifest in the nuclear threat, the constant increase in the number and power of deadly weapons and the readiness of some so-called patriots to start a war compared with which the holocaust will shrink into insignificance. It shows itself in the killing of nature and of "primitive" cultures with never a thought spent on those thus deprived of meaning for their lives; in the colossal conceit of our intellectuals, their belief that they know precisely what humanity needs and their relentless efforts to re-create people in their own, sorry image; in the infantile megalomania in some of our physicians who blackmail their patients with fear, mutilate them and then persecute them with large bills; in the lack of feeling of many so-called searchers for truth who systematically torture animals, study their discomfort and receive prizes for their cruelty.[6]

This was published in 1987—comments on the unrecognized dark side of a type of *metaphysics*. One's vision of the world is vitally important. Feyerabend summed it up: "The problem is the growing disregard for spiritual values and their replacement by a crude but 'scientific' materialism, occasionally even called humanism."[7]

SOME CONSCIOUSNESS ACTIVISTS

To set the stage before moving on to Joseph's life and times, we should cite some consciousness activists of today—among scholars and trained professionals—metaphysical whistle-blowers, so to speak. They come from different disciplines, outliers who encounter anomalies in their respective fields and dare to talk about them and even agitate for their recognition.

Anthropologist Mai Lan Gustafsson (2009), in her study of haunting and possession in contemporary Vietnam, had to deal with reports of "angry ghosts" she kept hearing about during her fieldwork. The violent sufferings caused by the American invasion, and the manner of death and displacement of millions, led to an epidemic of stories of spirits on the rampage. It was not a small question that Professor Gustafsson had to face: What attitude to adopt? How to listen to the Vietnamese people? Impose the interpretation that fits the investigator's Western belief system and by implication diminish or invalidate the stories of her informants?

Gustafsson chose to tell the story from the viewpoint of the victims of the "angry ghosts." She put herself in her informants' shoes and listened to their experiences. She ended by favoring the idea that something objectively real was causing the distress. Even the materialist Communist masters of Vietnam conceded there was a problem with the claimed hauntings and took steps to address it.

In scholarly studies, approaches to proscribed domains of discourse are sometimes indirect; one tiptoes around suspect subject matter (ghosts or stories of violent possession), reframes or rephrases them so as to distance oneself from the problem of the reality of things like ghosts. Eric Mueggler did a field study in a small area of Southwest China, focusing on a period called *The Age of Wild Ghosts*. These words (title of his book), we are told, are meant to capture the sense that life in this era was inflected by eruptions into the present of unreconciled fragments of the past, often personified as the ghosts of people (or spirits) who had met bad ends and who frequently possessed or killed their descendents.[8]

Terms like *spirits*, *ghosts*, and *possession* have been especially problematic since the eighteenth-century Enlightenment. But Mueggler, like Gustafsson, still writes about violent loss and haunting phenomena. The writers differ in their rhetorical stance: Gustafsson acknowledges the notoriety of her data and makes explicit her intention to tell the story from the viewpoint of the people having the experiences.

Mueggler deflects attention from the outlaw status of the ghosts and spirits said to wreak all the havoc, and defines and gives shape to a more abstract narrative about "unreconciled fragments of the past." No doubt it's easier to talk about "fragments of the past" in polite scientific society than about angry ghosts that attack and torment people.

Nevertheless, scholars and professionals in more than one discipline seem willing to entertain heretical opinions. Medical professionals, for example, since Raymond Moody (1975) have been questioning the nature of consciousness in studies of the near-death experience. The standard view that consciousness is a by-product of brain processes is difficult to sustain in light of certain facts about the near-death experience.

A Dutch cardiologist reported 150 cardiac arrests and near-death episodes (Van Lommel, 2002). It made the front pages of newspapers around the world. Why? The science was solid and came from the mainstream; and the paper challenged the belief that certain parts of the brain must be functional for *any* kind of conscious experience. Not only does consciousness persist after the brain goes dead, as many of these cases suggest, but it becomes more intense and richer in meaningful content.[9]

Another area of insurrection from within child psychiatry challenges mainstream views of consciousness; thousands of case histories of children who remember past lives have in fact been carefully studied and analyzed. The curious facts that need to be explained include more than memories from previous lives but also behaviors and bodily marks that documented cases show are carried from one life to another. The impressive mass of evidence collected by Ian Stevenson, Jim Tucker,[10] and others are at odds with mainstream reductive views of consciousness. The evidence seems to show that some of us display physical and mental traits that originate from previous lives.

In studies of religion, tension with the ruling ideas of what is real and possible seems inevitable. A good deal of academic writing on religion operates within standard reductionistic assumptions. But there are scholars of religion today who are decidedly open to the transcendent dimension. Jeffrey Kripal is among those in the vanguard of consciousness activists in this area; we will return to Kripal's religious futurism. Frederick Smith spent fifteen years writing a study of the phenomenon of possession in South Asia. Smith is bothered by methodologies that contract the limits of interpretation. Texts are all we have to work on, the cautious ones say, never immediate experience. This puts the subject under an academically certified cloud of suspicion. Smith is critical of this tinkering with the fundamental idea of experience: "The hermeneutic of suspicion on which rests much of value in our fields must not become a hermeneutic of mandatory, routine rejection."[11]

In 2001, New Testament scholar Craig Keener published an important (massively documented) two-volume study of "miracles." Keener, like Gustafsson the anthropologist, rejects the Humean assumption that "miracles" are impossible. Without defining miracle, he states that people today are reporting what they take to be miracles of the type described in the New Testament.

Keener argues that academic bias against miracles is an expression of rank cultural imperialism. He notes that despite the enormous popular interest, and the proliferation of anomaly claims and reports, rarely do qualified scholars take any of it seriously. He objects in particular to "scholars whose dismissal is dogmatic and lacks self-critical reflection about the historical origin and formation of their own beliefs."[12]

Keener's use of the word *supernatural* is not helpful. If there is no normal physical explanation of X, he seems to argue, X is supernatural. But that goes too far, and, in any case, the term *supernatural* needs to be unpacked. Suppose telepathy is a matter of fact but cannot be physically explained. Why should that lead us to regard it as something supernatural? At most we can add it to the list of facts of experience not understood by mainstream science.

By way of introducing the extreme case of Joseph, I'm citing recent authors who seem unfazed by the dominant ideologies of the possible. Some ethnographers have described very strange phenomena met in the field. Paul Stoller, for example, in his hands-on exploration of sorcery among the Songhay in Niger, was having strong impressions that something uncanny had entered his house. "I felt its presence and I was frightened," he said, and describes his encounter in considerable detail.[13]

Most of us would laugh at the idea of giant blobs materializing from the back of a woman in the course of a healing ceremony in Zambia; yet the ethnographer Edith Turner, who participated in the ceremony, reports observing precisely this: "Suddenly Meru (the healee) raised her arm, stretched it in liberation, and I saw with my own eyes a giant thing emerging out of the flesh of her back. It was a large gray blob about six inches across, opaque, and something between solid and smoke."[14]

Turner tells how the witch doctor worked on the blob until it shrank and gradually disappeared. All this was seen by others present at the ceremony. The report may be found in Young and Goulet, *Being Changed by Cross-Cultural Encounters*, papers about the anthropology of extraordinary experience. Turner lets us know what she wants: "My intention is to engage in dialogue with other anthropologists who have had such experiences in order to build up a reliable body of data on spirits and similar phenomena. . . . It would become possible to focus in a meaningful way on those rare events that are central to the life of many traditional societies."[15]

Indeed, if one combs available accounts, all sorts of surprising phenomena are being reported. And, as Turner rightly underscores, they are phenomena "central to the life of many traditional societies."

Consider another extraordinary report. Ethnographer Bruce Grindal writes that he witnessed the reanimation of a corpse during a divination rite in Ghana:

> What I saw in those moments was outside the realm of normal perception . . . .
> A terrible and beautiful sight burst upon me. Stretching from the amazingly delicate fingers and mouths of the goka, strands of fibrous light played upon the head, fingers, and toes of the dead man. The corpse, shaken by spasms, then rose to its feet, spinning and dancing in a frenzy.[16]

Modern documentation of such impossible phenomena is more plentiful than we might suppose. Even so, the mainstream wall of incuriosity stands as tall and erect as ever.

The spell of reductive materialism has penetrated the bastions of the Catholic Church. Consider the case of the twentieth-century stigmatic Padre

Pio. In his book on how saints are made, Kenneth Woodward describes the divisive cause of Padre Pio in the 1990s. About the now Saint Pio, Woodward writes: "Vatican saint-makers are skeptical of purported mystics. Indeed, even when the mystical phenomena are judged authentic, they have no bearing on the candidate's claim to sanctity."[17]

High officers of the Church were opposed to Padre Pio because he was an old-fashioned saint who performed miracles. They didn't approve of the stigmata, the scrutiny of hearts, the prophetic flair, the bilocations, or the odor of sanctity; they wanted a proper, tractable saint, not a real live comic book savior of the people. And they were as serious about getting rid of Padre Pio as the Grand Inquisitor in Dostoyevsky's *The Brothers Karamazov* was about getting rid of Christ.

In 1971, soon after the death of Padre Pio, Ennemond Boniface published a book that paints a grim picture of the opposition to Padre Pio within the church, characterized, he said, as an "enterprise of systematic destruction of the supernatural."[18] According to Boniface, the church persecuted the stigmatic because of the phenomena around him and the impact it had on the populace. Boniface even asserts there were attempts within the Church to kill Padre Pio.

For a more detailed account of Padre Pio and the politics of miracles, the historical study of Sergio Luzzato (2007) enables us to see one big similarity and one big difference between Padre Pio and Joseph of Copertino. Both were southerners, famous for highly visible charisms (levitation, stigmata), resulting in huge cult followings that led to their persecution, surveillance, and inquisitorial harrassment. That was the similarity.

The difference lay in how the Church dealt with the two mystical exhibitionists. Luzzatto makes it clear that the enemies of Padre Pio wanted to remove him from San Giovanni Rotondo and isolate him as much as possible from his followers. When they threatened to do so, it became apparent there would be a bloodbath, so the Padre remained in the Gargano for the rest of his life. During the seventeenth century the populace was more easily intimidated, and Joseph was severed from his followers again and again. The history of saintly politics reveals the dangers of mysticism accompanied by miraculous displays. Luzzato tells a nuanced story but abstains from committing himself on the "genuineness" of Padre Pio's advertised "miracles."

Ideological hostility to mystery is apparent in the most advanced of sciences. Bruce Rosenblum and Fred Kuttner write of the "skeleton" in the closet of physics, the enigma of quantum reality that lies behind the all-efficient, all-reliable quantum equations they say form the basis of one-third of the American economy.[19]

Graduate students in physics are instructed to concentrate on the calculative and instrumental side of their discipline. They are not encouraged to puzzle over what is *really* going on in the quantum world. Physicist Henry Stapp castigates this principled superficiality: "But this question has been suppressed by the new generation of quantum physicists trained to focus on calculations, and to refrain from thinking about the nature of reality."[20] Stapp, as we will see, believes that mind plays a central role in the fundamental reality of nature.

Signs of discontent with the reigning reductive paradigm are not rare. There is one big problem with the physicalist view of mind: people everywhere keep having experiences that contradict it! Close encounters with death have caused professional brain scientists to change their worldview; Jill Taylor, a professor of neuroanatomy, and neurosurgeon Eben Alexander had near-death experiences that instantly subverted their university-acquired worldview. As a result of a stroke, the thirty-seven-year-old Taylor claimed to experience reality freed from the filtering effects of her linguistic and rational brain. She compared her consciousness during this experience to "a great whale gliding through a sea of silent euphoria. Finer than the finest of pleasures we can experience as human beings, this absence of physical boundary was one of glorious bliss. As my consciousness dwelled in the flow of sweet tranquility, it was obvious to me that I would never be able to squeeze the enormousness of my own spirit back inside this tiny cellular matrix."[21]

Neurosurgeon Eben Alexander is similarly doubtful that mainstream conceptions can handle his own intensely transformative near-death experience. What struck Alexander was that just when the normal adaptive functions of the brain were knocked out of commission, the "impossible" happened; not only did he continue to be conscious, but the quality of his consciousness was exceptional—to use Dr. Alexander's word, "hyper-real." He found himself forced to let go of his "addiction to simplistic, primitive reductive materialism."[22] Another neuroscientist experiencer, Mario Beauregard, has written a book called *Brain Wars* (2010), in which he details reasons meant to disturb the dogmatic slumbers of neuroreductionists. All in all, we have a convergence of doubters from different fields; skeptical about the deeply entrenched dogma of physicalism—a dogma, in my view, that is by all its subterfuges *killing us*.

A DIFFERENT KIND OF SCIENCE?

The animus toward extraordinary experience can be pronounced: the need to whittle everything down to size, to force all human experience into the box of one ideology. What cannot be measured or reliably controlled is filed away as less than real and unworthy of serious attention, an attitude that to some is justified in light of all the great successes of modern science and technology.

Introduction 11

But consider a thought experiment that Henri Bergson suggested in 1913.[23] Instead of four hundred years of researching the science of matter, he said, imagine that we had behind us four hundred years of researching the inner world, the mysteries of mind, soul, and consciousness. What then? What if by now we had achieved four hundred years of a *different kind of scientific progress*? Suppose we had spent our mighty labors probing the great spectrum of mental phenomena, the normal mysteries of memory and consciousness, and the supernormal mysteries of the sort we canvass in this book?

Would it have led to different kinds of discovery—different morals, ideals, forms of thought? Would it have been, in the long run, friendlier to life in all its teeming variety? Made us happier, more reflective, creative, empathetic—*more human*? Could we have gained special insights into personality, social life, sense of community? Wiped out poverty, boredom, mass murder, war for profit, rape, psychotic greed? Evolved an ethics that enhanced not destroyed our planet, cherished not trashed the varieties of sentient existence?

Now to the story of Joseph of Copertino: a magnificent exhibit of Whitehead's transcendent side of imperfect religion.

NOTES

1. For the sources and original documentation of these controversial phenomena, the reader should begin by reading the appendix.

2. In their book they argue for charity, solidarity, and irony as marks of the religion of the future. This would be a religion for professors and postmodern scholars and not a religion that has anything to do with the people of history or with any of the saints, prophets, mystics, or ordinary seekers, pilgrims, or devotees associated with traditional spiritual experience. The religion of the future envisaged here is shorn of anything resembling enlightenment, transcendence, grace, joy, wonder, mystery, ecstasy, or self-transformation. Apart from this shortcoming, the book is worth reading.

3. The *New York Review of Books* has been the scene of recent critiques of facile reductionism from genetics and neuroscience. See, for example, H. Allen Orr on *The Social Animal* by David Brooks (August 18, 2011); and Colin McGinn on *Incomplete Nature: How Mind Emerged from Matter* by Terrence Deacon (June 7, 2012).

4. Geuss, 1981, p. 11.

5. See Stannard, 1992, *American Holocaust*, for a harrowing example.

6. Feyerabend, 1987, p. 313.

7. Ibid.

8. Meuggler, 2001, p. 3.

9. On near-death experience and Joseph, see discussion in subsection of chapter 6.

10. See Stevenson and Tucker entries in the references; their research extends our appreciation of the latent depths (albeit usually hidden) of the human personality.

11. See Smith, 2006, preface.

12. Keener, 2011, p. 13
13. Stoller and Olkes, 1987.
14. Turner, 1994, p. 83.
15. Ibid., pp. 86–87.
16. See Hunter, 2012.
17. Woodward, pp. 184–89.
18. Boniface, 1971, p. 159
19. Rosenblum and Kuttner, 2006, p. 4.
20. Stapp, 2012, p. 16, "Is the Universe Benevolent?"
21. Taylor, 2006, p. 133.
22. Alexander, 2013, p.156.
23. Bergson, pp. 157–175.

Part I

THE MAN AND HIS MARVELS

Chapter 1

Life and Times

If he had not existed, no one could have invented him. He is extraordinary even among extraordinary people. There is scarcely any saint commemorated by the Bollandists who is more baffling to human reason.

—Ernest Hello

Joseph Desa was born on June 17, 1603, in the village of Copertino, located between Brindisi and Otranto.[1] In the wake of a Renaissance in decline, and under Spanish occupation, the natives of the Kingdom of Naples lived in circumstances economically reduced and politically unstable. Life in Joseph's corner of the globe was brutal, nasty, and easily shortened. Much of Italy was plagued by bandits and *bravi* (hired guns); murder and intrigue in high and low places were not rare.

In the sixteenth century, Spanish Viceroy Don Pedro Alvarez de Toledo used brutal methods to convert the sprawling city of Naples into a quasi-orderly metropolis, expelling the Jewish merchants and meting out over 18,000 capital executions during his twenty-year tenure. Under the auspices of the new Society of Jesus and the Spanish Inquisition, the Church was in full reactionary gear, determined to uproot heresy and beat the Devil, reform the reformers and discipline malcontents and slackers in the Church hierarchy.

Belief in diabolic possession was at a high point,[2] adding legions of invisible enemies to complicate the climate of fear and suspicion that Jean Delumeau describes in such depressing detail in his massively grim *Sin and Fear: The Emergence of Western Guilt Culture* (1990). If Whitehead called it the century of genius, it was also a century of paranoia and vicious credulity. About this period Trevor-Roper[3] wrote: "Organized systematic 'demonology' which the medieval church constructed . . . in the sixteenth and seventeenth centuries acquired a terrible momentum of its own."

The worst period of the witch-craze in Europe coincides almost exactly with Joseph's lifetime (1603–1663). Though much less so in Italy, mass executions for witchcraft were prominent in Germany, England, and France. Natural disasters; plague; volcanic eruptions (Vesuvius in 1631); and popular uprisings against the Spanish occupation, like the one led by Masaniello in Naples and said to be inspired by the Madonna in 1648, were part of Joseph's world. The Counter-Reformation was in full swing, but at the same time new ideas, skeptical and scientific, were beginning to transform European consciousness. Beside the rise of the new scientific worldview ranged a popular credulity inflamed by fear, panic, and fanaticism. Instability was the breeding ground of psychic phenomena all over Europe. According to the German physician-historian Joseph Ennemoser: "At no time did more enthusiasts, visionaries, and prophets appear, than in the first half of the seventeenth century, and during the Thirty-years War, in which troubles of all sorts, sorrow and suffering, hunger and plague, overspread Germany."[4]

Into this psychically mobile world Joseph was born. Four agents of the law—wrapped in coats of mail, rapiers and pistols in hand—came pounding on the door of the house of Felix and Frances Desa. Warned of the impending visit, they had fled. The congenial Felix Desa ran afoul of debtors in a misguided attempt to help a friend. Employed and respected by one of the wealthy castle lords of Copertino, artisan Felix was known for his "sweet and liberal nature."[5]

The debt collectors dispossessed the Desas, and, to avoid prison, Felix abandoned his pregnant wife, went into hiding with friends, and sought asylum in the Church. Frances took shelter in a stable where she gave birth to Joseph, who was baptized in the church of Our Lady of the Snow. One might see in the reference to a *stable* a mere pious reference to the birth of Jesus. The Italian word is *stalla*—stable, stall, shed. Joseph being born in a *stalla* was a consequence of his mother being homeless and mateless. The Desas had already lost four children; the fifth, Livia, survived, and last came Joseph.

On Felix's side of the family, as on Frances's, there were several clergymen. Frances was severe and moralistic. Heartless or careless with her rhetoric, she was fond of saying she would rather see her children dead than watch them stray from virtue.

"I keep you here for the love of God!" she once told Joseph. "For charity! I found you in the woods and brought you home lest the wild animals eat you!"[6] G. C. Mattellini[7] describes Frances as ungiving, unforgiving, and "incapable of bending until death."

The mature Joseph made it a point of distinguishing his biological mother, whom he called his "nurse," from the Madonna whom he called his "true mother." Eventually, the "nurse" helped get him into the priesthood, but Joseph's beginnings were bleak and unpromising. His father was forced to abandon him before he was born, saddling him with debts and the threat of prison; his mother disowned him emotionally, broke sticks on his head, and mocked his gaucheries. But she was only harsh as the times were harsh.

Joseph's response was to retreat into himself, where he discovered the consolations of prayer and learned to explore his inner life. His was not unlike other stories of precocious religiosity—for example, Teresa of Avila or Catherine of Siena who at very early ages were seeking divine adventure.[8] As E. Robinson shows in his 1977 study, children can have profound mystical experiences.

If poverty drove Joseph toward his inner life, a long physical illness did the same with redoubled intensity. At nine he became bedridden from a growth on his backside; the damp, unhygienic living quarters led to infection and then gangrene, a condition that worsened and virtually crippled him for five years. Money and medical resources lacking, he was forced out of school; his sister, Livia, was all he had in the way of human support.

The growth on his backside, as "large as a melon," emitted a foul odor. His one respite from misery was to visit the church, and he begged his mother to carry him there as often as possible. She yielded to his repeated demands. Not happy about being forced to lug him back and forth, it fueled resentment and increased her moralistic perfectionism. The chroniclers left no record of maternal affection offered the boy during his ordeal. In later years, Joseph said he discovered the consolations of spiritual inwardness during the sufferings of his long boyhood illness.

Livia began to notice that Joseph was starting to fast in earnest. And Frances, a Franciscan tertiary, told him stories that awakened a powerful yearning to visit Assisi. The stories formed a large part of his education. He dreamed of seeing and touching the relics of the great saint enshrined there, but it would be years before he realized his dream, not before some curious turns of event. He was still bedridden and his future was uncertain.

After trying every available nostrum, Frances took the boy to a local hermit reputed to be a surgeon who offered to operate on Joseph. But when he started to heat up the cauterizing instruments and pulled out the silver forceps, Joseph's father, Felix, who had come out of hiding to oversee the operation, protested. He had no confidence in the so-called surgeon and asked him to go away. But Frances prevailed, and the operation was performed. The hermit excised an unseemly foul-smelling growth as Joseph screamed for help from St. Francis. The operation was miraculous in that Joseph was not outright killed.

The hermit subsequently applied some oil used in a lamp that burned before an image of Our Lady of Grace, rubbing it into Joseph's lesions, which somehow led to his recovery. Joseph was more receptive to the Madonna than to the hermit, and whether by miracle, placebo, or lucky break, he managed to regain his health and his mobility.

The first steps back on his life path were halting. The bedridden years had disrupted his psychomotor development, which soon became evident in his behavior, which at first was marked by a clumsiness and general disjointedness. It soon became clear that Joseph was ill-adapted to the ordinary business of life. Mattelini states that "at fifteen years old [Joseph] had the psychomotor skills of an eight year old."[9]

The impediment had impaired his ability to move about effectively; this in turn reinforced his tendency to slip into reveries and trances and to see visions. Motivated to escape from his diseased body and external circumstances, he made use of the psychospiritual tools at hand and explored his inner life. Bodily pain, arrested mobility, and the rapid shifts of state he seemed to experience, converged to push him toward introspection and spiritual life. Henri Ellenberger[10] has written about "creative illness," a condition that sometimes sparks the inspirations of shamans, artists, mystics, and the like. So it was with Joseph, forced to dissociate from his body, he learned to explore fantasy, visions, and budding ecstasies.

Making small altars relieved his physical suffering and furnished outlets for diverting his attention from the sordid reality he was compelled to endure. The church was his refuge and meant peace, safety, and cleanliness. The music surprised him with joy and raised up his spirits.

Unschooled, physiologically jarred to his depths, he was perceived as stupid. The future patron saint of students was a poor student, lapsing into trances, wandering from the gray trail of written words. He would stop in the middle of the street listening to church music and look up with his mouth open, thus earning the nickname *Boccaperta* (Gapingmouth). Apprenticed to a cobbler, before long he was pronounced useless and was fired.

He loitered around the neighborhood churches, offered to assist at Mass, and began to wear a hair shirt. The fasting intensified. He was fond of saying that for him it was always Lenten season. He abstained from meat and seasoned his few vegetables with wormwood, eating nothing for two or three days at a stretch. When questioned about this he'd shake his head and say he forgot to eat. He pardoned himself for being absent-minded and apologized for his fits of *stordimento*—the mystical daze into which he often seemed to lapse.

He was attracted to the Order of Conventuals, so he went to his paternal uncle, Fr. Francis Desa, a Franciscan cleric. Uncle Francis promptly rejected Joseph as unfit for the dignified calling of the priesthood. The reject then approached the provincial of the Capuchins and asked to be received as a lay brother. The request was granted. He received the habit in August 1620, was given the name of Stephen, and settled into the monastery at Martina Franca.

After eight months, he was censured because of kitchen ineptness. Bad at distinguishing wheat from rye bread, he dropped and broke dishes, and knocked over pots of boiling water when he threw wood on the fire. In penance for his maladroitness, he attached the broken dish shards to his hair shirt and endured the chafing.

Another friar told him that "spiritual" meant praying and meditating; so he stayed on his knees praying for hours on end until his knees got infected. He remembered how the hermit surgeon cut out the growth that had plagued him for years, so he grabbed a knife and blithely operated on his infected knee. As he was forced to lay back and convalesce from his self-administered operation, the novices thought he was shirking his duties. After eight months, the superiors at Martina Franca declared he was "absolutely not suited for Religion, thickheaded and neglectful, ignorant and unfit for society."[11]

Joseph felt particularly crushed having to give up his habit. He thought he had finally achieved an identity. With baroque panache, he said of the incident years later: "It seemed to me as if my skin was torn off with the habit and my flesh rent from the bone." Joseph departed in embarrassed haste from the monastery—it was ninety miles on foot back to Copertino. In the rush, he left behind his hat, shoes, and stockings. On the road, bandits tracked him and dogs harried him; he met a stranger, and, for no stated reason, bedraggled Joseph assumed the fellow was Malatasca—"Evil Pocket"—his nickname for the Devil.

He eventually bumped into one of his father's friends, who fed and put him up for the night. The following day, too ashamed to face his mother's scorn, he decided to seek counsel at Vetrara with his uncle, who was busy with the Lenten preaching. When Joseph arrived he prostrated himself and announced: "The Capuchin Fathers have taken the habit from me because I am good for nothing."

His uncle told him that his father had died and took him back to his mother, who received him with a touch of rare tenderness but had no material aid to offer him. Joseph was on his own; we see him for once in a completely indeterminate situation, without family, church, or friend. The sacristan of Grotella hid him in a garret in the convent bell tower where he remained sequestered for a long torrid summer. He might have ended up like his father, a fugitive hounded to an early grave, but eventually his mother managed to marshal help from Fr. John Donatus, who admitted him as a tertiary of the Conventuals in Grotella.

Assigned the lowly task of caring for the mule, Joseph began to ingratiate himself with his brothers and with the people during alms-gathering. He was learning to discharge his duties with increasing skill and dispatch and quickly displayed one of his more highly cultivated virtues—and the key to Church solidarity during the Counter-Reformation—flawless obedience.

Obedience, from Joseph's point of view, was (as he said) the *coltello*—the knife that kills the ego-centered self. For him it became part of a technique in service to self-mastery. The nascent religious also excelled in the department of ascesis; his hair shirt was not uncomfortable enough, so he donned an additional iron chain with cutting spurs that chafed his loins. He ate very little and slept very little on his three boards, old bearskin, and straw pallet. On June 19, 1625, he was received into the Order of Conventuals and began his novitiate for the priesthood.

The fact that Joseph made it to the priesthood was later treated by chroniclers as providential if not miraculous. The reason is that despite his winsome spiritual personality, his love of solitude, fasting, and meditation, he was a poor student. Not facile with theology or with the syllogism, deemed by his hero Francis of Assisi a wicked device of the Devil, he could not endure the casuistry or hair-splitting dialectics. He was such a bad student his teachers rebuked him regularly. His reply was unanswerable: "Have patience with me, you will acquire merit." The story is that Joseph knew just one passage in the Gospels that he could expound: "Blessed is the womb that bore Thee" (Luke 11:27). The examiner picked this very passage for him to expound, a coincidence that Joseph instantly perceived as signifying divine help.

He passed the first test toward the priesthood but had another, more daunting, exam to face; again he prayed for assistance from the Madonna. Again, by coincidence, Bishop Detti of Castro, the prelate in charge of giving the test, was forced to leave abruptly and waived the exam for Joseph and several others. Citing the first batch of novitiates as proving so competent, he assumed the rest would be equally competent. Joseph got the Madonna's help by not having to take the exam at all! This is the rather odd basis of his becoming the patron saint of students. Convinced the Madonna had answered his prayers, he was ordained on March 28, 1628.

He was now a priest in a sixteen-hundred-year-old religious organization. Returning to the monastery in Grotella, he said his first Mass. Struck by the sublimity of his office and seized with dread that he might fail, he "resolved anew to die entirely to the world and to lead a supernatural life."[12] He withdrew from his brothers and spent his time in a small room above the church vault or sometimes in an olive grove where he prayed and meditated ceaselessly.

The prolonged bouts of concentrated inwardness affected his behavior. Once ordained, it was as if he had obtained a license to pull out all the stops and abandon himself to ecstasy, which he did and which began to shade off into the more public form of ecstasy called levitation.[13] Strange phenomena were said to occur around Joseph—things very visible, very dramatic, and very disturbing. People began to notice and talk about him: some with awe and wonder, others with alarm and suspicion.

As for Joseph's temperament, besides a laudable spiritual stubbornness, he could be choleric and hot-tempered. In Bernini's early biography we read: "Once, on hearing a coachman curse God in an Osteria, Padre Joseph threw himself at the man and began to choke him, and might have killed him if he had not fainted and fallen to the ground in weakness, he himself a victim of pain for having offended the Most High."[14]

There are scattered reports of Joseph yielding to these outbursts of sudden wild emotion. Now and then a rough human being leaps out from behind the manicured picture we have of the saint. Some of his pious outbursts qualify as invasive. Bernini describes an occasion when Joseph divined that some locals were practicing some form of magic or sorcery in town. So he charged out of the monastery and stormed a private dwelling where folks were doing something "occult" and broke the whole thing up in a righteous fulmination.

Early in his priestly career he struggled to overcome attachment to worldly goods. Despite the vow of poverty, he retained a fondness for things some of his well-off relatives gave him—nice clothes, a fancy watch, and some paintings. Joseph would binge on these ordinary pleasures and then impulsively give things away. "But on the first occasion when necessity arose or when he would feel the pinch of poverty, he would go out and buy those articles he felt he needed," writes Parisciani.[15] This reportedly happened so often it became a standing joke with his confreres.

To make up for this weakness, he went barefoot in ragged attire, penitent and full of visible self-loathing; but these actions depressed rather than pacified his spirit. Bernini recounts how one day when Joseph was alone and sobbing in his cell, a mysterious personage appeared at his door and gave him a new habit. This happened in 1629 at the end of his second year as a priest; it appears that after this unexplained visit from a stranger, Joseph began to experience the benefits of poverty, the relaxed indifference to material things he was supposed to be feeling.

I am unable to make out from the written documents what really happened on this occasion. The boundary between dream and reality was never too sharp for Joseph. He was convinced that during his trial at the Inquisition, Saint Anthony of Padua was sitting in the audience and keeping a watchful eye on him. The moment, as Bernini recounts, a woman from the oldest profession appeared ripe for conversion, and gave a hint of contriteness, Joseph starts calling her "Mary Magdalene" and relates to her as Jesus would.

Still, his human, less-than-"perfect" side, was visible in different ways. I mentioned how he went for the throat of a blasphemer. By 1630, Joseph started to come out, as it were, with increasing signs of the various spiritual gifts he possessed, such as the ability to "scrutinize the hearts" and secret thoughts of the people around him. It appears from accounts that these newfound powers went to his head. He began to put on prophetic airs and set about hectoring people in public.

A painter suffering from a strange disease prayed to the Madonna, promising to paint something special to honor her if he got well. He got well. But when the painter failed to keep his word about the artwork, our saint threatened to cause a new illness in him and behaved more like a sorcerer than a saint. Another man broke his promise to commission an artist to make a painting of the Madonna. It turned out the painting cost more than he could afford. The fellow was a farmer, and Joseph coyly said to him: "It's of little importance to me—you promised it to Our Lady—*you'll see*!" The farmer immediately began to feel obscure pains in his body. Lo! In a transport of sudden generosity, he commissioned the painting.

Another fellow failed to say the breviary and Joseph proclaimed in public: "The breviary cries against you!" Another time he shouted: "There's a terrible stench in here since the arrival of this cleric!" Joseph could *smell* the cleric's offenses. Sometimes he *saw* dirt, muck, or black ink on the faces of the guilty ones, and he'd harangue them to get "cleaned up" in confession.

A certain Count don Cosimo Pinelli had an ongoing sexual liaison with the daughter of Martha Rodia; Joseph said that if the count didn't desist from his amours, he would go blind. This turned out to be what happened, and Joseph bragged about his prediction, but later restored the man's sight, this time getting him to leave the girl alone and pay reparations to the family!

Before long nobody in Copertino dared enter the company of the friar unless their conscience was squeaky-clean; otherwise they shrank in terror from the gaze of the black-bearded friar. People were getting fed up with Saint Joseph the sanctimonious bully and telepathic spy. Finally, his superiors commanded him under holy obedience to tone down his manner and try being more sensitive to the local sinners. Joseph took this to heart, and instead of using his powers like a black magician, got off his high horse and softened his rhetoric. He used politic phrases like "you must adjust your compass" or "you'd do better if you held your bow straight."

As his spiritual personality matured, he encountered different kinds of difficulty. For example, even though his fame as saint and miracle man was growing, he couldn't help any of his relatives suffering from the stagnant economy. Livia was tired of lofty advice and needed money; her husband, like Joseph's father, was wanted by bounty hunters and debt collectors. She went to Joseph for material help, but got nothing from him because, as he said, "I haven't anything. I'm poor."

When his own mother came begging for help, insisting on her maternal rights, he replied, "I have no mother." *His* mother, he clarified, is Our Lady in Heaven. She's everybody's mother, he explained, so go to her for help. The story is that when she got home, Frances found a loaf of bread in the cupboard that she swore had been bare.

Joseph had money problems not only with poor family relations but also with the friary. Whenever he cured people, especially members of the nobility, they were deeply grateful and offered gifts and financial rewards. But the friar, who was sworn to poverty, would accept none of it. His superiors reprimanded him for his callous largesse; the brothers were as economically wasted as his poor relations. But for Joseph to accept money was like getting into bed with "serpents."

What made all this especially annoying was that he would return after a day out with his habit torn to shreds by local admirers and relic hunters. The implacable, self-effacing mystic had no idea how to ward off his ravaging fans. But that meant the friary would have to defray the cost of a new habit. Joseph's response was to ask permission to remain in his cell and not venture into town.

Once he was ordained, the levitations began, and his life was never the same again. From 1630 to 1639 the astonishing effects became more frequent and more dramatic, and there was no way to keep them a secret. Two opposing forces came to rule his life. The first was that his name and all his personal effects and his living body would acquire the power to *attract people to him*. But a second, counterforce came from the Church, which did everything possible to keep him *away from people*. Caught between conflicting psychic vectors, the tension of this inner schism would intensify for the rest of his life.

The attraction is easy to understand. People began to see Joseph as a healer, a prophet, living proof of authentic divine power. But the Church felt the need to keep the miracle-hungry hoi polloi at a safe distance; it was coldly alert to any mischief the disarming Christ-clone might unintentionally cause. They had their eyes on him for any sign of worldly ambition or hints of doctrinal deviance or for any spiritual gaffes. Above all, they wanted to keep him out of the limelight; this, however, was very difficult to do.

The friar's behavior was completely unpredictable. A slight verbal or visual association might trigger an involuntary episode of ecstatic rapture and bring chaos to any scene, upstage any event taking place around him. If he stayed in a convent too long, the crowds would thicken and become restive. The policy of the Church was to relocate him, shunting him toward the boondocks, trying with limited success to prevent spontaneous public appearances. They also tried to stop him from saying Mass and hearing confessions, basic priestly functions that it now seemed he was unfit to perform.

He was grateful for the interventions of Rome insofar as they helped him obtain some much-needed solitude, peace, and quiet. In that solitude he delved deeper into his spiritual life, which to his acute embarrassment, often exploded in shocking aerial displays. This and related themes touched on in this chapter we will discuss later in more detail.

Joseph remained in Grotella for sixteen years, two of them in spiritual dryness and desolation. In response, he increased his ascetic regimen and tortured his body—"the Jackass"—into complete submission. He waxed inventive at the fine art of self-laceration. Bernini tells of a new "scourge studded with needles, pins, and star-shaped pieces of steel." He tightened the iron chain, which dug into his hair shirt. Joseph's disgusted superior found him covered with wounds, and ordered him to get rid of the new-fangled scourges. Meanwhile his fame as wonder-worker spread in Italy and beyond, and there was much excited talk about the new Saint Francis.

Then something went wrong. By 1634 he had gained such a reputation as prophet, healer, exorcist, and ecstatic that Father Antonio of Mauro had a brilliant idea. Antonio was in charge of the region in Apulia called Lecce, which included about sixty convents and conventinos. He had recently assumed his position of provincial, and it was the custom for newbies in his position to travel around and introduce themselves to the people. The big idea was to take Joseph with him on his self-introductory tour.

In spite of revulsion at the prospect of making a spectacle of himself, Joseph had no choice but to obey. Father Antonio offered him a horse of his own and money for food and lodging, but he turned them down, preferring to walk and to travel like a mendicant. Father Antonio later wrote with pride how he had conceived his plan: "Upon arriving at church with me, Joseph was immediately carried aloft in ecstasy. In sum, I visited and preached with words and he with deeds and life, which provided many of his brethren with occasions for self-reformation."[16]

The pious father provincial also stated, somewhat defensively: "Enamored of his great virtue, I chose him for my companion in a visit. I brought him with me through all these cities and places more to give a good example than to serve my ends."[17]

Companion Lodovico came along on this spiritual road show and to avoid crowds and the usual fanatics they traveled at night. Joseph was thirty-three years old—a number that was going to cause him difficulties. The little troupe would stay in each locale for a few days and move on; despite his discomfort with the project, the charisms in the course of that eventful year remained in full flower.

Toward the end of the itinerary, Signor Mauro stopped at a small town called Giovinazza in the province of Bari. Not everyone there was well disposed toward Joseph; the attention heaped on him caused heads to turn. Members of the clergy and nobility asked that he return to Giovinazza. They wanted to scrutinize the friar more closely, so they observed him say Mass, go into ecstasy, and rise into the air.

Apparently it was disconcerting for his brethren to witness this. A person with such charisma and such strange power might very well appear uncanny, sinister, and perhaps dangerous. A particularly dark suspicion crystallized in the mind of a Monsignor Joseph Palamolla, a Vicar Apostolic who presided over a near-empty diocese. Was he perhaps captious, suspicious, or feeling a little underappreciated? Whatever it was, something prompted him to compose a formal accusation of Joseph and send it to the Holy Office in Naples. Joseph, he declared, was posing as a "messiah." Palamolla accused Joseph of behaving with "affected sanctity" and of "abusing the credulity of the populace."[18]

Palamolla asked Joseph how old he was. "Thirty-three," was the reply. Bizarrely, the vicar took this as presumptuous—his age was much too suggestively Jesus-like! The more the vicar dwelled on the disturbing strangeness of Joseph, lanky and disheveled with dark eyes disposed to turn upward, the more alarmed he became. Yielding to an uncharitable impulse, he wrote a letter to the Holy Office in Naples: "Travelling from town to town is a man of thirty-three years who's acting like another Messiah, attracting the people to himself everywhere with prodigies at every turn. We must warn the authorities: a remedy will prevent future evils or future evils will grow beyond remedy."[19]

The ominous and threatening tone of this crafty letter found its mark. Before long, Joseph's superiors received a notice from the Holy Office. It was a summons for him to appear before the Tribunal in Naples (at the time one of the great cities in Europe). From being the reluctant star of a traveling spiritual circus, he now found himself under compulsion to appear before the Holy Inquisition. True, the Italian was not the Spanish Inquisition, but he still feared being imprisoned or possibly committed to the flames. Recently, three men were burned alive because they said Mass in public without having been properly ordained.

He was accused in solemn Latin: *Fratris Iosephi de Cupertino carcerati Neapoli ob affectatam sanctitatem et alia.*[20] "Friar Joseph imprisoned in Naples for affected sanctity and other things." There were pretenders who faked stigmata and affected signs of sanctity. But this was not Joseph's problem; no one questioned the reality of his reported phenomena. They were questioning his attitude, his being, or as Palamolla said, "ostentatious," or as the Latin statement had it, "affected" or "pretentious." He was acting like a "messiah," according to Vicar Palamolla.

It must have been distressing to see all the attention riveted on the dazed friar. Palamolla was obviously put off when he observed the following:

Celebrating the Mass at the major altar of the cathedral, arriving at the Memento of the living, he raises his hands, remains immobile briefly and then begins to tremble for another space of time and then screaming in a high voice, unfolds his hands and fixes his eyes on the Most Holy Sacrament resting on the altar, and launches himself in the air until he accosts the Guardian who was there serving the Mass. Then he (the Guardian) touched Joseph's ear and commanded him by obedience to continue with the Mass, and so he did.[21]

Palamolla, his accuser, was also an eyewitness to Joseph's anomalous movements. Some of the inquisitors had also witnessed Joseph levitate. That was not an issue for the accusers; it was an observed fact. The issue was whether these strange displays were signs of divine or diabolic influence. The concern was not with Joseph disrupting Mass but with whether he was intent on calling attention to himself.

The three inquisitors present at this trial had some questions they wanted answered. They wanted to know if he enjoyed the *moti* ("movements of his body"); if he could control them; and if he was proud of them. Joseph replied that he was not proud of them, but ashamed—in fact, embarrassed. He did admit that the *moti* were spiritually consoling but insisted they were the fruit of his self-mortification. As for controlling them, he said he prayed and asked his brethren to pray for them to stop at once. At first it seemed to work, but the benefits were short-lived. This unknown force, once fully aroused, could be irrepressible.

Some, driven by malice or honest skepticism, insinuated there was something contrived or exaggerated about Joseph's miracles. Others opined that the *moti* were of satanic provenance. Parisciani calls this Joseph's tragedy. At Naples the friar lost his innocence. From now on he would struggle with questions about his authenticity, wonder about the status and the meaning of his gifts. Was it perhaps all some evil delusion he was caught up in?

Doubt did not entirely dominate him; but he did often have to fight off waves of troubling, self-tormenting thoughts. He stumbled and irritated his interlocutors, but after a while they began to see someone who looked more like a gauche saint than a candidate for burning. Apparently Joseph's profound unfeigned humility defeated them.

A report of the proceedings in Naples had to be sent to Rome, where the case would be reviewed. All this was going to place its stamp on Joseph's life. After the Inquisition at Naples, he would never return to Grotella, the town that contained a small portrait of the Madonna so dear to his heart. He was attached to this painted image and had now to wean himself from it; it seems to have been his main psychic link to his feeling self.

Naples, a highly populated and thriving city of Europe, was overwhelming; all the young country priest could say was "Woe!" What may have driven him to cry "Woe!" was something recorded by an English diarist, John Evelyn, who was visiting Naples at the time:

> We went by coach to take the air and see the diversions, or rather madness, of the Carnival; the courtesans who swarm in this city to the number, as we are told, of 30,000 registered and paying a tax to the State, flinging eggs of sweet water into our coach as we passed by the houses and windows . . . who by a thousand studied devices seek to inveigle foolish young men.[22]

The sight of all those courtesans flaunting their wares in public must have terrified Joseph, who feared women more than he feared the Devil. No doubt he wished he were back home in Grotella, in some cave or olive grove, safely and serenely meditating on the Madonna.

The result of a long, tedious trial in Naples was to declare him innocent of all charges. The tribunal ordered him to say Mass before the nuns of St. Ligoria, and it wasn't long before he was raised in ecstasy above the altar. A great many were said to witness this posttrial flight in Naples. The public events and news of his appearance before the Holy Office grew Joseph's fame among nobles, clergy, and royalty. Persons of power and distinction were now even more curious about him and sought to meet him face to face. The Spanish viceroy, his wife, and court had asked him to say Mass in their private chapel. Joseph managed to escape this honor by the Holy Office ordering him to go to Rome.

The trip from Naples to Rome must have afforded him little relief. In Rome he was asked to give an account of his life before his superiors and various inquisitors. There was of course the unpleasant business he had just been through. When asked to explain what had happened before the crowd at Giovinazza, the performance he had given that prompted the need to face a tribunal in Naples, he said: "I don't remember what happened to me. There was a large crowd of people there; my superior directed me to go among them and I went reluctantly. I don't know what happened except that my superior spoke to me in a way that was humiliating."[23]

Again he found himself on trial in Rome, a procedure that required three stages and went on for months. In Rome, Joseph was also ordered to say Mass in public; and again, in spite of himself, was lifted off the ground in ecstasy—again, in the presence of inquisitors.

By trial's end, he had received a *monitio*—a warning! But for what? Surely it was a strange trial of a man accused of undergoing ecstasy and levitation before crowds of people *with the wrong attitude?* Some insinuated that his phenomena were tainted by diabolic influence or produced for cynical purposes. The *monitio* was a signal that the Holy Office was about to place him under surveillance. The otherworldly friar would from now on be moved about whenever and wherever deemed necessary—no questions asked, no respect for fairness or personal sensitivities.

Joseph did his best to embrace the abuses as signs of election to heroic virtue; around this time he had become depressed, and the ecstasies and raptures subsided. Hideous dreams and diabolic imaginings assailed him, which made him yearn for the Lady of Grotella whom he spoke of as his "Mama." If there is such a thing as lovesickness for the divine feminine, Joseph had a severe case. He experienced the image of the Madonna with great emotional intensity; the Madonna was perhaps his sole emotional connection to life, the world, to God.

The ordeal with the Inquisition, which lasted two years, took a toll on his health. The vitality of the youth who trudged all over Italy on foot was worn down. On the other hand, he continued to be subject to unknown forces, despite (or because of?) his life and his movements being increasingly constrained. The interlocutors from his trial decided to monitor him, as they did other mystics with extremist tendencies. Catherine of Siena also had to bare her spiritual self to the Inquisition and was placed under special surveillance by a guardian.

The prelates of Rome decided Joseph should live segregated from the general public. His epistolary life was curtailed. The purpose of imposing this isolation was to prevent the disturbances he caused when he was present at processions, ceremonies, or Masses. Another reason was to preserve him from being distracted by the populace so he could pursue his spiritual life in peace. His movements were so restricted, in effect he found himself under house arrest, his life increasingly solitary and regimented. He ate little, slept little, said Mass alone, meditated, read scripture and the lives of the saints—all mainly alone in a poorly lit cell, reciting, raplike, his own rhymed wisdom ditties.

Pope Urban VIII had sent him to be near the bones of St. Francis of Assisi. Upon arrival, the people who knew of his troubles with the Inquisition welcomed him. Upon entering the majestic basilica of the cathedral, he glanced high up at the face of the Madonna, which was painted by Cimabue. "Ah, Mama, you followed me here!" he cried out, and reportedly went into a tremendous rapture (chapter 3). It was a spectacular beginning to Joseph's tenure in Assisi.

By some odd twist, the custodian in charge there turned out to be Father Antonio of San Mauro, the man who caused his problems with the Inquisition. For obscure reasons, his old admirer Antonio turned against Joseph and went out of his way to persecute him for his first four years in Assisi.

Eventually, Antonio was himself called before the Inquisition and asked to explain his behavior toward Joseph. He must not have done a very good job, because the Tribunal now gave *him* a *monitio*. When he returned to Assisi he insulted Joseph, calling him a "hypocrite and flighty as a puppet, a mask of sanctity, liar and downright crazy." But when asked in Rome to comment on Joseph, he replied: "I can say nothing except that he was a saint who went into ecstasy continually and was adored by everybody."[24]

Did Antonio see something about Joseph others missed, or was it a case of spiritual envy? One wonders about Joseph's traveling companion, Lodovico, who spent many years as companion to the traveling friar but seems to have left few deposed impressions or memories of him. One day he insisted upon being sent to another convent, away from Joseph. Nothing is said about why he left his extraordinary companion so abruptly.

In 1644, the father general sent Joseph to Rome. He was summoned there at the request of Prince John Casimir Waza, brother of the king of Poland. The prince sought advice from Joseph about his future, and Joseph urged him not to become a Jesuit; he would have more important things to do; in fact, he became king of Poland.[25] After a brief stay in Rome, Joseph's spiritual aridity came to an end. He was sent back to Assisi and given a copy of the painting of the Virgin of Grotella he so loved. The people of Assisi were happy to have him back, and the city council conferred honorary citizenship on him; with fanfare, he was declared a "fellow-citizen of Saint Francis." Joseph was so smitten by this that "he was robbed of his senses and lifted in ecstasy almost to the ceiling." At Assisi, Joseph's fame for sanctity grew and the startling phenomena proliferated.

During Mass the flights took their most dramatic form. He remained for another nine years in Assisi. In 1647 he is reported to have wept from clairvoyantly witnessing scenes in Naples of the failed revolt against the Spanish occupation. He announced the death of Pope Urban VIII in Rome in 1644 before news of that event arrived and reportedly appeared at his mother's deathbed in Grotella.

Joseph was evolving. No longer concerned with material things or with what people thought of him, he now said, "The important thing is the inside, the interior is what counts."[26] He wearied of the endless visitors and dignitaries that kept him away from "the interior." In a letter, the Duchess of Parma spoke of Joseph as the "prodigy of our century." To hear things like that embarrassed and drove him to retreat more deeply into himself.

Then, without warning, on July 23, 1653, Padre Vincenzo, Inquisitor General of Perugia, arrived in Assisi with four armed guards. They came with the message that Joseph had to leave town immediately. The papal command from Innocent X was that he be brought to the town of Pietrarubbia.

"Are they taking me to prison?" he said when he heard they were coming.

Upon confronting the Inquisitor, Joseph kneeled down and kissed the intruder's feet. He was not happy to leave Assisi, so close to the remains of Francis, but departed in haste with Lodovico and two mules, again leaving behind hat, mantle, spectacles, and breviary.

Innocent X, uncomfortable with Joseph's ever-growing fame, decided to reexamine the charge of *affectatem sanctitatem* he was acquitted of in Naples. The pope was also annoyed by Joseph's relationship with the Infanta, whose

Savoy family was resisting repressive measures the pontiff had recently imposed. He might also have been jealous over all the European dignitaries vying for audience with Joseph, who, in any case, was sent to Pietrarubbia and confined to his cell.

But in Pietrarubbia he attracted even greater attention, and people came from Monte Feltro, Fossombrone, Fano, Pesaro, Rimini, Aricium, and Cesna, eager to see the holy man say Mass, hoping to get as close to him as possible, ask for his prayers, touch or be touched by him; the crowds were so great and so fervent they ripped tiles from the church walls and broke open holes so they could watch his ecstatic performances. Pilgrims built huts near the monastery or opened inns, causing groundswells of local business. The friar was good for the economy but bad for the tranquility of the more pedestrian religious.

Joseph lasted just three months in Pietrarubbia; next stop would be Fossombrone, by the Adriatic coast, a hermitage on a mountain overlooking the Metauro River:

> Confused rumors arose concerning the departure of Padre Joseph from Pietrarubbia. Without knowing who was spreading this news, it reached everywhere throughout the region. A few sought to know the itinerary of the voyage, kept secret by the vicar because he feared a riot and wanted to prevent people from seeing the friar publicly, even to keep him hidden from his own Capuchin brothers.[27]

The trip to Fossombrone left a trail of reports of strange incidents. On the way, Joseph and his retinue of Inquisitor and armed guards ran into a violent rainstorm. We are told that Joseph passed through this storm without being touched by a raindrop. Weather control and weather-creating phenomena are part of the lore of mystics and shamans, but I find no testimony backing up this claim. But there are other stories about weather control. Power to create deadly hailstorms was pivotal to Milarepa's conversion from sorcery to the mystical life.[28] In the twentieth century, anthropologist David Barker witnessed a shaman divert a rainstorm during a wedding ceremony, an observation that left Barker disoriented for two weeks.[29]

As Joseph was arbitrarily moved from convent to convent, prevented from forming attachments of any kind, the thought that God was everywhere came to life for him and helped him maintain equilibrium during the enforced moves and the dry patches of his interior life. If God is everywhere, he reasoned, then we can be happy anywhere; nothing can in principle block our contact with the divine reality. No matter where we are or what we are doing, the divine presence is accessible; it was an idea his difficult circumstances drove him to realize with dramatic intensity.

The journey to Fossombrone was supposed to be a secret, but everybody knew he was coming and hoped for a chance to meet him face to face. Said to have an uncanny sense of direction, finding his way on roads he had never traveled, Joseph was tranquil when he arrived at the new destination.

Fossombrone would become the scene of many ecstasies, raptures, and other strange events, and the word spread; the friars sometimes became so frightened of the massing pilgrims they fled to secret hideaways and stayed there incognito until they regained their composure. Joseph lasted for three years in Fossombrone before another visit from the Inquisitor became necessary.

In May 1656, when Alexander VII became pope, eight Conventual Provincials entreated him to restore Joseph to Assisi. Pope Alexander declared that one Saint Francis of Assisi was enough and decided to send Joseph to the Franciscan monastery at Osimo, located a short distance from Loreto and the Adriatic coast. Due to the plague, he was forced to delay his date with Osimo until July 6, 1657.

It was observed that he knew to the hour the arrival of the Inquisitor General and went to his window to watch him arrive. The father secretary arrived at half-past nine on that July evening. In the seventeenth century, we should recall, there were no technical ways information could be leaked, so there was no way Joseph could have known in advance of the father's arrival.

The need to impose isolation on Joseph at Osimo was perceived as acute. The stays at Pietrarubbia and Fossombrone had created so much excitement and disorder that the Church decided to take extra pains to isolate him from the outside world. The wild, unpredictable spectacle of divine power in action was something the Church found difficult to handle. Far from using the friar for propaganda in the Counter-Reformation, it tried to keep him away from an overly excitable public.

The pope's orders emphasized the need for isolation and were quite severe, as were the tactics used to enforce them, rigors enforced by a bishop who venerated Padre Joseph but loved being his custodian more than he cared about treating him well, is the way Bernini puts it, adding: "For this reason the *frate* was assigned a small apartment separate from the others so that God could liberally work His marvels through him without the distraction of extraneous people and the worries of daily life."[30]

During the last six years of his life, Joseph lived in profound solitude:

> From the day he arrived, he never left the convent, nor often even his little apartment, a place where for five months of the year not even the sun reached him. It was necessary to keep a little lamp lit night and day so as to distinguish his room from a tomb. Entire months would pass without him seeing anyone or

anyone seeing him; however, his home was so pleasant and his isolated way of living so blessed that to Padre Joseph, it seemed that he lived not in a city but alone in a forest Paradise.[31]

When the little Joseph caravan eventually arrived at Osimo, it paused before the city walls. An incident then illustrates Joseph's suggestibility, his proneness to hallucinate and create visions. People gathered on the porch of a nearby house, and a priest pointed out in the distance the cupola of the famous Holy House of Loreto, believed to be the house that Mary and Jesus lived in. The legend surrounding the itinerary of the Holy House has it being moved by unknown means from Palestine to the Italian coastal town of Loreto.

Joseph promptly claimed to see angels in flight over the city of Loreto, emitted his characteristic prelevitational shriek, and flew from the porch to the top of an almond tree, a distance of fifteen yards.[32] This reported and presumably well-witnessed event has been rendered iconic by artists, the most impressive being a painting by Ludovico Mazzanti.

Upon arrival in Osimo, and for the rest of his life, Joseph was officially segregated and placed under surveillance. Confined to the company of fellow religious brethren, he needed permission to do anything in public. Pope Alexander VII was determined not to let anybody "annoy" Padre Joseph. And the pope himself did not wish to be "annoyed" by the padre, who undoubtedly could at a moment's notice create public disturbances.

For Joseph, enforced seclusion and virtual imprisonment was (or at least seemed to be) perfectly fine—as he put it, a "forest paradise." After all the years of spiritual practice, he learned to navigate his mystical transports so well that his jail-like environs, even the wretched state of his body, ceased to affect him.

Moreover, the frequency of Joseph's ecstasies and raptures seemed to increase as time went on, and the approach of death did not diminish the force (whatever its nature) that enabled them to occur. About the last phase of his life in Osimo, Father Maccatelli testified (is he exaggerating?): "I can say that with my own eyes I have seen them take place in his room thousands of times."[33]

In Osimo, Joseph pushed mystical experimentation as far as he could. Parisciani writes: "Joseph's solitude became total: he never left his room, but felt serene and had more time to compose and sing his spiritual strophes."[34] The claims that witnesses, including the bishop of Osimo, made about the man were extravagant: some of his levitations lasted for hours, they said. I find little evidence to support levitations that lasted an hour or more. It is likely the references are to very long ecstasies.

But illness and the approach of death did not diminish his anomalous movements. If the friar had been sublimating his vital forces, you would expect a decline in the effect on the brink of death. But this seems not to have been the case. During his last Mass in which he celebrated the Feast of the Assumption, he was observed to levitate. As we will shortly see, he hovered over his deathbed even as the surgeon Francesco Pierpaoli was cauterizing his leg.

He died on September 18, 1663. Joseph's death was an extended performance, closely observed and carefully recorded. Here are the high points:[35] He had predicted and expected to die in Osimo. He said upon arrival, "This is the place where I shall rest." Toward the end he kept dropping hints and said things like, "I have to go on a long pilgrimage," or, "Don't you know that old people die in '63?" On August 10, he came down with a fever. When urged to pray for recovery, he said, "God forbid!"

When the doctor told him he had "double tertian," he remarked: "The jackass has now begun to climb the mountain." He viewed the process of his dying as climbing a mountain. He kept repeating his desire to "dissolve" and be one with God. The way to make this happen was through *nichiltà*—sinking into the great sea of mystical nothingness. By becoming *nulla,* nothing, he was free to embrace, be dissolved in, the infinite God.

On September 8, he requested the Viaticum; in the evening, he asked for Extreme Unction. While Father Buttari was anointing him, he heard Joseph whispering, "Oh, what light! Oh, what splendor! Oh, what fragrance! What taste of paradise!"

On the morning of September 12, at the sound of the bell announcing Holy Communion, Joseph leaped up from his deathbed and ran to and fro shouting to the priest, "This is my delight, this is my delight!," went into ecstasy for a quarter of an hour, then collapsed back into bed.

He repeated, "The jackass has already climbed half-way up the mountain." He grew weaker yet moved about restlessly. Suddenly he cried out, "Take away my heart! Burn it! Cut it out! Rip open my chest! . . . Oh, love, love!"

He kept talking about the "jackass" wanting to rest; finally, on September 18, he smiled, said "Amen," and died.

This is a strange picture of a man's death, a picture of ecstatic expectation, impatience as if for something wonderful. Can it really be that behind the veil of ordinary perception is something to make one scream with delight at the nearness of death?

The end of a saint's life is also a new beginning. In the Catholic Church, the saint must prove himself after death before receiving the supreme accolade. A quasi-democratic procedure has to be followed. Admirers establish a cult or cause, leading, sometimes very slowly, to a trial or process (evidence-based) for beatification and canonization.

In Joseph's case, eyewitness testimonials from living witnesses concerning his life, virtues, and special gifts were obtained in Nardo within a few years of his death. His first biographer, Roberto Nuti, and his diarist, Arcangelo Rosmi, had already deposed much collected testimony.

On February 24, 1753, Pope Benedict XIV (a friend of Voltaire) solemnly beatified Joseph. The pope, previously Prosper Lambertini, as "devil's advocate," had examined the evidence for Joseph's whole life and affirmed the case for his "prolonged flights." Lambertini was a pioneer in the study of what today we call parapsychology.[36] Using the latest science of his day, he tried, whenever possible, to explain alleged miracles naturalistically.

Because of the extreme strangeness of Joseph's case, Lambertini introduced "strong animadversions" to his beatification. These were overcome by evidence that the friar exemplified heroic virtue. Finally, he was canonized. Three additional healing miracles, produced postmortem by appealing to the dead saint, were solemnly decreed by Clement XIII on July 16, 1767, and Joseph entered the canon, the great list of saints.

The fashions of sainthood change in history. In the early days of the Jesus movement, just believing and proclaiming your faith made you a "saint." The faith of the first saints was a provocation to the established civic cults. Some gave their lives for their faith and became martyrs, or saintly witnesses. The tomb or remains of a martyr or saint and their relics were used as gathering places for believers; and the cult of the saints was a cult of friendship with unseen helpers.[37]

Some achieve sainthood by being great organizers, teachers, or peacemakers—the social saints. The desert saints of the Thebaid in the fourth century preferred the ecstasies of isolation and desolation.[38] The earliest saints—like Jesus—were wonder-workers. Are they going out of fashion? According to Kenneth Woodward, there is a shift nowadays away from the medieval criteria of sainthood that focused on miracles. Today a model of sainthood based on heroic virtue is preferred, which makes room in the canon for an Edith Stein, a philosopher, or an Oscar Romero, who was assassinated by the corrupt rulers of San Salvador.

Woodward states that the heroic virtue proponents go out of their way to ignore or invalidate the traditional emphasis on miracles. For historical and fashionable reasons, talk of miracles today is more likely than not to be viewed as retrograde, reactionary, and irrational. Miracles are not only suspect in the eyes of reductive scientists, but also in the eyes of official religionists, intimidated by the scientific priesthood. In Sergio Luzzato's historical study of Padre Pio, a great deal of evidence is presented showing how, within the Church, antimystical and antimiracle sentiment was especially high during his career, culminating in Pope John XXIII, who did not see anything holy about the friar's stigmata and refused to meet him face to face.

According to Luzzato, Pope John, before becoming pope, doubted there was anything supernatural about the padre, and, in fact, "had a distaste for

Padre Pio's spirituality" (119). He was disturbed by the "fanaticism" of people who seemed to deify Padre Pio. He distinguished between what he called "local" and "global" sanctity, and disapproved of the local kind that is based on a relationship with a "special Christian," someone like Padre Pio or Joseph of Copertino. Fear of cultish enthusiasm, a breeding ground of fanaticism and irrationalism, was thus the motive behind the need to deconstruct claims of the miraculous.[39]

In the context of a hierarchic structure like the Catholic Church or in different hierarchic academic and scientific structures, miracles or anomalies are always ambiguous; they seem to signify something important, divine power or herald of a new paradigm. But they may also be perceived as problematic and treated with extreme caution and suspicion and sometimes placed under intellectual arrest and persecuted.

On the other hand, ordinary people, not wed to reductive ideologies or bullied by hierarchy, are more likely to respond with curiosity and wonder to the idea of miracles, which they may see as signs of something that might heal or save or transform their existence. Nobody would rave much about Clark Kent if he were just a reporter and a nice guy; the secret appeal is that behind the nice-guy façade is a hidden Superman. Heroic virtue by itself isn't enough for the fully active religious imagination; there is an attraction to the idea of enlightened beings who are endowed with extraordinary powers.

NOTES

1. For a basic account of Joseph's life and times, I have relied on Bernini's early *Vita* of Joseph (noted for its eyewitness testimony) and on the books of the preeminent twentieth-century scholar Gustavo Parisciani. For discussion of the documentation of Joseph's life and times, see the appendix.
2. Levack, 2013.
3. Trevor-Roper, 1968, p. 91.
4. Ennemoser, 1970, vol. 1, p. 225.
5. GP, p. 4.
6. GP, p. 13.
7. Mattelini, 2003, pp. 11–13.
8. Weinstein and Bell, 1982, pp. 19–47.
9. Ibid., p. 18.
10. Ellenberger, 1970, pp. 447–48, 672–73.
11. Chiappinelli, 2008, p. 39.
12. Pastrovicchi, 1980, p. 11.
13. References to sources for these and other extraordinary claims are provided in detail in chapters 2, 3, and 4.
14. DB, p. 143.

15. GP3, p. 12.
16. Parisciani, 1996, p. 27.
17. Chiappinelli, 2008, p. 71.
18. GP, 1996.
19. GP, p. 65.
20. Roma. Arch. Sant'Offizio, Decreta 1639.
21. GP, p. 68.
22. Lancaster, 2005, p.119.
23. GP3, 25.
24. Chiappinelli, 2008, p. 93.
25. See Parisciani, 1988.
26. GP3, p. 38.
27. DB, p. 113.
28. Evans-Wentz (1928). See chap. 3, pp. 75–79, for discussion.
29. See Barker, 1979.
30. DB, p. 124.
31 31. Ibid., p. 126.
32. Pastrovicchi, 1980, p. 107.
33. Testimony from Apostolic trials in Osimo, 13-XI-1688.
34. GP, 1996, p. 248.
35. All the subsequent quotes on Joseph's death are from GP3, pp. 57–63.
36. See Haynes, 1970.
37. Brown, 1981.
38. Lacarriere, 1963.
39. See Luzzato's discussion, 2003, pp.118–20.

Chapter 2

A New Force

> These experiments appear conclusively to establish the existence of a new force, in some unknown manner connected with the human organization, which for convenience may be called the Psychic Force.
>
> —Sir William Crookes (1871)

Having presented an outline of Joseph's life, I want next to review a spectrum of miscellaneous mind-body interactions before discussing his famous levitations. Levitation is bound to strike the unprepared reader as too bizarre to take seriously. Placed, however, in the context of a spectrum of interrelated mind-body phenomena, levitation, at first so incredible, might begin to appear more intelligible. In short, the purpose of this chapter is to put Joseph's strangest phenomenon in context.

Sir William Crookes (1832–1919), the Victorian physicist and chemist, was president of the Royal Society from 1913 to 1915; he invented the radiometer, discovered thallium, devised the Crookes tube, and had a gold-medal reputation as physicist and chemist. He also famously performed experiments with D. D. Home, a medium known for his extraordinary phenomena—including levitation.

A brief comparison with Joseph seems in order. D. D. Home is reported to have levitated out of a window several stories above ground and then back in through another window in the presence of Lord Dunraven and other English gentlemen. Frank Podmore, a credible skeptic, thought the stagy way Home's levitation was produced—the dim light and heightened expectation—*could* explain it as a group hallucination. The philosopher Stephen Braude wrote a more detailed and reliable account of Home's phenomena,[1] and, I should add, offers a crisp summary of Joseph's levitations, brushing aside as "glib" the attempt to play down the evidence.

Home and Joseph shared certain characteristics: deprived of normal family life, exposed to poverty, they found themselves at the mercy of the political and social powers around them, attracting but also repelling many important people. Robert Browning unfairly satirized Home in his poem "Mr. Sludge, the Medium." The provincial, Palamolla, falsely denounced Joseph to the Inquisition for posing as the messiah and abusing the credulity of the gullible.

Their gifts disrupted the society around them; people were fascinated and suspicious; they made loyal friends and nasty enemies. Browning's wife, the poet Elizabeth Barrett, embraced as authentic D. D. Home, as did a good part of European royalty. Like Joseph, Daniel worried about being spied on by secret agents who suspected him of political machinations; both had little control over their most dramatic gifts, being subject to the whims, or secret logic, of the subliminal mind.

The differences between the two were marked. Joseph spurned celebrity; Daniel exploited and made a living from his celebrity. Joseph was an obedient Catholic; Daniel flirted with Catholicism, but, preferring his picaresque lifestyle, was expelled from Rome by the Church. Joseph was an ascetic extremist; Daniel had a wife, children, refined tastes, and definite material needs. He was fond of jewelry and other gifts received from royal admirers; Joseph fell apart if someone gave him a pillow or new set of underwear. Finally, failing health diminished Daniel's powers, but Joseph's survived to the day of his death.[2] What they had in common was more important than their differences; both behaved in ways that seemed to defy the assumptions of mechanistic materialism.

The experiments Crookes performed with Home caused uneasiness among his scientific friends. Darwin wrote Sir Francis Galton in 1872: "Have you seen Mr. Crookes? I hope to heaven you have, as I for one should feel entire confidence in your conclusion."

In a letter to Lady Derby, Darwin wrote: "I cannot disbelieve Mr. Crookes's statements, nor can I believe his results."

Galton replied to Darwin that Crookes "was thoroughly scientific in his procedure . . . the affair is no matter of vulgar legerdemain."[3] Darwin, however, recoiled when confronted with an opportunity to witness a demonstration of physical mediumship. Darwin's cocreator of the theory of natural selection, Alfred Russell Wallace, *did* take the opportunity to witness the phenomena.

I want here to review various types of evidence for the "new force" that Crookes claimed to discover; the new force may be inferred in various ways. Levitation was one of the effects observed that led Crookes to claim its existence.[4] What kind of a force? The Latin etymon for the word *levitate* is *levis*, according to my Latin dictionary, meaning "light," as in light-armed; in movement, rapid, swift. The term also carries the sense of fickle, capricious, unstable. *Levis* is related to *levare*, which means "to make light" and therefore "to raise and lift up." It is a force that makes light and lifts up, and it does so in a sense that is both subjective and objective.

As the accounts of his life amply show, Joseph (in various ways) was devoted to "making light" of himself. Elements of levitation appear in more subtle psychological forms than the ostentatiously physical; for example, in the case of flying dreams. There is of course a controversial sense of this term, which refers to the movement or raising of physical objects in space, without recourse to any known physical force; sometimes the object is one's body, a form of endosomatic (in the body) psychokinesis (PK).

The concept of PK (literally "mind moving" or "mind changing") covers quite a bit of territory that ranges from the ordinary to the extraordinary. In my view, levitation is an extreme manifestation of something entirely normal and ordinary. A protean capacity, PK refers to any *direct* mental effect on physical events, living or nonliving. Defining it like this, we are forced to consider a curious implication. There is a very normal type of PK, according to this definition, which occurs whenever our minds affect our own bodies, as, for example, in the deliberate way I am typing the letters of these words on my computer keyboard. I decide I want to write a sentence; my thoughts, via the motor neurons of my brain, direct the muscles of my arms, hands, and fingers, and I watch my intentions materialize on the screen, word by word, phrase by phrase. Some researchers call this "endosomatic" PK; "exosomatic" PK would involve direct mental action on external bodies, as in a dice-throwing experiment or distant healing effect.[5]

We of course take for granted the common form of PK in which our thoughts and feelings affect our own bodies; we don't use the word *psychokinetic* to describe stirring a cup of coffee or pointing at the moon. On the other hand, some materialists do find problematic the idea that our minds can freely and selectively act upon our bodies.[6]

A problem with both forms of PK, according to the materialist, is how any mental event *not in space* could affect any physical object or event *in space* such as brain events or falling dice. On this point I agree with Hume; experience is the sole arbiter of what we judge to be "real," occurrent, or causally efficacious. There are no *a priori* limits on what can happen in nature; and anyway we all know from experience that there are connections between some of our thoughts and some of our bodily actions. I feel embarrassed, and I blush (involuntary); I resist my inclination to indulge and retract my hand from the cookie jar (voluntary). I am often variously inclined strongly to perform an action; but I know from experience that I can yield to or resist the inclination. So we have two forms of endosomatic PK, involuntary and voluntary, and sometimes a blend of the two. Ascetics and athletes, people given to extraordinary effort, or victims of psychosomatic disorders, know about endosomatic PK from experience.

The more unusual mind-body effects may be harder to accept as "real" because they are unusual, and because they occur in unaccustomed ways—for example, man flying. If our minds are inherently psychokinetic, we are probably "emitting" various kinds of influence all the time, on our own bodies and perhaps on other bodies, unconsciously, no doubt, and inconspicuously. So we seem to have two kinds of PK, the normally unobvious and the spectacular, and a great deal, I believe, that lies between.

In a sense, then, levitation is no more remarkable than the ability to twirl one's thumb; in both cases, some intangible mental agency within us directly causes bodies to move or otherwise change. The rareness and theatricality of levitation ought not to distract us from its humble roots in the mundane struggles and movements of everyday life. As we have defined the term, levitation would be a very extreme effect by comparison with ordinary voluntary movements, and so is bound to seem freakishly anomalous. I want now to suggest another sense in which levitation is closer to ordinary life than we might suspect.

FLYING DREAMS

Most of us are acquainted with the subjective sense of levitation through flying dreams. Although not common, most people will report occasionally having had such dreams. Flying dreams are dreams of levitation. Levitation of course is a physical event; a dream of flying is purely mental. But flying dreams are real experiences, even if they occur in a different kind of space than the shared 3-D space our public bodies occupy. According to dream researcher Robert Van de Castle,[7] flying dreams are associated with lucid dreams, and typically leave people feeling exhilarated.[8] I can personally testify to this from my own flying dreams, my favorite being a dream of myself mounted on my 1914 Haines virgin-silver soprano flute; in my dream I flew ecstatically into a clear blue open sky.

Medical anthropologist David Hufford studied a case in which Genevieve Foster had a flying dream that preceded a prolonged mystical experience in which "her world was flooded with light."[9] The juxtaposition of these experiences suggests their complementary nature, as if they were aspects of a single mode of being pressing to reveal itself.

In flying dreams we experience a subjective but intensely real sense of freedom from the usual constraints of gravity. The majority of people who have ecstatic experiences do not levitate, but ecstatic flying dreams, more common than levitation, *feel like* levitation. I am trying to show that what seems remote and bizarre may be more familiar and ordinary than we may at first suppose.

One way then to probe the mystery of Joseph's levitations may be by exploring certain facets of our dream life.[10] According to Kelly Bulkeley's study of dreams, there is a downward vertical spectrum that represents the dark side of gravity. This is the cause of those dreams we have of being heavy, blocked, paralyzed. Bulkeley thinks our struggles with the weight, mass, and constraints of physical existence cause many of our "bad dreams."

But there are also dreams that express the counter-gravitational impetus of the ascending spirit, the most prominent being the flying dream:

> At the upper end of the elemental axis are mystical dreams. Mystical dreams express the human capacity to envision a transcendental freedom from the oppressive limitations of gravity, entropy and death. These include flying dreams, which give the dreamer a vivid physiological experience of being liberated from the shackles of earthly existence.[11]

Nobody really knows for sure why we dream; we are entitled to speculate. If Bulkeley is on the right track, flying dreams may be thought of as anticipations of a higher mode of existence—pointers to a new stage of evolution on earth or pointers to life in a postmortem environment. If flying dreams are about achieving "unshackled existence," as Bulkeley suggests, they underscore what Joseph's levitations suggest: something within us can or wants to transcend our gravity-bound terrestrial existence.

Is there a practical link between flying dreams and levitation? In the case of Joseph, the levitations always emerged from an ecstatic state. Dreams and ecstasy, profoundly inward states of mind, seem to be the portals we have to enter if we hope for insight into the mystery of levitation. There seems to be a connection: The anomalous movements in the outer world of sense point toward realities of inner space; conversely, our inner levitations may point to a realm of outer space.

AN EXPERIMENT IN QUASI-LEVITATION

A partial answer to why I'm curious about levitation is that I once conducted an experiment in which I witnessed a quasi-case of it. It occurred during a class on personality development a colleague and I were teaching at New Jersey City University in the 1980s. In discussing shamanism and Eastern spiritual practice, we got around to discussing certain "damned" and "excluded" phenomena that intrigue psychical researchers and other academically independent thinkers.

We decided on one occasion to try an experiment, based on a game a student played when she was a girl. Breathing and humming in unison, four young girls each put two fingers under the knees and elbows of a fifth, sitting in a chair. Then they would hold their breath and then say in unison, "lift," and without effort, the fifth person would lift into the air by the mere touch of their fingers.

I suggested we perform a similar experiment. Four young ladies volunteered to participate, and a two-hundred-pound ex-marine offered up the solid mass of his body for the experiment. The ex-marine sat in a chair; the four young ladies assembled around him, touching him with their fingers under his elbows and knees. They took a deep breath in unison, repeating his name in unison, and after a while I said, "Lift!"

Much to everybody's astonishment, we observed the ex-marine lifted up as high as the ladies could reach with their outstretched, slender and unmuscular arms; from what I could see, they were not making any effort. I will never forget the startled but strangely thrilled look on the face of the man who was lifted up. There was also fear in his eyes. The experience lasted a few long seconds and down he came, quite gently. When I questioned them, the students confirmed my impression; no muscular effort was exerted to lift him; their fingers were in contact with his body, but that was all.

The man reported feeling very light and, as I said, seemed a bit shaken. I was never able to replicate this experiment. I believe the success was due to the particular group of students and the rapport we developed from meditating and chanting together for about ten weeks. My comment about this informal experiment: If a group of students could manage this little marvel, think what a seasoned religious community, under intense psychic pressure, might be able to accomplish.

SYNCHRONICITIES

Another common type of experience suggests the action, or at least the presence, of unknown mental influences. Carl Jung and Wolfgang Pauli thought that certain kinds of intensely meaningful coincidences can have power that C. G. Jung confusingly called *acausal*. It seems rather that with certain meaningful coincidences, a *different kind* of causation comes into play.

The term *coincidence* refers to the chance intersection of two or more events. All experience is "coincidental," wherever we are, and at every moment, things are changing and coinciding, juxtaposing, shifting into new patterns. Most of the time the changes and coincidings are so slight that we fail to notice them. But sometimes they come together in ways that suggest meaning, some bit of closure or revelation.

Jung tells of a patient who was describing a dream she had had about a golden scarab. Jung then heard something tapping on the window behind him; he opened the window and caught a golden beetle as it flew into the room. "Contrary to its usual habits," Jung remarks, the creature "had evidently felt an urge to get into a dark room at this particular moment."[12] Jung and his patient were astonished; the coincidental appearance of a golden beetle seemed freighted with meaning, and the strange manner of its arrival was uncanny.

Striking coincidences of this sort might *seem* to indicate a mysterious presence of mind shaping the course of events. In these occurrences, no ordinary forms of causal influence are involved, nothing, at any rate, mechanical. The agency we suppose may be at work appears to communicate meaning through symbols and archetypal imagery.

In Jung's case, the scarab was viewed as a symbol of immortality, and made a startling impression in the therapeutic context. In synchronicities, the causality is obscure, but the meaning is vividly felt. Meaningful coincidences are fairly common. Sometimes they throw a ray of mystery and enchantment into the mix of mundane existence.[13] They seem to hint of forces that secretly envelop and shape our existence. In the next type of mind-matter interaction, the effect is more defined, more blatantly puzzling.

PLACEBO EFFECT

Measurement in scientific method is good for detecting subtle effects, slight but significant deviations from chance. Use of placebo (chemically inert substances) is a procedure for producing therapeutic results by appealing to the eminently mental attitudes of hope, trust, and positive expectation. It has been demonstrated that *belief and confidence* in some supposed therapeutic procedure can *by themselves* have marked healing and therapeutic effects.[14]

"Belief," of course, was the cornerstone of Joseph's worldview; but with Joseph belief meant a highly charged, emotional trust, with complete openness to the idea of an active transcendent power. His consistent recommendation to anyone in distress was to remain *allegro*, in "high spirits," and trust completely in that transcendent power of the Madonna.

Perhaps the most spectacular case of the so-called placebo effect involved a man dying of cancer who came to believe in a new experimental drug, Krebiozen. A pseudonymous Mr. Wright of the mid-fifties was dying of cancer of the lymph modes, his neck bulging with orange-sized tumors. Wright begged his doctor, Philip West, to try the new drug on him.

After taking it, the "tumor masses melted away like snowballs on a hot stove," and the patient was discharged from the hospital ten days later. Later,

Mr. Wright read a report declaring the medicine was ineffective. In two months all the symptoms of cancer returned. Doctor West, deciding to improvise, persuaded the patient that the newspapers were wrong and that his relapse was due to inadequate dosage.

Wright recaptured his hope and enthusiasm, and West this time injected him with distilled water, telling him it was the proper dosage, noting that the patient was "ecstatic" in his expectation to be healed. Mr. Wright was convinced he was ingesting a miracle drug and again the symptoms of cancer disappeared, and again he was described as "the picture of health."

And so he remained until he read an announcement from the American Medical Association: "Nationwide tests show Krebiozen to be a worthless drug for the treatment of cancer."[15] In a matter of days, Mr. Wright was a dead man. This is a remarkable story that proves the amazing self-healing—and self-destructive—potential of the human mind. We should note that the speed of the healing matches the reported healing speed in the Joseph stories. The intangible living belief, as long as it lasted, appeared to have had a miraculous effect on Wright's body. Ironically, the AMA's pronouncement is what killed him.

As we'll see in chapter 4, when people were "treated" with an object they believed had been touched by Joseph, some were said to have been immediately healed or even brought back from the brink of death. The modern case of Mr. Wright (one of many) shows how we have underrated the healing power of the human mind and is consistent with "miracle" healing stories in the seventeenth century. The story of Mr. Wright reminds me of Joseph's reported healings, where the belief was strong and the healing sudden and complete.

Placebos—chemically inert belief-inducers—are as effective as antidepression drugs.[16] The belief that one is going to be lifted from depression can be as effective as ingesting a drug designed for that purpose. One wonders if depressed people stay depressed because they can't imagine anything that *could* raise their spirits. Is depression an illness of the imagination, an impoverished sense of possibilities?

INTERLUDE OF HYPNOSIS

In a spectrum of interactions, hypnotic suggestion can also work "miracles," a word you might use to describe A. A. Mason's famous cure of a victim of ichthyosis (fish-skin disease) in which the afflicted is covered from head to toe with hard, black, fishlike scales, a rare genetic condition.[17] Mason's hypnotic treatment (gestures and verbal suggestions) reversed the effects of this *congenital* disease. Again, we are talking about a man making mental suggestions to another man suffering from a genetic mishap of hideous consequence, and over a period of time almost completely reversing the disease. This seems to me as shocking as levitation. What is more unlikely *prima facie*? That something purely mental could warp gravity or that something purely mental could reverse a genetically caused disease? Both are surprising, unexpected, and call for more thoughtful research.

SPORT, BALLET, AND PSYCHOKINESIS

In sport, athletes push against their physical limits and once in a while break into transcendent performance, as described in Rhea White's and Michael Murphy's *The Psychic Side of Sports*.[18] Is there a link between sport and saintliness? Joseph was an extreme ascetic. According to the Greek lexicon, the word *ascetic* is from *askesis*, meaning "exercise, training, esp. of the life and habits of an athlete." Ascetic mystics, like athletes, exercise and train their minds and bodies, mystics in order to achieve union with ultimate reality, athletes to excel in sport and be canonized in the Hall of Fame.

Rhea White and Michael Murphy argue that like mystics, yogis, and shamans, athletes experience extraordinary states that exceed the limits of ordinary life. In every human capacity we find a spectrum of performance, from the highest to the less striking and more common. Cases from different sports—martial arts, baseball, sailing, mountain climbing, and so on—report sensations of detachment and acute well-being; of floating, flying, weightlessness, freedom, power; of peace, calm, and immortality. The experiences occur suddenly, usually briefly.

People have observed great dancers linger in the air in a way said to be dreamlike or bordering on levitation. Nijinsky was well known for this. According to Nandor Fodor, Romola Nijinsky said of her deceased husband:

> I often asked him how he managed to stay up in the air. He never could understand why we could not do it. He just took a leap, held his breath, and stayed up. He felt supported in the air. Moreover, he could control his descent, or could come down slower or quicker as he wished.... When once, in admiration, I told him what a pity it was that he could not see himself; he answered in all seriousness: "But I do. I always see myself. I am detached. I am outside. I make myself dance from the outside."[19]

Two things to note here: the first is the role of breath control, similar to Yogananda's claim that levitation is possible through *pranayama*;[20] the second is reminiscent of Joseph, for Nijinsky seems to have been ecstatically beside himself when he danced. More recently it was written of another dancer, Mikhail Baryshnikov: "The most exquisitely chilling weapon in the arsenal of this complete dancer was his *ballon*, his ability to ascend in the air and stay there, defying gravity, especially in the double *tour en l'air*, in which the male dancer revolves two full turns before landing."[21]

White and Murphy document types of experience in which individuals exert themselves against tremendous obstacles, not unlike those hardy athletes of consciousness we call mystics.

One story of a long-distance run suggests a resemblance to ascetic life. Bill Emmerton had run six hundred miles to Land's End through snow, rain, and fierce winds blowing from the North Sea, and was exhausted. "Then, all of a sudden," he said, "I had this *light* feeling, I felt as though I was going through space, treading on clouds." Emmerton, like others in similar circumstances, described becoming conscious of a warm, helping presence: "I didn't know what it was, but I heard a voice saying, 'We're here to help you,'" after which he communed with what seemed like his ancestral spirits.

The authors of this unusual book make an important observation I will take up in detail later. They point out that some sports "seem to draw back a curtain that ordinarily screens out all intimations of immortality, thus revealing a reality that has been there, unguessed, all the time."[22]

A greater psychospiritual reality permeates and encompasses us, or so it sometimes seems. But except for rare moments when the right conditions are in place, the presence of this reality eludes us. Joseph, like Emmerton the long-distance runner and indeed all athletes who push against the limits, needed to exhaust his sense of "self" before opening to the available possibilities. Michael Murphy has collected accounts of what he calls "ecstatic walking," which points to another stage on the spectrum we are sketching. Finally, for accounts of being pushed to the edge where breaking beyond one's limits becomes possible, have a look at the intriguing study by John Geiger.[23]

EFFECTS DISTURBING AND NEGATIVE

We are glancing (by way of prelude) at documented examples of mind acting in unexpected ways on matter. Sometimes an extended influence can be cruel and destructive. Here are two examples related to childbirth. One is technically called *pseudocyesis* and refers to women who falsely believe they are pregnant and exhibit specific physiological symptoms of pregnancy, sometimes deceiving trained physicians.

The symptoms are gradual abdominal swelling that mimics the tempo of real pregnancy, disruptions of normal menstrual flow, impressions of fetal movement that others can detect, nausea, and other physical symptoms. In a review of this material, psychologist Emily Kelly reminds us that scientists have no idea "how the specific idea of pregnancy can trigger the specific physiological systems necessary to produce the symptoms."[24] What strange abilities the human mind possesses to reshape reality.

Take another example, also related to childbirth. An unsettling mystery of psychophysical influence concerns *maternal impressions*. A pregnant woman, usually during the first trimester, sees something that impacts her with intense emotion—an infant in some way maimed—with the result that the traumatic image is *physically* impressed on the embryo and the baby is born mutilated in ways that correspond to what the mother saw during pregnancy. But there are no neural connections between mother and fetus. Even if there were, there would be no physical explanation of how a specifically idiosyncratic image in the mother's mind could reproduce itself in the body of her newborn.

The phenomenon has a history of instructive controversy, and shows how the belief that something is impossible can prevent professionals from noticing it, or from taking it seriously, despite its scientific importance. The American psychiatrist Ian Stevenson published a review of fifty cases of maternal impressions that are difficult to dismiss as merely coincidental.[25]

A few grisly examples will suffice. One pregnant mother saw a child who was born with a missing left hand and wrist. Her child was born with a missing left hand and forearm. In another case, a pregnant woman saw a person who visited her frequently with a deformed left index finger that resembled a lion's claw. The unfortunate woman gave birth to a child with a deformed left index finger whose nail appeared clawlike.

However surprising this is, responsible physicians find an unexplained mental influence at work here. The cases that exist—the precision of correspondence between what the subject sees and how the offspring is deformed—force us to add maternal impressions to our list of perplexing mind-matter interactions.

With regard to the reported flights of the friar, we reduce cognitive dissonance by showing there is a spectrum of interrelated mind-body effects, ranging from normal volitional effects to decidedly abnormal maternal impressions, on into the realm of poltergeists or perhaps the odor of sanctity and thus by degrees leading us to confront outré levitation.

Some of the puzzling effects are intelligible: somebody's hair suddenly turns white after a shocking event; or a person dies soon after his or her spouse dies. Some people seem able to postpone the time of their death until a certain anniversary, birthday, or other important and meaningful event. Occasionally they die at a symbolically satisfying time, as Thomas Jefferson and John Adams apparently did when they both expired on July 4, fifty years to the day after they signed the Declaration of Independence.

Belief can work negatively as well as positively, as we saw in the case of Mr. Wright and his suicidal disbelief in Krebiozen. An aborigine who believes "the bone has been pointed at him" may die in perfect health unless some protective counter-belief takes hold of his easily spellbound mind.[26] The physician J. C. Barker, in his disturbing study *Scared to Death* (1968), enumerates case histories of individuals in fine fettle who died because they became convinced they were going to die: caused by a supposed curse, a broken taboo, or a fortune-teller's prediction.

In a written report, a nurse told me of the strange way her husband met his end. Once when he was a teenager at a carnival he sat down with an old fortune-teller. She gazed at his palm and said, "You are going to have a wonderful life," but after a pause, added, "but you will die at the age of thirty-five." He pushed what she said out of his mind at first, but as he approached his thirty-fifth birthday he grew unaccountably ill, and on the day of his birthday, he died. The coroner could not identify the cause of death—a frightening illustration of the power of "auto-suggestion."

Barker's book is full of unsettling tales of death by autosuggestion. Could the belief that you are going to die—due to a hex pronounced by a sorcerer—cause you to die? Cannon's classic paper (1942) on "voodoo" death explained how one's vital organs can shut down and result in death from the sheer power of expectation. Cases of "hex death" have been reported in Zaire and elsewhere well into the twentieth century. To self-destruct physically by means of our own mental powers is a form of endosomatic PK.

Although the diagnostic use of the concept of hysteria is nowadays clouded by controversy, it is still used to refer to symptoms of blindness, paralysis, anesthesia, amnesia, and aphasia that cannot be explained neurologically or organically. Recent attempts to understand hysteria have not been successful, despite the new brain-scanning technologies. Hysterical symptoms appear and disappear in accord with purely psychological variables and not in accord with neurophysiology. The symptoms of hysteria occur in the complete absence of any physical pathology.

Another puzzling interaction is as follows. Persons who display multiple personality or "dissociative identity disorder" show that different "alters" have different physiological signatures. A new personality seems to crystallize with new physiological characteristics. For example, alter 1 may be allergic to wheat, but not alter 2 or 3. Handedness sometimes changes, and in fact studies indicate that alters exhibit altered sensory and organic responses to stimuli.[27]

New personalities emerge with their own physiological signature, a sign of the plasticity of the psychophysical organism. Scholar Frederic Myers saw the human personality as naturally "multiplex," with hidden selves ("chains of memory" he said), poised to come to life and manifest under favorable conditions. We should, Myers urged, creatively exploit our multiplicity; aim to dissociate from the inferior versions of oneself and refashion a higher synthesis. In a Romantic conceit, Myers, like Keats, viewed his "self" as if it were a poem that could be revised and perfected.[28]

POLTERGEISTS

The next class of spontaneous effects is odder and more blatant than the previous. Thurston said that poltergeists, like levitation, involve *some form* of PK, quoting the physicist Sir William Barrett, one of the founders of psychical research:

> The movement of objects (referring to poltergeists) is usually quite unlike that due to gravitational or other attraction. They slide about, rise in the air, move in eccentric paths, sometimes in a leisurely manner, often turn round in their career, and usually descend quietly, without hurting the observers. At other times an immense weight is lifted, often in daylight . . . crockery is thrown about and broken, bedclothes are dragged off, the occupants sometimes lifted gently to the ground.[29]

Poltergeists generally seem to be guided by a whimsical but not a darkly destructive intelligence. *Poltergeist* is a German word that means "noisy, disturbing spirit," and the poltergeist is a global phenomenon. In cultures that believe in spirits, the unexplained movements of objects are interpreted as mischief made by prankster spirits. The modern view, based on field research and careful analysis, suggests that most but not all of the time the spooky irregularities are psychokinetic projections of emotionally disturbed adolescents.[30]

It might have helped the zealous demonologists of old if they had known that such effects were no more than the objectified psychic energies of people in emotional turmoil.[31] The antics of the poltergeist show how PK differs from mechanical movements; the poltergeist displays an expressive dynamic, an emotional, symbolic intelligence at work.

In Bavaria, in 1967, Hans Bender documented a poltergeist case. The scene was a lawyer's office in the town of Rosenheim where in late November of that year something brazenly surreal invaded the everyday work world. The physical machinery of the office was disrupted: light bulbs exploded, neon ceiling lamps went on and off; caught on camera, overhead lamps swayed violently to and fro. Light fixtures unscrewed themselves from sockets and fuses blew. Sharp noises came from nowhere and copying machines broke down.

Something kept dialing the phone number requesting the time, sometimes at a rate of six times a second. Work at the office became impossible and the call went out for help. Engineers from the phone company and physicists from the Max Planck Institute came on the scene, as did Bender, a parapsychologist from the Freiburg Institute.

After a thorough investigation, it was concluded that a nineteen-year-old employee, Annemarie S., was subconsciously causing the disturbances.

Events occurred only when Annemarie was present; bulbs exploded and fell *toward her*. The effects seemed weaker as distance between Annemarie and the objects increased.

Physicists from the Max Planck Institute, F. Karger and G. Zicha, concluded that the phenomena defied physical explanation and were "performed by intelligently controlled forces (e.g., the telephone incidents) with a tendency to evade investigation." The agent, Annemarie, became agitated after the investigation and the phenomena intensified; she had a breakdown and was forced to take a leave of absence.[32]

Like most cases of levitation, poltergeist outbreaks are involuntary. But in a British report, a young man, Matthew Manning, learned how to gain control of the force that was producing the anomalous effects. Unlike Annemarie, he taught himself to sublimate the "force" into more productive outlets like automatic writing and automatic drawing, and as long as he wrote and drew, the externalized havoc ceased. Like Joseph of Copertino, Matthew Manning displayed a variety of talents, and consciously sought to train and to some degree control them; and, fortunately, reliable observers were available to record his phenomena.[33] Now look at a phenomenon similar to poltergeists.

TELEKINETIC ENUNCIATIONS OF DEATH

Liminality is the mother of strange mind-matter manifestations. Ernesto Bozzano collected cases involving unexplained physical phenomena that occur at the moment of death: paintings or photographs that fall inexplicably off walls, clocks that stop at the exact time of their owner's death, mirrors that break, bells that ring, pianos that play by themselves, flowers that wilt or bloom without known cause.[34] The reported coincidental signals of distant death vary.

Although infrequently observed, the phenomenon is worldwide. The stunning correspondences are what F. W. H. Myers called "enunciative." How to make sense of these parting gestures that Bozzano describes? Minimally, they qualify as "meaningful coincidences." In the act of being severed from life, as so many case histories in Bozzano's collection illustrate, a force seems to imprint parting farewells on the material world of the living. The significance of this is ambiguous. Is it a last convulsive "farewell forever!"? Or a signal of transcendence, a drum roll before passing into the next dimension?

MAKING PK HAPPEN

Some people, it is believed, can consciously exploit their latent "psychic force": yogis, shamans, magicians, and mystics, for example. The Gospels

(Matt. 8: 23–27) say that Jesus calmed a storm at sea, an impressive psychokinetic performance, if it were true. There are contemporary reports of shamans commanding the elements. John Neihardt in 1972 claims he witnessed Black Elk conjure rain from a cloudless afternoon sky "during a season of drought, one of the worst in the memory of the old men."

Anthropologist David Barker was in Dharamsala, India, on March 10, 1973, when he observed a Tibetan priest-shaman, Gunsang Rinzing, stop a rainstorm to permit a festival of mourning. The shaman had built a large fire and for twenty hours recited mantras with intense concentration. Barker writes: "The rain had diminished to a drizzle, and by 10 o'clock it had become only a cold fog over a circle with a radius of about 150 meters. Everywhere else in the area it continued to pour, but the crowd of six thousand refugees was never rained on." Barker observed that the atmosphere had an "airless" quality and reports feeling disoriented for weeks after the experience.[35]

There are several fantastic tales of weather magic in the lore of Joseph but none that I found were backed by satisfactory testimony. Nevertheless, modern accounts such as the one just cited should serve to keep our minds open to the possibility.

We find an experimental attitude in some traditions: yogis of the school of Patanjali, for example, and many Christian mystics. Patanjali's yoga sutras discuss at length the *siddhis* or "attainments." Catholic mystics may be recipients of *charisms* or "gifts" from God. Slightly different metaphors are used: *siddhi* suggests one can play an active role in attaining the effect; *charism* (gift) stresses the need for the right kind of receptivity.

As stated in Patanjali's sutras, if the yogi puts all his attention on something light like a cotton ball or a feather, and becomes so absorbed in the object of his meditation that he forgets himself, he will become physically light and thus might levitate. This resembles the practice of Joseph, absorbed in his thoughts about heaven, ecstatic and self-forgetting. According to the sutras, the main practice for achieving *any* siddhi or "attainment" is simple in concept. It is expressed by the term *samyama: sam*, an intensifier, and *yama*, "restraint, inhibition." The method consists in holding one's attention on the goal to be achieved until the sense of effort and self-awareness fade away. In such states of self-oblivion, the siddhis or extensions of capacity are said to manifest.

Here are two reports of unusual attainments produced by modern yogis. The first is from a publication in the *American Heart Journal*.[36] In the experiment, a yogi was buried in a very tight underground pit for eight days, connected to an EKG. Once the pit was closed up, the yogi's heart began to beat very rapidly (250 beats per minute). The tachycardia went on for twenty-nine hours and then quite suddenly the EKG tracing flat-lined. Witnesses thought the yogi had died and wanted to stop the experiment.

The yogi's attendant assured the scientists it would be all right, and the flat-line continued for five days until just before the experiment was supposed to end. The tachycardia started up again and persisted for two hours, after which the yogi returned to his normal heartbeat and was taken out of the pit. It was determined that there was no manipulation or breakage of equipment. The scientists who conducted the experiment were unable to account for the EKG results. It was difficult to believe that the yogi voluntarily stopped his heart for five days *and did not die.* The ability to flat-line one's heart for so long, then revive and walk away, admittedly sounds incredible. Incredible—but it may also be true, unless the experiment be proved a fake.

INEDIA

Inedia, living without eating or drinking, is a feat often reported of Christian mystics. Prahlad Jani claims to have lived without food or water since 1940. At the age of eight he saw a vision of the Hindu goddess Amba, who touched his tongue, whereupon he states that he ceased to need, or want, to eat or drink. He claims to be nourished by sun and air and drops of nectar received directly from the goddess Amba. Living as a hermit in a rainforest cave near the Gujarat temple in Ambaji, he wakes at four in the morning and begins his daily meditation.

To test his claims, the eminent neurologist Sudhir Shah and thirty-five other scientists from the Indian Defense Institute and the Sterling Hospital in Ahmadabad, India, conducted controlled experiments with Jani in 2003 and again in 2010. They kept him under surveillance in a sealed room continuously, once for ten days and once for fifteen days, using closed-circuit TV cameras, blocking the toilet, plying him with a battery of physiological tests. They videotaped him whenever he moved from his room to do some test. Jani was provided one hundred milliliters of water to use as a mouthwash, which was measured after he spat it out to make sure that he drank none of the water.

The Ahmadabad Association of Physicians issued a statement that no water entered his body for the period of the experiment; however, some urine did form in his bladder but was reabsorbed by the bladder walls. In both tests, they concluded there was no evidence that he ate, drank, or eliminated. All the medical tests performed produced results within the range of normality. The experiment was conducted in hopes of learning how to help military personnel and astronauts in critical circumstances; no specific mechanisms explaining the inedia were found.

Physicians and the press who took no part of these experiments reacted with simple disbelief; in their view of the world, Jani's reputed inedia was impossible, and therefore the experimenters had to be making the story up. They also asserted that Jani's disciples were somehow providing the eighty-year-old hermit with food and drink. This was pure speculation. It is of course impossible to certify that Jani had not eaten or drunk anything for seven decades; but results of the tests of 2003 and 2010 remain unexplained. Jani's inedia is another part of a spectrum of physical phenomena, at the far end of which are Joseph's levitations.[37]

MATERIALIZATION

If what we are calling the "new force" exists, it might produce effects that come under the heading of materialization. This is perhaps the most counterintuitive of reported phenomena; indications that the mind can transform itself into material manifestations. For example, some people are said to impress their mental images directly onto light-sensitive film.

The phenomenon in which "some unknown cause has produced a material, chemical change in the substance of the film" has been around since the invention of the daguerreotype in 1849. For an early history that details the failed court trials of the photographer Mumler, who was accused but acquitted of fraud in this regard, see *Photographing the Invisible* (Coates, 1973). More recently, the psychoanalyst Jule Eisenbud took extraordinary pains to rule out fraud with his star subject who "worked with more than three dozen scientifically trained observers—physicians, physicists, physiologists, engineers, and others—under a variety of conditions. During this period (1964–1967) over 400 normally inexplicable images on over 100 different themes were obtained."[38]

The importance of Eisenbud's work, besides the precautions he took against fraud, lay in the careful effort to rule out virtually any conceivable form of energy transfer in producing the effects of psychic photography. Crookes's new force might apply to photography as much as to levitation; the force in question seems capable of modifying gravitation *and* light.

Eisenbud's subject, Ted Serios, a Chicago bellhop, was apparently able to project mental images directly onto Polaroid film. One wonders if this ability is related to the effects of maternal impressions discussed above. The description of the physiological state of Ted Serios that preceded the production of his phenomena is worth noting:

> When about to shoot, he seemed rapidly to go into an intense state of concentration, with eyes open, lips compressed, and a quite noticeable tension in his muscular system. His limbs would tend to shake somewhat, as if with a slight palsy, and the foot of his crossed leg would sometimes start to jerk up and down a bit convulsively. His face would become suffused and blotchy, the veins standing out on his forehead, his eyes visibly bloodshot.[39]

This is reminiscent of Joseph struggling with the onset of ecstasy, resisting what seems from all the descriptions like a great force. Both men were given to altered states, Ted Serios relying upon alcohol. The saintly monk and the drunken bellhop, the one acting upon gravity, the other upon light, appear to have drawn on an unknown force, each understanding it in their own way.

There are other, more traditional accounts of materialization. One thinks of stories of the multiplication of loaves and fishes or perhaps of the claimed first miracle of Jesus at a marriage banquet in Cana of Galilee (John 2, 1–11) where scripture says he turned water into wine. Thurston provides eyewitness accounts as late as the nineteenth century of saints multiplying grain and other foods in circumstances of inadequate supplies for the needy.[40]

Of special interest are the detailed records of several materializing mediums.[41] Marthe Beraud, known as "Eva C.," a physical medium of saintly patience, was sponsored, cared for, and studied by Madam Bisson, artist and psychic investigator. Eva's chief investigator, however, was the systematic Baron von Schrenck-Notzing, who spent four years, sometimes working with Nobel Prize–winning physiologist Charles Richet as well as with other scientists of the day, photographing Eva C. extrude from her body a malleable white substance he called *teleplasm*, named *ectoplasm* by Richet. There are hundreds of photographs of gobs, strands, and clouds of the Baron's teleplasm that turn, stage by visible stage, into features of a face, hand, or whole figure.

Figures of women and men appear in these flat materialized forms that researchers photographed, forms that look like fake two-dimensional cartoons. Eva C. is supposed to have materialized these curious artworks for brief periods of time—long enough to be photographed—before they retracted from the visible plane.

Were they produced fraudulently? The medium had to submit to Schrenck-Notzing's (or Mme. Bisson's) internal body searches before every experiment; he exercised complete control over her person during the experiments. Nothing suspect was ever detected. The photographs reveal a variety of effects in different stages of apparent materialization.

This performance *could only be faked* through collaboration of the investigators; the medium alone could not have put on such a show, having neither the means nor the knowledge. Charles Richet and Gustave Geley independently investigated Eva; she produced similar manifestations for them, so the Nobel Prize winner would also have been in on the trick. All the scientists would have had to be in on the game. Schrenck-Notzing's work with Marthe Beraud drew much frenetic criticism. The historian Andreas Somer has detailed the career of this remarkable pioneer of two tabooed domains of research—sexology and the physical phenomena of mediumship.[42]

The gifts of the Icelandic medium Indridi Indridason (1883–1912) surfaced in 1905 and continued to manifest until 1909, a brief career but one crammed with many unexplained phenomena: odor and light, singing voices and musical instruments playing themselves, materializations of different degrees, levitation of objects including the medium's body, and so forth.

The uneducated Indridason produced these effects under controlled conditions. Unfortunately, his career was cut short; he contracted typhoid and died at the age of twenty-nine. Like Joseph, he was entranced when phenomena occurred; he believed they were the work of spirits that he saw around him. He quickly became a celebrity in Iceland; many of course simply "knew" his feats were impossible and heaped scorn and derision on him.[43]

When Indridi was invited to join a table-tilting experiment, the table immediately shook vehemently. His séances were transformed into a public, interactive theater; nevertheless, the researchers resolved not to be imposed upon. The open space where Indridason performed was isolated from everybody outside by a finely woven net no hand could penetrate. The entire building was scanned for suspicious materials and the medium was undressed and examined before and after every séance.

Many of his most extraordinary phenomena occurred spontaneously in unexpected venues. Like Joseph's, Indridi's gifts were irrepressible. And like Joseph, he learned to channel the form of his phenomena in accordance with what he was taught from *his* spiritualist tradition. The Icelandic investigators claimed that Indridason learned to obtain results in every category in which they set out to instruct him. The cultural worlds of seventeenth-century baroque Catholicism and the Icelandic spiritualism of the early twentieth century differ sharply; still, Joseph and Indridi saw visions, went into trances, believed in spirits, produced strange fragrances—and both were seen to levitate.

The reports describe the levitation of various objects and of Indridason's body. In Kvaran's account of Indridason's alleged first levitation beginning in a darkened space, someone observed the medium's head resting on the edge of a table, then someone saw his feet resting on another table. A match was lit "and we all saw him in this position, with nothing else holding him off the floor."[44]

In another, rather clever, example, a large number of sitters placed the medium in a special basket chair whose slightest movement emitted audible creaks; they moved their chairs and surrounded the medium in such a way that he could not physically move outside the circle. They put out the light. Professor Nielsson, the chief watchman of the proceedings, later wrote:

> Very soon the medium was levitated in the basket chair at a great distance from the floor—the creaking in the chair being heard while it glided . . . *above our*

heads—and was eventually rather noisily deposited on the floor behind the chairs. Then the light was immediately lit and there sat the medium unconscious (in a deep trance) in the chair.[45]

In 1905, when Indridason first learned how to do automatic writing, he fell into a trance and seemed frightened by shadowy presences. He screamed at spirits that wanted to impose their will on him. These "spirits"—forces of Indridason's unconscious?—prompted poltergeist phenomena and powerful levitation effects during the winter of 1907. These began to occur in the bedrooms of what the researchers called the Experimental House. The events were so disruptive and invasive that the public séances were halted. The young medium was terrified when a force began to pull his bed around. He called for the company and protection of the researchers. Those who tried to help Indridi became the target of poltergeist blows, and objects were thrown at them, but most swerved, nearly missed, and were shattered.

Finally, Thorlaksson and Oddgeirsson were called to help the medium. Thorlaksson wrote of this event:

> Then Indridi screams for help once more. I run into the bedroom. But then I see a picture that I shall never forget. Indridi is lying in the air in a horizontal position, at about the height of my chest, and swaying there to and fro, with his feet pointing toward the window, and it seems to me that the invisible power that is holding him in the air is trying to swing him out of the window. I don't hesitate for a moment, but grab the medium, and push him down on the bed and hold him there. But then I notice that both of us are being lifted up. I scream to Thordur Oddgeirsson and ask him to come and help.[46]

Once again we think of Crookes's claim of a new force; whatever it is, and whatever terminology is used to describe it, a significant body of observation points to its existence. In the above, the reader should notice the investigator Thorlaksson, in trying to control the medium's levitation, says that "both of us are being lifted up." As we'll see, Joseph on several occasions was witnessed lifting other people up. And for further comparison, I would note that the reported "poltergeist" attacks on Indridason correspond to the alleged diabolic attacks on Joseph. The "force" has a dark, contrarian side, difficult to explain. One never quite knows when it will decide to go on the attack.

PSYCHOKINESIS IN MORE CONTROLLED SETTINGS

Moving from the wild world of Icelandic mediumship, we should cite a few experimental PK studies.[47] The effects we find are mostly small and seemingly trivial, but their significance may be greater than we suspect. In one kind of experiment, the target is inanimate, like tumbling dice; J. B. Rhine's dice-throwing experiments are landmarks in the field. Another high point would be H. Schmidt's (1974) PK research with random event generators where agents try to influence microphysical targets.

According to Dean Radin, a meta-analysis of dice-throwing experiments—covering a mass of studies—reveals a positive effect, small, but with a probability astronomically against chance. Radin reviewed more recent types of PK experiments where the agent tries to mentally influence automated, quantum-driven target systems. Helmut Schmidt designed a target system for PK experiments using the random decay of beta particles. Once again, a small but definitely real effect displays itself; it is "a widespread ability distributed throughout the population," according to Radin.[48]

Could such small deviations amount to anything of practical interest? With Joseph in mind, one wonders whether the small, diffuse effect that Radin infers from the experimental data may become concentrated and intensely directed in some special cases, so that an effect normally inconspicuous or masquerading as a coincidence might from time to time reach a crescendo and localize so that a poltergeist, a physical healing, or a case of levitation becomes evident.

The PK force we are discussing may be amplified in special group settings. Kenneth Batcheldor (1984) conducted group studies demonstrating this. In group settings, individuals are freed from so-called "ownership inhibition." The slightest doubt or hesitation, Batcheldor found, would inhibit the desired effect. It may exasperate rationalists to say this, but firmly held beliefs, even absurd ones, might facilitate the attainment of one's goals, *even goals that at first seem impossible*. In Batcheldor's experiments, the challenge was to forge on the spot the attitude of unwavering confidence that one could succeed in the PK task.

This will seem to many of us like a difficult task. It will seem especially impossible to anyone with a rigid cast of mind. Perhaps a new kind of agility in the way we hold our beliefs is called for, if we hope to advance the study of these subtle mental abilities. Common sense suggests that some beliefs should be held lightly or firmly, depending on the context. But there might be special contexts where we decide to maintain a belief in something seemingly impossible, and toward that end inhabit a role as an actor inhabits a character for an evening's performance.

Radin meta-analyzed an extensive database of random number generator (RNG) studies produced at Princeton University over a period of years. Again "the effects were small but consistent across individual trials, and across different people." Findings in the Princeton database suggest a simple way to magnify the PK factor. There seems to be an additive effect when two or more come together before a random event generator. "The effect size was more than four times that of individuals," observes Radin.

This is similar to Batcheldor's findings that a well-formed group working harmoniously, without ownership inhibition, magnified the intensity of the psychokinetic effects. Similarly, Joseph, and other levitators in his tradition, operated in a cohesive religio-social network, with a common belief-system and shared emotional lability. They were not bothered by ownership inhibition. They assumed without question there were powers beyond themselves that could do extraordinary things—God, the Madonna, a calendar of versatile saints.

Batcheldor instructed his group to maintain an absolutely confident expectation of success. The smallest flicker of doubt would ruin the process. A Canadian group, drawing on Batcheldor's ideas, performed an experiment in which they tried to psychically create a ghost.[49] They came short of that specific aim, but the group did produce interesting effects: "What are we entitled to claim concerning the Philip experiment?" asked the authors:

> We feel we have proved that the collective thought of a group of people can produce physical effects that are expressed either in the form of noise (the raps) or in movements (of the table). We have proved that group telepathy exists, and that it can be directed via this force to poltergeist outbreaks. We believe that we are only a step away from producing a ghost, hallucination, or apparition.[50]

The shared story, quasi-ritual setting, and unwavering confidence and expectation of success suggest how religious movements may start; especially if they are accompanied by unusual phenomena, real or imagined. The phenomena are perceived as confirmation of the truth of their beliefs. And of course Joseph was very much an expression of the group dynamic he inherited. The link between how he felt for a whole array of sacred symbols and his ecstasies was pivotal. Cases then run from a thread of PK capacity in the general population to the dramatically expressive, sometimes seemingly miraculous, effects produced by mystics, shamans, and yogis.

LEVITATING AROUND RELIGIOUS HISTORY

Levitation—the event, if it occurs—is undoubtedly rare. Yet we find references to it in diverse traditions.[51] The prophet Ezekiel (8:3) reports: "He put forth the form of a hand, and took me by a lock of my head; and the Spirit lifted me up between the earth and the heaven." That sounds like a description of levitation. And, of course, famously, Jesus is said to have walked on water and even imparted the power to Peter briefly. Unfortunately, Peter lost his *pistis* (trust) and had to be rescued as he began to sink (Matt. 21: 25–31). And we are told by Luke in the last words of his edition of the Good News: "Then he took them out in the outskirts of Bethany, and raising his hands, he blessed them. Now as he blessed them, he withdrew from them and was carried up to heaven."

The Ascension, the cornerstone of Christian belief, would be a very spectacular example of levitation, to Christians for sure, the most important in human history. Christians today might see in Joseph proof that ascension to the heavenly realms might be more than magnificent metaphor. The vision of divine flight, of radical transcendence, is universal. Accounts of levitation are found in Asian religions. The modern Indian sage Yogananda wrote a chapter titled "The Levitating Saint" in his autobiography. A disciple states that he witnessed a yogi, Nagendra Bhaduri, levitate before his eyes. Yogananda accepts the word of his disciple as true, holding that Bhaduri's experience can be explained by his mastery of pranayama, a refined technique of breath control. In a long footnote, the well-informed Yogananda summarizes the story of Joseph's phenomena, and remarks: "St. Joseph exhibited a worldly absentmindedness that was really a divine recollectedness."[52]

Here is a more suggestive story. In Rechung's biography of the Tibetan yogi Milarepa, we read: "Having obtained transcendental knowledge in the control of the ethereal and spiritual nature of the mind, he was enabled to furnish demonstration thereof by flying through the sky, by walking, resting, and sleeping in the air."

Sleeping in a levitated state sounds like a tall tale, but Joseph is sometimes described as being "out of his senses," in a state like sleeping. Also similar to Joseph's practices are the solitude, heroic asceticism, and constant meditation. Milarepa recounts a period of his life in which he studied sorcery with a master of the black arts in order to exact vengeance on the men who hurt his mother and robbed him of his patrimony.

He raised a hailstorm that destroyed the house of his enemies, killing thirty-five people; at further insistence from his mother, Milarepa tells how by sorcery—it took him two weeks of chanting—he raised deadly hailstorms that destroyed all the crops and remaining assets of his victims, depriving the few survivors of food and basic necessities.

But Milarepa says he repented his actions, assuming he performed them as he says he did, and resumed his way on the road to higher spiritual evolution. The power marshaled in the creation of hailstorms would now manifest through his prodigious flying siddhi. He describes two stages of development. In the first, he ranged over inward flights and visions; then, he states, his powers were expressed externally as bodily flight. "By night in my dreams, I could traverse the universe in every direction unimpeded," he is quoted as saying, adding:

> Thenceforth, I persevered in my devotions, until, finally, I actually could fly. . . . Once, while thus flying, I happened to pass over a small village, called Longda, where a brother of my uncle's deceased daughter-in-law happened to live. The son saw me flying and said, "See, a man is flying." And he left his work to look at me. The father said, "What is there to marvel at or to be amused about in the sight?"[53]

Another woman and her husband were frightened by the long shadow of the flying yogi passing over them. The woman dismisses Milarepa as a good-for-nothing, but the son of this curious couple says: "If a man be able to fly, I do not mind his being a good-for-nothing; there can be nothing more wonderful than a man flying."

Milarepa then reflects on the fact that having been seen flying by "several persons" who knew who he was, it would be wise for him to go elsewhere, for "if I continued here, worldly folk would flock to me, praying for protection from harms and the fulfillment of selfish desires."

Milarepa escaped to a more remote cave and along the way broke into pieces his last worldly possession, an earthen pot. To celebrate his now total poverty, he composed a hymn to impermanence; the broken pot, he says, became his guru.[54] As with Joseph, the aerial oddities attract unwelcome attention and become a burden. Joseph and Milarepa end their lives in solitude. Despite the lack of eyewitness testimony to any of this—beside the word of Milarepa himself—the account has a weird verisimilitude.

In line with possible Tibetan parallels to Joseph, Alexandra David-Neel's observations of quasi-levitational speed-and-endurance walking in Tibet deserves to be cited.[55] The intrepid explorer, a Parisian-born scholar from the Sorbonne, describes various psychophysical practices she observed in her travels to Tibet. They "combine mental concentration with various breathing gymnastics" to produce *lung-gom-pa*, which she observed three times: a kind of extraordinary walking, strangely regular, like gliding or jumping, performed in a trance, sometimes nonstop for several days.

Another psychic practice involved so-called *tummo*, techniques for generating heat from their naked or thinly clad bodies in the freezing fastness of mountainous Tibet. Another practice, cited as a "psychic sport" was sending messages "on the wind," or, as we say, by telepathy ("feeling at a distance"). Alexandra David-Neel observed one *lung-gom* devotee walking with heavy stones tied to his ankles, meant to stop him from floating away!

In more recent times, we find accounts of supposed diabolic possession where levitation has reportedly been observed. A scholar in Semitic languages, Malachi Martin, published a study of five cases of possession in twentieth-century America. He lists as observed unexplained physical effects:

hideous stench, sensations of freezing, distortions of facial skin, immobilization of the possessed person, sensations of pressure and suffocation, doors slamming violently open and shut, and levitation. In one case, an American psychologist, said to be possessed, levitated in view of others: "His body lifted off the couch ever so slightly; it remained suspended in midair without touching the couch, and returned by itself to the surface as Carl (pseudonym) returned to normalcy."[56] Part of this scene is said to have been videotaped, but not the levitation.

In another case, whole-body levitation was reported. Thus, in a history of spiritualism, we read:

> Mr. Henry Gordon, a medium from Springfield, Massachusetts, first exhibited in New York the astonishing feat of floating in the air. After the first manifestation of this kind, the marvel was frequently repeated in the person of this same medium, and his transit through the air for a distance of sixty feet at the residence of Dr. Gray, in Lafayette place, occurred in the presence of a large number of unimpeachable witnesses."[57]

An encouraging statement, especially the allusion to "unimpeachable witnesses," but unfortunately the narrative suddenly stops; no written testimony is presented.

An American case from Salem, Massachussetts, 1693, involves Cotton Mather accusing a young woman, Margaret Rule, of being a witch; the grounds for the accusation were that different people saw the woman levitate. Margaret would levitate from her bed to the ceiling, and witnesses would reach up and try to pull her down, as was the case with the Icelandic medium, Indridi Indridason; they were unable to do so. Cotton Mather obtained six written statements from persons who witnessed these levitations. Among them was Samuel Ames, who testified that Margaret Rule was

> lifted up from her bed, wholly by an invisible force, a great way towards the top of the room where she lay. In her being so lifted she had no assistance from any use of her own arms or hands or any other part of her body, not so much as her heels touching her bed or resting on any support whatsoever. And I have seen her thus lifted when not only a strong person hath thrown his whole weight across her to pull her down, but several other persons have endeavored with all their might to hinder her from being so raised up, which I suppose that several others will testify as myself when called unto it.[58]

So in the same witch-obsessed and devil-haunted century as Joseph's, possession and levitation were being reported in America. Joseph was suspected of being a warlock but managed to make his levitations acceptable to the Church; in America Margaret Rule was not so fortunate. On the other hand, the story about Margaret Rule seems to imply that the force keeping her airborne was quite strong.

The phenomenon of levitation is still reported nowadays. For example, there is the case of Father Aloysius Ellacuria, a Claretian priest from Southern California who was observed on more than one occasion by several Carmelite nuns and laywomen to levitate during Mass. In 1975, one witness wrote in Paris: "We were in the Rue de Bac chapel . . . excited that Father Aloysius was saying mass for us there . . . when suddenly at the offertory Fr. Aloysius cried out, 'My God!' Naturally everyone looks up and there is Father Aloysius lost in ecstasy and a good four inches off the floor. You could see the space under his shoes."[59]

I was lucky to obtain an eyewitness report of a levitation that occurred in the 1990s, in which two women observed a Spanish nun levitate. Carol de Herran, late director of The Monroe Institute in Central Virginia, wrote this account for me:

> Sometime in the early nineties when I lived in Jerez de la Frontera, Spain, in the old section of town, I received a visitor from Sweden. Since many cloistered convents were located in the area around my home, I thought it would be quite different from anything she had experienced in Sweden, so I accompanied her to visit the Convent of Reparadoras, about one block away. A beautiful brick Mudejar style church is attached to the Convent that is occupied by a group of nuns founded in the twentieth century, called the Slaves of the Eucharist. Each nun spends at least two hours per day, one in the morning and one at night in prayer before the altar. Except for two hours per day of recreation time, after lunch and after dinner, the rest of the time is spent in silence and sewing articles to be used in church services.
>
> On the day of our visit, I had closed my eyes in meditation, while my visitor was looking around the church. She suddenly became very disturbed. I watched as the nun at the altar waved her arms slowly, as if about to fly, and then seemed to float upwards about three feet from the pew where she had been kneeling. After a short while, maybe two or three minutes, she floated back down again. I was awestruck but my visitor looked very distressed, at the point of fainting. It was necessary to take her outside to help her recover.

Joseph, of course, came from a Christian tradition in which miracles and charisms have until recent times figured prominently. To illustrate the range of this, I will describe the content of Herbert Thurston's classic study of the physical phenomena of mysticism.[60] All together, the book contains seventeen chapters that revolve around one great theme: *bodily metamorphosis*.[61]

The phenomena are interrelated in a coherent way, and an image emerges that suggests a new stage in the evolution of the human body.[62] Let's look at this image, drawn from Thurston's study of Catholic mystics and their physical phenomena.

The first chapter deals with levitation. We are told that there are about one hundred and fifty to two hundred cases of reported levitation in church history, that is, reports for which there is written testimony. Levitation would appear *temporarily* to free the body from constraints imposed by a fundamental force of nature—gravity. In fact, all of the so-called charisms (sacred gifts) exhibit a reduction of the physical constraints normally associated with embodied life.

The next chapter deals with *stigmata*—the re-creation of the wounds of Christ—a demonstration of the power of imagination over physiology. In the chapter titled "Tokens of Espousal," female disciples mystically espoused to Jesus produce "rings" that betoken this espousal, rings that form themselves from the skin and blood of their hands and appear on their fingers.

As with stigmata, the body is transformed into an instrument that expresses an idea, and for which there is no genetic coding. It appears that a mental agency, subliminal to be sure, is using the materials of biology at hand for its own purpose of symbolic display and expression.

Chapter 4 of Thurston's book, titled "Telekinesis," features some strange behavior of the Eucharistic host. The host is reported to fly from the hand of the priest to the tongue of the eager communicant, released from the grip of gravity.

The next two chapters exhibit the new body under the aspect of supernormal light and heat: enraptured mystics radiate light and appear incombustible, adding more details to the image of the metamorphosis. Another discussion comes under the heading of *incendium amoris*—or "fire of love." Once more the physical phenomena express an idea: in this case, that divine ardor *really* generates tremendous heat. We are given images of saints on fire with love, flinging off their clothes in freezing weather, ablaze with ecstatic adoration.

Whatever the agency at work behind these psychophysical manifestations, it wants to reverse the symbolism that links death with entropy and decay. So chapter 9 of Thurston's book describes the odor of sanctity, which Bernini illustrates in detail in Joseph's case. The odor of sanctity is encountered at the tombs and among the mortal remains of the holy ones. The deposed reports of unexplained fragrances deconstruct the association of death with the stench of decay. The unexplained odors convey the freshness of spring, life, blooming youth. This is followed by three parts of a long chapter on bodily incorruption. The dead bodies of saints seem to snub their noses at mortality as they make a show of resisting the onset of putrefaction. It appears as if something is causing their dead bodies to preserve their lifelike appearance.

In Thurston's chapter on "The Absence of Cadaveric Rigidity," evidence is presented to show how the bodies of the dead friends of God behave in totally contrarian ways. There are, for example, sworn depositions stating that saintly bodies do not stiffen after life departs from them; they are said to remain pliable and flexible long after the time that rigor mortis is supposed (officially, as it were) to take possession of the corpse and make it rigid.

As I interpret the constellation of effects, it signifies a symbolic insurrection against the finality of death.

The next chapters add to the chorus of protest; for example, two of them cover the paradoxical effect of "seeing without eyes." Documented reports exist suggesting that perception is not locked into a single organ system; the rare individual in a rare context appears able to exercise visual perception through the ear or surface of the stomach. If, as William Blake said, we see not with but *through* our eyes, it might then be possible to see *through* our ears or stomach. This effect, if real, would imply that perception uses the nervous system, but is not identical with or physically produced by it.

Finally, the last chapters of Thurston's book present more imagery of bodily transformation. The theme of the next charism is living without eating, drinking, or eliminating. This kind of siddhi (recall the case of Jani) speaks to the idea of breaking free from the biosphere and, to complement this, levitation implies freedom from the fundamental glue that binds us to Earth. Finally, inedia points to freedom from the form of nature where everything eats everything to survive, the driving appetite for consumption that marks the essence of animal life.

The summary is meant to show that the charisms of the saints described in Thurston's book may be read as prefiguring the transformation of the human body. If there is a "new force" unknown to mainstream science, as Crookes believed, it may be part of our biological heritage and a pointer to higher stages of human evolution.

Ian Wilson noticed that people with stigmata show other strange effects, such as the ability to live without food or drink (inedia). Physical changes he notes include flesh that assumes the shape and color of iron nails, limbs that acquire incredible elasticity and length, tongues and breasts that temporarily become huge, or heads that shrink and cave into the shoulders as bodies are sculpted into a ball. "There is a good case for believing that the inner mechanism which triggers stigmata is the key to the heightening of a series of other potentials of the human body," says Wilson, also suggesting that some of the queer phenomena that turn up in religious history may in fact be clues to a further stage of human evolution.[63]

Before we move on to testimony for Joseph's levitations, we should consider that levitators other than Joseph are on record from this critical period of the Catholic Counter-Reformation. One thing consistently appears to be the case: levitators are ecstatics, but few ecstatics are levitators. The state of "being beside oneself" typically precedes the rapture; for example, the

Sienese Capuchin nun Passitea who died in 1615. Her biographer, an Arabic scholar with a keen sense of evidence, wrote:

> According to the violence of the ecstasy she was lifted more or less from the ground. Sister Felice deposed that she had seen her raised three *braccia* (arms-length), Sister Maria Francesca more than four *bracchia* and at the same time she was completely surrounded with an immense effulgence of light. This lasted for two or three hours. On one occasion at Santa Fiori in the house of the Duchess Sforza, when she was present with a crowd of other people, Passitea was surprised by rapture, under the influence of which she remained raised from the ground at the height of a man. The Duchess, witness of the occurrence, caused an attestation of the fact to be drawn up, which was signed by all present.[64]

Or consider the sworn testimony from Brother Jerome da Silva, describing what he saw when he tried to deliver a message to Francis Suarez:

> As the curtain which shut off the working room was drawn, I saw through the space left between the curtain and the jambs of the door a very great brightness. I pushed aside the curtain and entered the inner apartment. Then I noticed that a blinding light was coming from the crucifix, so intense that it was like the reflection of the sun from glass windows, and I felt that I could not have remained looking at it without being completely dazzled. The light streamed from the crucifix upon the face and breast of Father Suarez and in this brightness I saw him in a kneeling position in front of the crucifix, his head uncovered, his hands joined, and his body in the air lifted three feet above the floor on a level with the table on which the crucifix stood. On seeing this I withdrew, but before quitting the room I paused in a state of bewilderment, as it were, beside myself.[65]

In each of the two preceding examples, the phenomenon is seen from a third-person perspective. For an account of *what it feels like* to be levitated, here is Teresa of Avila, as described in her autobiography. The rapture once it commences is irresistible, she says, and

> often it comes like a strong, swift impulse before your thought can forewarn you of it or you can do anything to help yourself; you see and feel this cloud, or this powerful eagle, rising and bearing you up with it on its wings. . . . When I tried to resist these raptures, it seemed that I was being lifted up by a force beneath my feet so powerful that I know nothing to which I can compare it, for it came with a much greater vehemence than any other spiritual experience and I felt as if I were being ground to powder.[66]

At first she feels fear and tries without success to resist the force, noting an interesting aftereffect: "The favor also leaves a strange detachment." Not only her spirit but also her body felt "a new estrangement from things of earth." This causes a kind of distress or uneasiness. With Joseph, as we'll see, distress and uneasiness were much intensified and complicated his life.

Enough. We have looked at a range of mind-body interactions, from "normal" motor behavior to matters abnormal and supernormal. There is a great deal we do not understand about the human mind. For example, there is the story of Joseph of Copertino's levitations. In the next chapter we survey some of the reports.

NOTES

1. Braude, 1991. For an analysis of D. D. Home's effects, see pp. 70–107. See also Braude's short but incisive discussion of Joseph's levitations, pp. 161–69.
2. Burton, 1948.
3. Medhurst and Goldney, 1963, pp. 25–156, for Darwin, esp. 41–46.
4. One memorable example was Home's observed ability to play an accordion at a distance, without touching it. For an absorbing account of these credible absurdities, see Braude's *Limits of Consciousness*.
5. For this distinction, see Thouless and Wiesner, 1946, pp. 107–19.
6. For a critique of so-called determinism, see Kelly, 2003.
7. Van de Castle, *Our Dreaming Mind*, 1994.
8. Personal communication.
9. Foster and Hufford, 1985.
10. See discussion of dreams and levitation in chapter 8.
11. Bulkeley, 2011, p. 17.
12. Jung and Pauli, 1955, p. 31.
13. See psychiatrist Bernard Beitman's *Connecting with Coincidence*, which explores the varieties of everyday coincidence touching on many facets of human experience.
14. IM, pp. 139–49.
15. Unknown.
16. See Petersen, 2008, and Kirsch, 2011.
17. Mason, 1952, pp. 422–23.
18. White and Murphy, 1978.
19. Fodor, 1964, pp. 24–29.
20. 1975, p. 76.
21. Ibid., p. 46.
22. Ibid., p. 33.
23. Geiger, 2009. Again, we are dealing with a relatively rare phenomenon but one that definitely represents a recurrent pattern of response to life-threatening crisis.
24. See chapter 3 in IM, 117–239.
25. Stevenson, 1997a, pp.104–38.
26. Cannon, 1942, pp. 169–81.

27. IM, p. 169.
28. Myers, 1892.
29. Barrett, 1912, p. 378.
30. Roll, 1972, a fascinating study of the poltergeist.
31. Ibid.
32. Bender, 1974, pp. 131–34.
33. Manning, 1975.
34. Bozzano, 1948.
35. Barker, pp. 52–55.
36. See Kothari et al., 1973, pp. 282–84.
37. See the extraordinary documentary by Austrian film critic Peter Straubinger, first shown at the Cannes Film Festival in 2010. See also mataji_case_study.pdf for a summary of the two experiments performed on Jani.
38. Eisenbud, 1977, p. 419.
39. Eisenbud, 1967, p. 25.
40. Thurston, 1952, pp. 385–95, on the multiplication of food. In these accounts, the food never materializes out of nowhere. The pattern recounted is of small supplies that are distributed from various containers but whose supply is never quite exhausted until all needs are provided for. If these stories are true, they suggest a very discreet, understated "miraculous" agency.
41. Schrenck-Notzing, 1920; Imich, 1995.
42. Somer, 2009, pp. 299–322.
43. Gissurarson and Haraldsson, 1955, pp. 47–98.
44. Ibid., p. 61.
45. Ibid., p. 64.
46. Ibid., p. 71.
47. See Krippner, 1977.
48. Radin, 1997, p. 143.
49. Owen and Sparrow, 1977.
50. Ibid., p. 179.
51. See Leroy, 1928, *La Levitation*. Juvisy: *Les Editions du Cerf*. This book is not easy to find, but Cendrars (1949/1996) quotes very large portions of it in his study of Joseph, *Sky Memoirs*, citing examples of levitation as reported from the eleventh to the twentieth century.
52. Yogananda, 1975.
53. Evans-Wentz, 1928, p. 210.
54. Ibid., pp. 211–14.
55. David-Neel, 1971.
56. Martin, 1976, p. 363.
57. Harding, 1869, pp. 73–74.
58. Brown, 1970, pp. 238–39.
59. Treece, 1989, pp. 253–54.
60. Thurston, 1952, passim.
61. In the interest of brevity, I will not reproduce or consider in detail the evidence for these claims; the purpose of this section is to describe the central idea of

Thurston's book; the image of bodily metamorphosis ties the phenomena together into a coherent bundle.

62. For an extensive treatment of this theme, see Michael Murphy's *The Future of the Body*.
63. Wilson, 1989, p. 110.
64. Thurston, 1952, p. 29.
65. Ibid., pp. 26–28.
66. Peers, 1960, p. 191.

Chapter 3

The Case for Joseph's Levitations

> The levitations of Saint Joseph, striking mysteriously at the root of man's nature in a way that even the discoveries of Darwin, Freud, and psychical research have failed to do, have been put into a permanent stall.
>
> —Jule Eisenbud

In this chapter, I want to take Saint Joseph's levitations out of "stall." But I think it fair to begin with a caveat: Anyone inclined to suspend judgment on the factual basis of the levitation claims would be justified on two grounds. The first is that the events described occurred in the seventeenth century, and exaggerations, distortions, and outright fabrication cannot in general be entirely ruled out. The second is that no matter how compelling the accounts may appear, the utter rareness and elusiveness of such phenomena today may for many serve as grounds for suspending or refusing belief.

Nevertheless, there is a large quantity of eyewitness documentation of Joseph's reported phenomena. We shall review some of the documentation that bears on his levitations in this chapter. Whatever one makes of these testimonies, they are part of the story of an extraordinary man. To avoid being tedious, I won't in every instance qualify statements by saying the "alleged" or "claimed" or "reported" account of this or that; but in all cases that is implied. Nor do I wish to fixate on any single item, despite its spectacular nature, in the story of Joseph. My broader concern is with the implications of a spectrum of reported extraordinary phenomena. If even a fraction of such accounts are well founded, there is a great deal to think about with respect to the nature of mind.

As for mystical *rapture*, the Jesuit scholar Herbert Thurston, who wrote extensively about the charisms of saints, fixes on Joseph as the strongest case history; we have multiple witnesses, he says, observations in daylight, letters, diaries, records from the Inquisition, numerous written depositions, and a thirty-five-year-long career. Thurston wrote: "From the time of his ordination St. Joseph's life was one long succession of ecstasies, miracles of healing and supernatural happenings on a scale not paralleled in the reasonably authenticated life of any saint."[1] The reader may look at the appendix for the primary sources of testimony for Joseph's extraordinary phenomena.

I first read about the friar in Eric Dingwall's scholarly collection of essays, *Human Oddities*.[2] Dingwall, known for his skepticism, describes the levitations, basing his narrative on the original Italian sources. He notes the difficulties in trying to obtain many of these documents. Dingwall relied on Bernini's biography, praising it because it closely follows the *processi*, the proceedings from trials where evidence was deposed under oath. Swearing under oath was especially serious business then, since belief in one's immortal soul and postmortem judgment were more solidly entrenched in the conscience of the culture. There was, moreover, what Jean Delumeau (1990) described as the black pall of sin, fear, and guilt that draped itself around seventeenth-century Counter-Reformation Europe; these were not feelings or attitudes conducive to lying under oath.

Bernini's *Vita* is useful because of its copious transcription of eyewitness testimony based on the earliest documents. The primary sources that Gustavo Parisciani draws on for his 1963 magnum opus include thirteen volumes in the Vatican Archives, trial records, biographies, diaries, letters, and official church documents originating in the different cities and convents Joseph lived in or visited, like Grottela, Naples, Rome, Assisi, Pietra Rubbia, Fossombrone, and Osimo. Parisciani is emphatic about his intention to present the reported facts of Joseph's life.

Bernini's *Vita* describes Joseph's ecstasies and raptures. The reports show that the *ratti*, the rapturous upliftings in space, always emerged from the *estasi* (ecstasies), during which he was absorbed in some heavenly scene, state, or personage. Existentially, as described, the levitations seemed inseparable from the ecstasies, the former being a dramatic expression, a literalization of the latter. "Heaven" was the object of his ecstatic uplift: a psychological space at right angles from the concerns of earthly existence.

The *estasi* had their bodily markers: eyes upturned, body insensible to witnesses poking, burning, stinging, or pushing various parts of his body. Flies trekked across his glazed eyeballs during ecstasy. Joseph's body appeared *as if it were dead*—cold, stiff, unresponsive. Accounts that liken the appearance of ecstasy to a kind of death are found about mystics of all traditions.[3] According to Bernini: "The trial papers are full of testimonies regarding the raptures that Giuseppe experienced, which we would find incredible if they had not been authenticated by the authority of the *processi* from which we have faithfully extracted this testimony."[4]

This shows a modern attitude. Recognizing that extraordinary phenomena require eyewitness testimony, he quotes, paraphrases, and summarizes accounts from the *processi*.

During Joseph's sixteen years at Grotella, it was publicly deposed that he levitated seventy times, after which the diarist Arcangelo Rosmi[5] stopped recording new cases. After seeing something seventy times, especially something so attention-grabbing and obvious as a man unnaturally raised up in the air, it seemed to Rosmi there was enough evidence to establish the effect as real. Still, with something as rare as levitation, one would prefer to collect as much testimony as possible.

We find reports from every town and city in Italy where Joseph resided. People swore they observed him aloft in Grotella, Assisi, Rome, Naples, Perugia, Osimo, Fossombrone, and Pietrarubbia—in churches, convents, and conventinos all over Italy. Wherever he went he created a sensation and left a trail of haunted, aroused seekers who wanted, often desperately, to see, touch, or consult with him. People from all walks of life were affected, some very distinguished like John Casimir Waza, a spiritual son of Joseph who became the King of Poland;[6] the Duke of Brunswick (the employer of Leibniz); and the passionately spiritual Infanta Maria, the Princess of Savoy, in the end rebuffed by Joseph.

AN EMBARRASSMENT OF RAPTURES

There was a time of great aridity in Joseph's life in Assisi from 1645 to 1647, after which his mystical life flourished. Drawing largely on Arcangelo Rosmi's diary of that period, Parisciani wrote:

> To enumerate and catalogue the ecstasies and the levitations that occurred in Assisi in this decade would not be worth the trouble. In days of fervor, Padre Giuseppe might leave his senses several times. During a single Mass one could verify three or four cases of levitation. It would be impossible to narrate one by one the mystical manifestations, which were the daily joy and the daily torment of Joseph.[7]

The force that overpowered Joseph aloft was irresistible, as it was for St. Teresa; his prayers and those of his confreres could delay but not stop it. He once repeated to don Arcangelo: "It was a great force that, it was a great force, it was a great force."[8] His body would tremble when he resisted the onset of ecstasy while saying Mass and he had to support himself on the altar. At such times he was unable to break the host, which felt rigid like a piece of iron. When he broke it, he would drop one piece in the chalice and remain immobile "like a statue" with the other piece in his hand.

Joseph told don Arcangelo that the ecstasies stopped him from performing his priestly tasks. Throughout his life this force never seemed to abate in its intensity. A mystery and a wonder perhaps, but not altogether a positive experience. The *moti* caused him shame and embarrassment—*un male que pativa*, "an evil that he suffered." Typically, after a seizure, he would excuse himself as being sleepy or otherwise indisposed, cover his head with his hood and hasten back to his cell. The ills came from the reactions of onlookers to his behavior, forcing him into a "battle against indiscreet curiosity." But apart from these untoward reactions, the ecstasies were for him "a taste of the true glory of paradise."[9]

In trying to explain the erratic movements of ecstatics, Joseph said, using the third person: "People who love God with their hearts are like drunkards who are beside themselves (*che non stanno in se*) and thus sing, dance and do suchlike things." When the joyous side of ecstasy took over, his spirit would lift him in spectacular ways. Antonio Cossandri, the Maestro di Cappella of the Sacred Convent, brought three young singers of outstanding talent to Joseph's room to perform. Upon hearing the boys sing, he immediately went into ecstasy, falling into a kneeling position, then rising and floating above the ground. To confirm what they were seeing, all three boys "put their hands between Joseph's tunic and the ground."[10]

The strange performances took place more readily during holidays and festivals. Times of ritual remembrance of Saint Francis or the Madonna were powerfully charged with the kind of meaning that could enrapture him instantly. For Joseph, the entire sacred calendar was a standing invitation to ecstatic projection. Remembrance of the birth, miracles, crucifixion, death, resurrection, and ascension of Christ occasioned many remarkable ecstasies and queer wanderings in the air.

Saying Mass was perhaps the most reliable inducer of exaltation. So intensely dramatic was his Mass that his superiors stopped him from celebrating it in public. It could last for three or four hours; he would go into ecstasy, his body assume the form of a cross, become immobile, then rise and float, sometimes his toes hovering inches above the ground. He came back to himself spontaneously, or when commanded to under holy obedience. Almost anything could throw him into a state, but certain moments of the Mass were major triggers: the memento, for example, remembering the living or the dead, or the moment of consecration and elevation of the host—the moment that for Joseph signified the supreme miracle, the incarnation of the divine.

Joseph had a favorite wax doll of the Christ child that sent him into ecstasies. The brothers feared he would crush the baby Christ doll with his love, but luckily he never did. He invested the doll, as he did the relics of St. Francis, and the painting of the Madonna at Grotella, with enrapturing significance. His personal perception of sacred meaning triggered the ecstasies and hence the raptures. Rosmi noted that the mood and spirit of Lent or Easter were reflected in the form and tempo of his levitational dances. During Mass on Good Friday, for example, he was prone to experience the pains of the crucified one.

C. G. Jung had described the Mass as a method of ritual transformation of consciousness.[11] The Graeco-Roman rites, like the Catholic Mass, were meant to awaken experiences of divine power, divine presence. The normal functions of personality went into abeyance. There were many ways to trigger ecstasy and enthusiasm: vigil and fasting, contemplation of sacred symbols, music, drumming, whirling dances, pain, inhalation of fumes—whatever it took to break through the barrier to the greater consciousness. The Catholic Mass may not have customarily induced ecstasy and enthusiasm for the ordinary celebrant, but it did for an excitable mystic like Joseph. The essence of Joseph seems captured in Proclus's description of celebrants of the Mysteries "going out of themselves to be wholly established in the Divine and to be enraptured."[12]

Back to Joseph's calendar of charisms: around Good Friday, the dark side took over, and he now was seen to levitate backward. Rosmi asked Joseph about the backward levitations. He replied that they arose "from the humility of the soul, seeing the greatness of the Lord." They signify "the supreme desire of the soul to unite itself with its beloved object," and it is "like a small bird in a cage when it goes looking everywhere to see if it can get out and fly away." Joseph said that flying forward and backward were simply a kind of agitated by-product of his quest for the "beloved object." Curious about what the *moti* inwardly signified to Joseph, Rosmi keeps asking why he's raptured forward *and* backward. And why so intrusively at the most solemn moments of the Mass?[13]

Whatever was causing the movements, it seemed to be playing with Joseph: threw him down and raised him up, bounced him forward and yanked him back. He also remarked that feelings of worthlessness sometimes determined the vector of certain *moti*. He once explained his flights as the effect of being tantalized by the "rays" of divine splendor. When the rays "draw back," he stated, he felt a surge to unite with the "beloved object." As Joseph described it, the backward levitations were the rebound from a violently felt divine flirtation.[14]

Rosmi's diary recounts how the liturgy affected the form of the phenomena, expressing and reflecting the shifts of theme and tone. Joseph identified with all phases of the liturgy and immersed himself in each motif, bringing it to life in himself with uninhibited emotional intensity. Joseph was a master at playing various roles that as a priest he was called on to enact. The ecstatic enactments must have facilitated the raptures.[15] Take this extreme example of identifying with a role that Rosmi recorded: the friar apparently thought so deeply about the fall of Adam that he got sick and vomited blood.

When he had to identify with the suffering Christ, he looked upon himself in the worst light, and felt unworthy of his vocation. Wrapped in black penitential thoughts, the host in his hands would feel unbearably heavy. Unable to break or even hold it, he would fall heavily to the ground, weep, sob on his knees, and levitate backward, enacting and displaying his humble self-deprecation.

The movements observed by Rosmi were under the sway of a saturnine, crucified-obsessed consciousness; he was now supernormally weighed down, slammed down, driven backward. The movements were expressive and responsive to mood and circumstance. When it was time to celebrate the Easter resurrection, Joseph became jovial and expansive, and the levitational force raised him unabashedly upward. For a description of one of his Masses, Parisciani selects a case for its "minute particulars." It was during the Easter liturgy in 1647, and Joseph was saying Mass on the Day of Purification.

> He began to tremble at the memento of the living, after three profound sighs. At the elevation, he tried without success to raise the host three or four times. Then the tremor grew until the ecstasies lifted him backwards through the power of an act of humility. He remained with his eyes fixed on the Sacrament. In a sudden rapture (levitation), he was then at the predella, and remained there with outstretched arms. Screaming three times, he repeated the backward flight, until he finished his sleep. Then he got up with reverence in order to continue the Mass. This time he succeeded with the elevation. In a rapt state he rose with his whole body, remaining for a long time only on the tip of one toe. Then the host and his body were slowly lowered. At the height of his chest, his hands again halted. All trembling the host reposed. A new ecstasy at the memento of the dead, but without making noise. Instead he cried out breaking bread and flew back and forth four or five times. A jump and a shout. Then he was immobilized over the predella for a long rapture. At the end, he fell face down on the ground and wept bitterly.[16]

It goes on; again he struggles to raise himself but weeps and is flung face down on the ground. A glance at an image of the Madonna and up he goes again; finally, he concludes the Mass. One can see why the Church felt obliged to keep him at a safe distance from a restive congregation.

MULTIPLE TRIGGERS

Joseph's anomalous movements were observed under various circumstances, not only while saying Mass. Almost anything might inspire him with awe and prompt an ecstatic foray. This caused problems in public venues. One feast day he was instructed to hear confessions, but as the crowds swarmed around him, he "couldn't hear their confessions because as soon as he entered the confessional he went into ecstasy, offering all those present a spectacle of wonder rather than judgment and absolution."[17]

He was, in short, sometimes unable to perform as a priest—say his beloved Mass or hear confessions—because of the involuntary ecstatic seizures. Unable to control his internal eruptions, his priestly profession was severely compromised. In a sense, he was as bad a priest as he was a cobbler, and both for the same reason: he couldn't keep his mind on the job. As Bernini was fond of saying, the friar had already inwardly established his residence in heaven. The best he could do was try to minimize the rapture and not attract too much attention: "For Padre Giuseppe it was normal for his body to rise up in the air during celebration of the Mass: he would rise with his feet barely touching the ground—only the tip of his big toe touching, a position not only unnatural but incredible. He continued this way until the end of the sacrifice."[18]

With this discreet levitation he was able to make it to the end of the Mass. The passage goes on: "Even so he was either out of his senses or flying backwards and looking like death, or would rise up a few hands' widths from the ground or act in a way that all could see was completely with God."

The image of the Madonna probably affected him most powerfully. He responded in a spectacular way to Cimabue's painting of the Virgin in the basilica of Assisi when he first arrived there on April 30, 1639:

> After stepping inside the Church, Giuseppe glanced at a painting of the Holy Virgin located in the vault above the wooden frieze of the altar of the Immaculate Conception, a Madonna painted with the Baby Jesus in her arms in a way that strikingly resembled the Madonna of the Grotella. At the sight of her, Padre Giuseppe gave a huge scream and flew about thirty meters in the air and, embracing her, said, "Ah, Mamma mia! You have followed me!" It all happened so quickly that those present were filled with sacred terror, marveling to each other, and remaining in a stupor over the Padre's performance.[19]

According to a more detailed account of this incident, the rapture upon arrival at Assisi "sustained in him such a shattering emotion that it prompted a flight higher yet than any on record." (Fr. Martelli; first biographer, Nuti; and Fr. Roncalli are cited in the *Summarium* for the claim that Joseph rose on this occasion to a height of "thirty meters" [*trenta metri*].)[20] The Cimabue painting was similar to the image of the Grotella Madonna, soulfully leaning her crowned head on the head of the divine son.

Heads and shoulders touching, mother and son make an icon of loving union, the exact opposite of what Joseph experienced with *his* mother, who threatened to throw him to the wolves. Roberto Nuti, confrere and first biographer, wrote: "He made me understand that his first ecstasy was in a church of the monastery of San Chiara in his country on the occasion of admiring an image of the most beautiful Virgin."[21] Moreover, as we read from the *Acta Sanctorum*, "In the very last Mass that he celebrated, on the festival of the Assumption (of the Virgin), 1663, a month before his death, he was lifted up in a longer rapture than usual."[22]

Any reference to the sacred could cause him to dissociate and be thrown into full-blown uplift. The thought or the sight of the pope could do it as well as calling to mind Filippo Neri, an admired compatriot also known for his ecstatic flights. Joseph venerated Saint Catherine, whom he called his "advocate"; thinking of her might induce spasms of ecstatic levitation. Joseph responded to music, dance, and artistic expressions that celebrated Christmas, Easter, Good Friday, or other sacred times.

He was particularly responsive to relics, and was surrounded by them, tangible links to persons or places of heavenly import. At Assisi the veil of the Holy Madonna and the shoes and robe of Saint Francis were publicly displayed on special occasions. The veil seems to have produced some strong effects: "Once he had kissed it, again he flew backward eight paces, landing on his knees, and then again he flew forward above the table where the reliquary of the Sacred Veil stood between two torches, and he went into ecstasy with his arms spread wide."[23]

His hands were suspended over the flames but were not burned. Similar flights occurred. Confronted with the shoes of St. Francis, in the presence of foreign delegates and others: "He flew backward for three paces and the flight was so high that he flew over the heads of two of the delegates and fell to the pavement behind them on to his knees."[24] Apparently, "many times he was found collapsed on the ground of the church and was bodily carried as though a corpse back to his cell, returning to life again only after a command of obedience by the Custodian."[25]

Joseph was eight years old when he began his ecstatic career and made the transition to full rapture when he became a priest at the age of twenty-five. In the beginning, he appeared clumsy and stupid, earning, as noted, the moniker, Boccaperta—"Gapingmouth." Bernini speaks of the first ecstatic forays as the larval condition of later developments: "But those ecstasies and elevations of a mind fixed on God were mere foreshadowing of the rapturous flights that Padre Giuseppe experienced after he became a priest. The raptures were in fact much more powerful than the ecstasies, because they carried away not only his mind but also his body—the inner *and* outer man."[26]

The raptures were always preceded by a scream (*grido, urlo*). A sudden need to express himself is announced—a breakthrough of accumulated force—a herald of violent transport. Was the scream a cry for consummation? for a break from prolonged psychical tension, release from "mental excesses"? Asked about the screams, he replied: "In the same way that gunpowder makes a loud bang in the barrel when one shoots, so does my ecstatic heart shout out when it has access to the love of God."[27]

Joseph's levitations are *explosive* and scream for release from the pressure of an unbearable love.

The only way back to his mundane self was by holy obedience. Otherwise, pulling, poking, or shouting at him would get no response. The Guardian of the convent of Capuchins in Fossombrone witnessed Joseph in ecstasy and testifies that he had to call him back:

Afterward, the Guardian asked Giuseppe if, during the ecstasy, he had seen or heard anything through his senses. Giuseppe said he did not. The Guardian asked how had he then heard and understood the order to return to himself. The Padre explained that while in ecstasy he never heard the words to return to himself, but God would hear the holy order and make the vision that occupied his soul disappear; the soul would then return to his body and senses.[28]

This is an interesting exchange. According to Joseph, consciously he heard nothing, but his subliminal mind—he said God—did register the message and the ecstasy was disrupted.

Everything appears to Joseph as if an intelligence outside of himself is addressing, commanding him; and so it is, whether we call it God or the subliminal mind, there is something bigger than the conscious Joseph that seems to be pushing, molding, and directing him. Bernini notes a strange thing about the ecstatic's clothing:

His priestly robes or his daily tunics, always remained very composed, both as he flew from the air or as he fell to the ground as though dead, thrown by the force of the Spirit that moved him. It in fact appeared as if an invisible hand wrapped itself around him and shaped the clothes appropriately . . . every part of his dress was as it should have been (as if he were motionless), a thing that seemed miraculous, given the way his body thrashed during the ecstasies and raptures, as recorded in the *processi*.[29]

Peter Brown recounts the story[30] of female demoniacs levitating upside down at the tombs of prophets in the Holy Land; in spite of gravity, the skirts of the demoniacs remained "composed" and stayed in place, like Joseph's tunic during flight, as described above—a curious confirmation of what seems like the altered space around ecstatics and demoniacs, as we'll see in our discussion of the physics of levitation in chapter 8.

During ecstasy his body would assume the form of a cross; it appeared that something was propelling Joseph to mount a display of himself, as if he were a living artwork—a vision to be framed, admired, venerated. But note this peculiarity: "If he was saying Mass when rapture occurred, he would return to the altar and pick up right where he left off, and to the exact syllable; without repeating or skipping a single word."[31]

This is comparable to the twentieth-century medium Pearl Curran, said to channel a so-named seventeenth-century "Patience Worth." Patience (the entranced Pearl Curran) was famous for her literary "stunts," and one of the less spectacular was her ability to interrupt her automatic writing of some poem or story, leave it and return later to pick up exactly where she had left off—not unlike what Bernini says Joseph did.

In some psychical sense, he appeared to reside in another world, and suffered from his bondage to earth. He was like an exile, an alien visitor; and no one could predict what would catapult him into rapture. Bernini relates that one day Joseph saw three crosses being carried toward him in a procession as he was walking with two of his brethren from Copertino. Suddenly, the thought entered his mind:

> "Brothers, if it were to happen that you found Christ crucified on these crosses and each one of us were able to touch and kiss him, on what part of the body would you have kissed him? You, for example, Donato Antonio?" And Donato Antonio replied that he would have kissed him on the soles of his feet. "And you, Father Candeloro?" Padre Giuseppe asked the old priest. Brother Candeloro said, "I would kiss him on his most holy rib-cage, from which the seven sacraments originated."
>
> Then Padre Giuseppe began to respond, as the two brothers say in the *processi*: "I . . . I . . . and I" swelling up more and more as though he could not say another word, but instead let out a great scream and all of a sudden flew from the brothers all the way to the cross, embraced it, and landed on his knees supported by the cross-beam about three meters from the ground. At the sound of the scream even the brothers of the convent, along with the two priests traveling with Giuseppe, stopped to contemplate and admire him in his ecstasy for a good long while with tears in their eyes.
>
> As sunset was approaching, the Superior arrived at Calvary and ascended toward the Cross and stood on tiptoes, stretching out his hand to touch the hem of Padre Giuseppe's tunic and to command him, by virtue of holy obedience, to return to himself. Then Padre Giuseppe, as though he had awakened from deep sleep, recognized the danger he was in and began to cry. He turned toward the cross and embraced it, gradually making his way on the ground and looking a bit stupefied. The other brothers pulled down the hoods of their robes and went away.[32]

Bernini continues:

> A similar thing happened during a procession made from Copertino to the Grotella. Seeing the three crosses from far away, Padre Giuseppe exclaimed three times, "Oh, Oh, Oh!" and let out a powerful scream, then flew through the air a great distance, posing on top of one of the three crosses in ecstasy. The people that were participating in the procession were terrified. Those who heard the scream and saw him fly above the people in ecstasy to the top of the cross became so agitated that the procession became a huge confusion.[33]

A simple sensory experience of the sky could trigger the experience, and once again Joseph proves a most unusual aviator:

> Fr. Antonio Chiarello, while walking with Padre Giuseppe through the orchard of the convent, at a certain point gazed up into the heavens. "Padre Giuseppe, what a beautiful sky God has made!" These words seemed like an invitation for Padre Giuseppe to fly up into the sky, and so he did, letting out a loud cry and bounding from the ground to fly up to the top of an olive tree where he landed on his knees on a branch that kept shaking. One reads in the *processi* that it was as though a bird were perched on the branch. Padre Giuseppe stayed up there about a half hour and finally came back to himself, asking the priest how to get down from the tree. The priest had to get a ladder and in that way he descended from the olive tree.[34]

Esthetic sensations, church music, or the sound of violins carried him away. Once around Christmastime he invited some shepherds to bring their pipes and trumpets into the church. Entering the nave he began to sing and dance, and the excitement grew. The shepherds later deposed (under oath) what they observed:

> Padre Giuseppe was so delighted that he began to dance in the center of the nave and, at the sound of the pipes, suddenly sighed and loudly screamed and flew up in the air like a bird, halfway to the ceiling, *where he continued dancing above the main altar*, and went to embrace the tabernacle that was a considerable distance above the main altar. This was all the more marvelous because the altar was filled with flaming candles and he rested between the candles without knocking over even one. He stayed that way with his knees above the altar, embracing the tabernacle with both arms, for about fifteen minutes and then returned to himself without having done any damage whatsoever. His eyes were full of tears and he said, "Praise God, brothers." We all remained in awe; I said to myself, "This is truly a miracle."[35]

Bernini, obsessed by the ecstasies and raptures, injects precise references and rapid-fire summaries throughout the biography. For example, in chapter 4, he gives a snapshot summary of Joseph's ecstatic history during his sixteen-year tenure at Grotella. Joseph was seen in the Church

> now going to the altar, jumping onto the last step of the pulpit; now (on Holy Thursday) launched in the air from the floor all the way to a sculpted sepulcher of Jesus Christ; now on the feast day of San Francesco, carried through the air to the saint's altar; now on the feast of the Madonna of Carmine, rising in ecstasy from the earth; now reciting the litanies, intoning the *Sancta Maria,* and flying up to the main altar and out of the Church; now in his cell where every time he would say devotions he would go up; or now, contemplating the mysteries, up in the air, climbing up high with burning embers in his hand. And causing sacred terror to all present, from his seat in the refectory he flew in the air with a sea urchin in his hand; and in the nearby countryside flew from the ground up above an olive tree; and another time flew above a great cross.[36]

There are accounts of chance events precipitating embarrassing raptures, a random exposure to a sound or association that catapults him into sudden rapture. His reported upliftings varied in length of time, from mere seconds to fifteen minutes of sustained floating, with some accounts of more prolonged excursions. Prosper Lambertini was the devil's advocate who examined the documents and spoke of the "prolonged" flights of the saint. Later, when Lambertini became pope he submitted "strong animadversions" to Joseph's beatification because of the strangeness of the friar's behavior but finally agreed to it in 1753. This was due to Joseph's heroic virtue. The charisms corroborate his close relationship to God.

As to the duration of Joseph's levitations, short or long, they seem to point to the reality of an unrecognized force of nature, the new force of nature that, as mentioned in chapter 2, William Crookes claimed to discover. The crucial point is that the flights lasted long—ten minutes or half an hour—enough to render implausible the claim that they were tricks of perception.

According to witnesses, Joseph sometimes imparted immunity to gravity to others, as in this incident where the trigger for Joseph seems to have been irrepressible high spirits:

> Padre Giuseppe was very happy to see them (fellow friars) in the convent and became so full of joy that he lifted one of them off the ground with great vigor of spirit, using only one hand under the arm, and swinging him around as though he weighed nothing, even though he was surely stronger, taller and heavier than Giuseppe himself. He did this to show how much joy he felt in seeing them back at the convent.[37]

In another joint-flight report, levitation is deployed therapeutically with a mentally disturbed person:

And so it happened, that the Knight, Baldassare Rossi, struck by a disease that affects the mind, thought everyone else was crazy and believed that he alone was sane. In the end, the man's relatives tied him to a chair and brought him before the Padre, asking to cure his mental infirmity. Rossi, with great difficulty, was untied, and forced to kneel before Padre Giuseppe, who rose to his feet from where he was sitting and putting a hand on the demented man's head, said: "Knight Baldassare, don't have doubts. Entrust yourself to God and His Holy Mother." Saying this he pressed down with the hand that was on his head. Meanwhile, the sick man was pulling on his own hair.

Suddenly, Padre Giuseppe's usual scream broke forth, "Oh!", and he went into a rapture, rising from the ground up high, and bringing the madman with him. They were both suspended in the air for almost ten minutes. Who knows what they did while up there? When they returned to earth, Padre Giuseppe was heard to say to the man, "Stay happy, Knight!" who now seemed perfectly sound of mind and went home, praising God for the wonder of the day.[38]

This may be the only example on record demonstrating the psychotherapeutic potential of levitation.

In the following famous example, there is a hint of the adaptive potential of Joseph's peculiar talent. In 1646 his superior asked the friar to talk with a troupe of distinguished admirers. Bernini's account reads as follows:

[T]he Admiral of Castile came to Assisi from Rome with his wife and children, attracted by Giuseppe's fame, and met with the Padre in his cell. Afterward, the Admiral told his wife that he had seen and spoken with another St. Francis. The wife, also wanting to talk to Giuseppe, asked the Custodian (*con spagnolesca veemenza*) if she could speak in private with the holy one. The Custodian, anticipating the repugnance of Padre Giuseppe in having to deal with this woman, asked him to go into the church to meet with her and her companions for the sake of obedience. Padre Giuseppe smiled and said that he would obey but did not know if he would be able to speak to them.

Apparently, he foresaw that he would not be able to speak because the greater force of the Immaculate Mother of God would transport him elsewhere. After leaving his cell, he entered the Church through a small door in front of the altar on which a statue of the image of the Immaculate Conception had been erected. The moment he entered, he looked at the statue, screamed, and flew a distance of twelve steps *above the heads of the Admiral and the women*, to embrace the feet of the statue of the Queen of Heaven.

Then, after remaining in that pose of adoration for some time, he gave another scream and, still flying through the air, returned near the little door where he bowed in reverence to the Mother of God and kissed the floor, his head inclined so that his hood fell over his face. He then walked away back to his cell, leaving everyone dazed if not traumatized. The wife of the Admiral fainted and the Admiral had to revive her, splashing water in her face and holding smelling salts to her nose; the Admiral himself raised his eyebrows and, opening his arms, stupefied, did not faint, but became weak-kneed and flustered.[39]

The eyewitness testimony of Padre Provenzala[40] contains more details. The statue of the Immaculate Conception, he says, was not placed at ground level but stood above the ground, *più di un uomo*—"more than a man's length."[41] So when Joseph embraced the feet of the statue and held a pose of adoration, he would have been hovering midair. "Many others" attested to this, among them Francesco Allegretti, lieutenant of the Assisi Lancers.

Joseph's abilities also came into play in the course of everyday life. An incident to recount extends the idea of what Crookes's force could do. Fra Placido was a carpenter, sculptor, and carver of intaglios. Joseph, who had few needs, was longing to take a certain painting of Christ back with him to his cell. He had to ask Placido, who could remove it from the predella, but Placido refused to. Joseph promptly went to one of his superiors and asked for the painting, and it was granted. Placido failed to remove the painting, so Joseph then leaped upon the predella, broke the painting loose, and took it back to his cell.

When Placido discovered this clumsy maneuver, he became furious and shouted: "I'll kill him! I'll kill him!" and grabbed from among his tools the biggest knife in sight. He mounted his horse and charged after Joseph, brandishing the knife. When Placido appeared in a red-faced fury, Joseph just smiled at him. "From ten meters, an invisible force slammed Placido to the ground," Parisciani reports in his study of Joseph and the Inquisition.[42]

By the time the dazed Placido managed to pull himself up off the ground, he had a change of heart. He wept and trembled, loudly confessing it was *il demonio* who put the idea of murder in his head. Joseph corrected him and said he had been instructed to give him the painting and that he had disobeyed. It was only because of that infraction of his will that the demon had gained authority over him. The two men embraced and became friends. Parisciani cites three written depositions attesting to this comedy, including Joseph himself who told it to his diarist Arcangelo Rosmi.

An "invisible force" knocked Placido off his horse. We have seen how the space around Joseph during ecstasy seemed to freeze or bracket ordinary physical constraints like gravity, combustion, pain, atmospheric effects, mechanical damage, and so on. In the incident just described, the preventive barrier seems to have extended ten meters, becoming proactive and stopping Placido from getting into trouble with his knife.

Now a report with a political twist. Bernini, the enthusiastic papalist, dwells on the story of the German Duke of Brunswick, which shows the powerful impact on those who witnessed Joseph in action:

The most marvelous conversion to the Catholic Faith involved John Frederick, Duke of Brunswick-Luneberg. This German Duke arrived in Assisi from Rome in order to see with his own eyes the friar who in Germany was said to be a great saint. He was staying in the Sacred Convent by direct order of Pope Innocent X. Secretly, a letter had been sent from Rome to the Custodian in which the Pope ordered him to make the Duke speak to Padre Giuseppe so the Padre's prayers and persuasive powers would make him convert from Lutheranism. The conversion would be a great advantage for Catholic religious affairs in many countries, not only a direct advantage for the Duke. The Duke asked permission to speak to Padre Giuseppe, saying he would leave Assisi immediately after.

The morning of the following day—it was a Sunday—the Duke and the two Counts were led down a secret stairway to the door of the chapel near the old novitiate where Giuseppe usually celebrated Mass. No one knew anything about their coming, least of all the Padre, who had not been informed of their arrival or purpose for being there. All three assisted with the Mass.

In trying to break the consecrated Host, Giuseppe began to wail and gave a great scream and flew into the air *backward in a kneeling position*. He then returned to the altar and remained in ecstasy for some time. He found the Host difficult to break; it was necessary to apply force to divide it. He deduced that some hard-hearted person was present at the Mass. The Duke wanted to know the reason for Padre Giuseppe's unexpected torrent of tears and asked the custodian, who explained that Padre Giuseppe was not inclined to speak about personal matters.

The Custodian, however, in deference to the Duke, did speak to Padre Giuseppe and was told: "These men you have sent to Mass this morning have a hard heart; they do not believe in the things that Holy Mother Church believes. For this reason, the Host went rigid in my hands and I cannot break it."[43]

The combined spectacle of the friar's ecstasy and the divination of his Lutheran scruples caused the duke to change his plans and stay on to talk in private with Joseph, setting the stage for his eventual conversion. The friar's impact may be seen in another way:

One of the two Counts, not respecting the miracles that God was performing for the sake of the Duke, said: "Curse the moment I came to this country! I had a peaceful spirit in my country. Now pangs of conscience and agitations of spirit are always troubling me." The Duke, however, did not share this reaction, because he was greatly moved by the evidence of the miracle and the effect of grace on him.[44]

For the count, the tacit inference was that if Joseph could fly backward, he must be privy to a divine force that can so mock and override nature. An encounter with Joseph could destroy all intellectual resistance. The unhappy German count finally converted to the Catholic faith in 1653.

Interestingly, we have confirmation of the duke's story from the pen of the philosopher Leibniz,[45] who was employed by the duke at the time. As far as I know, Leibniz never commented on Joseph's aerial talents. Church officials recognized in his marvels a possible tool for advancing political aims, but this is the only example I know of.

> Unfortunately, Leibniz does not seem to have written much about the marvelous events which hastened the steps of his noble patron into the Catholic fold. It is true that he bluntly says that the Duke went to Assisi and was there converted to the Roman Catholic faith by the wonder-working Father Joseph, but he appears to think it was wiser not to comment on the nature or explanation of these wonders.[46]

Church officials recognized in Joseph's marvels a means for advancing political aims, but the friar was too unpredictable to be harnessed as a tool of such intrigues. Recall that when he was asked to charm the Spanish ambassador's wife, he reportedly flew over her head, causing her to faint in terror.

The surgeon Francesco Pierpaolo, who attended Joseph on his deathbed, deposed that on four occasions he observed Joseph lifted up; in one striking case, he was operating on the ailing holy man:

> During his last illness, in the act of cauterizing the right leg by order of Doctor Giacinto Carosi, while he sat in his chair with his right leg propped up on my knee, I began to operate on him with instruments. I realized he could not feel a thing that I was doing during the operation. He sat there with his arms spread, his eyes open, his face turned toward heaven; the mouth was slightly open without giving a sign that he was breathing and I noticed that Padre Giuseppe was rising up into the air about a palm's length from the chair. He remained in the position he'd been in before, completely out of his senses. Moreover, I noticed that a fly was on the pupil of his eye and it kept returning even when I'd shoo it away. I got on my knees to better observe Padre Giuseppe, as did the doctor, who was also present, and we both verified that not only was he entirely out of his senses but he had also floated above the ground into the air in the way I've said. Seven or eight minutes passed with him in this state. Silvestro and the brothers of the convent who saw this said to "Call him by name!" And in holy obedience he returned to himself, with a smile on his face, and sat again in the chair as he had been sitting before, telling me to continue with the cauterization. I told him that it was done and he, not believing me, insisted I was teasing him. I let him see the leg already tied. He remarked that he hadn't felt any pain at all.[47]

Joseph's flying talents apparently showed no "decline effect." What kind of force could remain undiminished by rapidly declining health and near death? Joseph's strange bodily movements seem to have had something to do with displaced sexual desire, according to Bernini. But the sex drive must be at low ebb on one's deathbed. According to Bernini: "For more than 35 years his superiors would not let him participate in the choir or in processions or in the refectory because he would disrupt any event with his ecstasies and raptures." This obviously argues for the reality of something extraordinary manifesting in Joseph's life. So disturbing was the sight of the airborne friar that Church officials moved him around a great deal, always aiming to stem the tide of gawkers and followers who gathered around him. It is hard otherwise to explain the way the Church secretly kept moving him from convent to convent.

The external itinerary of Joseph's life makes little sense without a strong presumption that he powerfully impressed large numbers of people in ways that are consistent with the extant records. The cause of all the commotion was mainly Joseph's ecstatic flights, so obvious, so shocking, and so memorable. The chronicles describe fans digging holes in church walls, prying off roof tiles, so they could observe his impossible behaviors. It must have seemed the chance of a lifetime to behold living proof of supernatural power—a saint who could fly!

SUMMARY OF EVIDENCE AND POSSIBLE OBJECTIONS

Joseph's story is exceptional in many ways. The rareness of levitation is no doubt due to the rareness of just the right conditions necessary to produce the effect. Nor in fact are we certain about what those conditions are, except for the one constant variable, a state of ecstasy or possession, a state in which our ordinary functioning mindset is virtually displaced.

As I tried to show in chapter 2, levitation is just a very spectacular manifestation of mind acting on body. Among mind-body interactions, we can imagine a spectrum running from normal voluntary bodily movements to the abnormal (psychosomatic illness) and the supernormal (stigmata, poltergeists, levitation). But levitation, why is it important? I'll answer with a question: Who would have guessed that sparks of electricity would turn out to be part of the basic fabric of physical nature?

We may now ask: What are the points that favor the claim that Joseph went into ecstasy and indeed levitated (let us say) many times?

I would begin by pointing out that the ability to depose evidence for levitation is simple. No special skills or knowledge are needed to observe a human body rise from the ground and then to describe what one has observed. There could be circumstances where it was difficult to be sure about what one was seeing; but in normal daylight, in everyday circumstances, perception ought to have been, apart from the strangeness, simple and straightforward. The case of the surgeon Pierpaolo as witness is a good example; the critic has to claim that the surgeon and his assistant lied under oath or were in some way hallucinated as they operated on Joseph and noticed him floating above the operating chair.

Crucially, let me underscore: Joseph's case doesn't depend on a few good observations, one or two scenes that so-and-so mentioned, but on thirty-five years of roughly continuous eyewitness testimony. About 150 sworn eyewitness reports have been deposed, according to Parisciani—ordinary men and women, masons, surgeons, artists, popes, cardinals, ambassadors, theologians, inquisitors, dukes, kings, and princesses from all over Italy and parts of Europe.

The number cited refers to written testimony; the actual number of witnesses had to have been far greater. Given a public life of thirty-five years, at Mass, at trials, at festivals, on holy days, in his cell, and so on, many hundreds would have witnessed the phenomena, if not thousands.

In preparing for the beatification of Joseph in 1753, Prosper Lambertini (later Pope Benedict XIV) critically examined these documented observations.[48] As devil's advocate, Lambertini made a distinction between ecstasies and raptures that are God-inspired, natural (e.g., caused by illness), or caused by diabolical possession. In his treatise on beatification and canonization, Lambertini wrote:

> When I was Promoter of the Faith, the cause of the venerable of God, Joseph of Copertino, was discussed in the Congregation of Sacred Rites, on the doubt about his virtues, which, after my resignation of the office, was happily solved; in which unexceptionable witnesses deposed to the most frequent elevations and great flights on the part of that ecstatic and rapt servant of God.[49]

"Unexceptional witnesses" and "frequent elevations and great flights" constitute a strong endorsement. Lambertini studied the crucial documents, had formulated the rules and procedures of beatification and canonization, and was a master in handling evidence from his experience as devil's advocate.[50]

To quote a more recent statement from a writer decidedly unfriendly to the Catholic Church, Norman Douglas:[51]

> It might be urged that a kind of enthusiasm for their distinguished brother monk may have tempted the inmates of his convent to exaggerate his rare gifts. Nothing of the kind. He performed flights not only in Copertino, but also in various large towns of Italy, such as Naples, Rome, and Assisi. And the spectators were by no means an assemblage of ignorant personages, but men whose rank and credibility would have weight in any section of society.[52]

The way the Church treated Joseph is consistent with the reports of his levitations. The displacements of Joseph from convent to convent, his being summoned several times to appear before Inquisitors, and his exile to the most remote regions of Italy are all consistent with the written testimonials of witnesses to his startling aerial behaviors.

These spectacular performances caused a variety of problems for his superiors and for the church hierarchy. The troubles with the Inquisition, the displacements from place to more inaccessible place, being accused of acting like a messiah, all of this supports the reality of the levitation testimonials. Apart from something spectacular *like them*, one is at a loss to explain the Church's treatment of Joseph. Joseph is even said to have levitated before Pope Urban VIII and before the Inquisitors in Rome.[53] Were they all deceived, and what could have driven so many people to invent wild tales about a flying monk? There would be nothing to gain from collectively concocting such a story if it were not true.

Arguments suggesting that the effects were due to trickery, expectation, or illusion-inducing circumstances like stage props, or inadequate lighting, or deliberate dupers, have nothing to support them; Joseph's levitations occurred in daylight, suddenly, without warning, all over Italy. The ecstasies and flights occurred often while he was saying Mass in the presence of numerous people. Public life was so disrupted by them that his superiors were often forced to protect him from unruly crowds. Joseph suffered from the public reactions to his involuntary behaviors, and he was completely unable to suppress them. If the levitations were illusions or hallucinations, they were massive, coherent, and persistent—strangely, as realistic as reality itself.

Against the large body of deposed documentary evidence—history, letters, diaries, biographies, sworn testimonies at trials of beatification and canonization—what can the resolute disbeliever say? One could dogmatically assert that levitation is impossible, in which case belief in it would be based on magical thinking, wish fulfillment, projection, misinterpretation, hysterical fabrication, papist propaganda, and so on and so forth. One could simply refuse to look at the evidence on *a priori* grounds, like the philosophers who refused to look through Galileo's telescope.

But to explain the whole mass of reports and claims as pie in the sky, we would have to assume that large numbers of people were having the same illusion, systematically misinterpreting the movements of one friar for thirty-five years, and that all grades of people were swearing in public that they saw things they only imagined. We would have to assume that numerous Church authorities were lying or exaggerating and for some unknown reason hiding and shunting around a completely innocent, nonlevitating friar. One would have to posit an incredible amount of mendacity and stupidity on the part of Rosmi, Nuti, Bernini, Lambertini, and all the *processi* deposers who recorded their observations.

Resistance to the idea of levitation shows up in odd ways. There's a discussion of St. Joseph in volume 10 of S. Baring-Gould's *Lives of the*

Saints. Baring-Gould, an erudite and witty Anglican priest, strongly resists (but cannot ignore) the accounts of Joseph's flights, citing Pastrovicchi, Bernini, and other sources, and fully respecting the friar's piety. His entry on Joseph is long and dwells on the reported levitations, but is inaccurate in the descriptions. He speaks of the "extraordinary bounds into the air in which he indulged."

First of all, "indulged" is scarcely the right verb. He misrepresents Joseph as "jumping" or taking a "flying leap" to the top of an olive tree or cross or tabernacle above an altar! In a footnote, he writes: "At Protestant Dissenting Revivals similar extraordinary leaps and dances are not infrequent. The Jumpers and Shakers also make these nervous hysterical capers."[54]

Baring-Gould says nothing about the prolonged character of Joseph's flights, which could not be described as hysterical leaping and jumping but consisted of involuntary upliftings of the body always somehow emerging from ecstatic states and molded around delicate internal (*not* violent muscular) movements. Moreover, when people "jump" into the air—on top of an olive tree?—they normally fall back down. Joseph was repeatedly seen to remain aloft for "prolonged" periods of time.

Here I should mention an objection I heard from a philosopher who doggedly believes, without so much as referring to any of the testimony, that I should withdraw any factual claims concerning levitation because that would "violate" the law of gravity. But this appears to be a mistake. If I throw a ball up into the air I'm not violating the law of gravity; I'm exerting a mechanical force that briefly countervails the normal effect of gravity. Levitation, too, involves a force that temporarily does the same thing. But with levitation we don't understand the nature of the force, first recognized by the physicist William Crookes who studied the effect with D. D. Home. Again, Crookes, from the epigraph of the previous chapter: "These experiments appear conclusively to establish the existence of a new force, in some unknown manner connected with the human organization, which for convenience may be called the Psychic Force." The philosopher's fear is unfounded: levitation would not "violate" or invalidate any physical laws; but it would imply the existence of a "new force" that science needs to acknowledge and try to understand.

We should mention some recent criticism of the value of eyewitness testimony. There is a popular video-based experiment in which viewers are asked to describe the number of plays performed on a basketball court.[55] A figure dressed like a gorilla wanders on the court and, in the experiment, is often not noticed by observers. This is supposed to prove the grave limitations of eyewitness testimony, and you might be tempted to conclude that the reports of Joseph are suspect.

But the little contrived gorilla set-up is not comparable to the situation of witnesses repeatedly seeing Joseph levitate for thirty-five years in towns all over Italy. In Joseph's case, there were no prearranged instructions to look at something to distract the viewer from an object introduced into the viewing field. The gorilla experiment was about *not* noticing something present; in Joseph's levitations, something extraordinary was very much noticed. The gorilla experiment may be invoked to explain why people do not notice something, or do not take seriously evidence for certain taboo phenomena *like* levitation. Something is *not* noticed or examined or taken seriously because the dominant culture forbids you to believe it is possible. We are carefully misdirected, slyly induced to look away.

To sum up the main points that suggest the historical reality of Joseph's levitations: the simple and unambiguous nature of the evidence, the reported frequency, the numerous credible witnesses and sworn depositions, the steady recurrence of the phenomenon over thirty-five years, and the convoluted way the Church dealt with the friar. This last includes periods of intense scrutiny by the Holy Office and Inquisitors in Naples and Rome, the postmortem trials of his beatification and canonization, animadversions of a rationalistic pope, and testimony of Church officials who began by charging him with "offenses" that could have cost him his life, but which were all dropped as false. All this could give a resolute disbeliever in levitation a serious intellectual headache.

NOTES

1. Thurston and Attwater, 1980, vol. 3, p. 588.
2. See pp. 68–90.
3. See Arbman, 1968, *passim*.
4. DB, p. 27.
5. Rosmi's *Diaries* (see appendix).
6. Parisciani has written an entire book about Joseph and a man who did not want to be king; Joseph talked John Waza out of becoming a Jesuit, predicting he would have a more important role to play in the history of Europe. See Parisciani's book about Joseph and Poland, 1988.
7. GP, 1963, p. 442.
8. Ibid., p. 438.
9. Ibid., p. 440.
10. Ibid., p. 443.
11. Jung, 1958, pp. 203–95.
12. Angus, 1925–1975, pp. 100–101.
13. GP, p. 447.
14. GP, p.448.
15. For further discussion of this point, see chapter 7.
16. GP, p. 468.
17. DB, p. 150.
18. DB, p. 60.

19. DB, p. 62.
20. Sebasti, 2003, p. 96.
21. Ibid., p. 92.
22. Thurston, 1952, p. 16; *Acta Sanctorum*, Sep. vol. 5, pp. 1040–42.
23. DB, p. 155.
24. DB, p. 156.
25. Ibid.
26. DB, p. 147.
27. DB, p. 149.
28. DB, p. 201.
29. DB, p. 152.
30. See Brown, 1981, *The Cult of the Saints,* p. 107.
31. DB, p. 152.
32. DB, p. 47.
33. DB, p. 148.
34. DB, p. 150.
35. DB, p. 26.
36. DB, p. 30.
37. DB, p. 128.
38. DB, p. 72.
39. DB, chap. 11.
40. A.S. 2037, f. 72 verso.
41. Sebasti, 2003, p. 97.
42. P. 112.
43. DB, p. 85.
44. DB, p. 86.
45. Leibniz, 1843, p. 9.
46. Dingwall, 1962, p. 20.
47. DB, p. 134.
48. Haynes, 1970, pp. 116–37.
49. Pope Benedict XIV, 1850, *Heroic Virtue* (vol. 3): *A Portion of the Treatise of Benedict XIV on the Beatification and Canonization of the Servants of God*, p. 116.
50. For a discussion of Lambertini's critical role as "devil's advocate," see Haynes (1970), pp. 25–43.
51. See *North American Review*, 1913.
52. See also a separate account in Douglas's *Old Calabria*, pp. 84–89.
53. Haynes, 1970, p. 35.
54. Baring-Gould, 1914, p. 297.
55. Chabris and Simons, 2010.

Chapter 4

A Complement of Talents

> From the time of his ordination St. Joseph's life was one long succession of ecstasies, miracles of healing and supernatural happenings on a scale not paralleled in the reasonably authenticated life of any other saint.[1]
>
> —Herbert Thurston

The historical documents on Joseph contain reports of various remarkable phenomena. The epigraph, from the habitually precise and cautious Thurston, is our warrant for this chapter. To grasp the range of the friar's impact on people wherever he went, I want to recount in brief some of his other reported "supernatural happenings."

Like the shaman, medium, or diviner, the local saint typically is a multitasker. In modern society, the type of versatile saint or well-rounded shaman is replaced by specialists: counselor, psychotherapist, priest, sage, exorcist, pharmacist, psychiatrist, philosopher, theologian, mythographer, entertainer. Joseph was not quite that versatile, but in addition to the reported gravity immunities, he displayed other extraordinary talents or, as they are termed in Joseph's tradition, charisms.

Bernini's *Vita* contains reports of the odor of sanctity, exorcising demons, healings, claims of "infused wisdom," penetrating the secrets or forgotten thoughts of others, prophecy or precognition, and power over animals and natural forces. Let's have a look.

ODOR OF SANCTITY

Since the martyrdom of St. Polycarp in the second century, supernatural fragrance has been linked to heroic sanctity and sexual purity. It was prominent with Padre Pio (now canonized), who was said to make his presence known to distant persons through various odors.[2] In Joseph's weirdly expressive world, moral qualities were said to assume a material presence. They radiated atmospheres. Bernini wrote:

> Padre Giuseppe was rewarded with the gift of this mystical perfume, *which everyone could smell*. It penetrated his body and his clothes and his cell and everything belonging to him—a smell so pleasant that it astonished all who knew it. There are many testimonies.[3]

From one deposed witness in the *processi*:

> I know that the cell where Padre Giuseppe lived and his clothes exuded a perfume that must have the fragrance of heaven because it could not possibly have been natural. In fact, it smelled just like the perfume that came out of Saint Clair's Breviary in Assisi, which is kept in the reliquary at the church in San Damiano. I have had first-hand experience of that smell.
>
> And when I returned to the Convent and the cell of Padre Giuseppe, the other Religious would ask me if I was also wearing perfume. I would respond that personally I would not use perfume but had been with Padre Giuseppe, who smelled that way. His smell would stay with me for two entire weeks even though I washed my hands daily. This happened despite not touching anything that belonged to Giuseppe, but only sitting in his cell in conversation with him.[4]

Another witness reported that Joseph's odor resembled one that came from the tomb of Saint Anthony of Padua. We should note the suggestive power of odors; there is nothing visible and defined we can use to contrast one odor from another. Still, witnesses insist on the odor of sanctity being in a class all its own. Thurston tries to score a point against the Spiritualists because, in his view, their mystical perfumes seem more mundane than paradisal. This sounds like Thurston's bias at work, but as with levitation, he would be right to insist on the robustness of the reports of unexplained saintly fragrances. Joseph's was not an odor easily washed out, according to Padre Angelucci:

> A certain Bernardino had given my mother a dirty cape of Padre Giuseppe's to wash, but it so happened that this cape, even though washed in hot water with soap, continued to emanate the perfume that one smells in the cell of the Padre. I know it well because I smelled it during the entire time I spent at the Sacred Convent with Padre Giuseppe.[5]

The odor in question appears to stay attached to physical objects like capes that touched his body and it apparently could survive a good washing with soap and hot water. The deposition of Cardinal Spinola is brief but striking:

When I entered in that little cell, the sweet perfume would cheer me up and I could compare it to nothing in nature or in the art of man. But one thing is certain: while the smell of most perfumes would eventually make me ill, the perfume of Padre Giuseppe brought me the greatest pleasure and seemed even to heal my body.[6]

The smell produced therapeutically joyous emotion. These experiences could not be explained; the idea of the friar sneaking around and dousing himself with perfume has no merit. The application of ordinary perfumes would have disgusted him. In fact, he often used tobacco in hopes of *concealing* the real odor he emitted. The odors, like the raptures, were making his life difficult; they attracted too much attention. Another experiencer of the odors, Father John from Fossombrone, said:

For all the time that I conversed with Padre Giuseppe, I always found him to be an extremely pure person. The perfume that emanated from his body was very strong and pleasant, it pleased everyone who entered his cell that, although tiny and almost always dark, always smelled so delightful and you could always find him because of the perfume of his cell.

That perfume spread through all the cells and lingered on in clothes which, though washed often with soap and lye, never lost the fragrance. The same thing happened with the priestly robes that the Padre used; not only did they smell like the perfume but it spread through the armoires and the other robes kept the smell. The same thing happened to those he touched.

Giulia Bentivoglio, whose daughter Padre Giuseppe had given a rosary, said that for an entire year the rosary produced a most wonderful odor and that even now one could smell it, though faintly.[7]

According to Bernini, Joseph's perfume lingered in his cell for about thirteen years after he died at Osimo. Any attempt to account for the odor of sanctity would have to explain how what seems an abstract virtue like purity could materialize into a presence of the atmosphere, invisible like thought yet pervasive like perfume. Or, I suppose, the odor might be due to changes from ascetic practice, a biochemical phenomenon, but I'm not aware of any evidence to support this view.

The Renaissance scholar and magus Marsilio Ficino sought to blend art and religion into a therapy of the imagination.[8] Ficino thought the aromas of nature were spiritually nourishing and have the power to lift us out of our ordinary selves:

By means of this fragrance, as though it were the breath and spirit of the world's vitality, they nourish you and refresh you. Indeed, I would say that your own spirit is very much like these fragrances, and through this spirit, the link between your body and soul, these fragrances refresh your body and wonderfully restore your soul.[9]

The fragrances said to emanate from Joseph seemed to do what Ficino said were the high purpose of the senses, which is to raise us into another dimension of consciousness.

PENETRATING SECRET THOUGHTS AND FUTURES

Joseph displayed a type of *charism* or "gift" nowadays called *extrasensory perception* (ESP)—in other words, *direct* awareness of other minds or the external world. In Joseph's culture, telepathy was called "scrutiny of hearts." The modern term *clairvoyance* ("clear-seeing") would correspond to the visionary faculty. Bernini reports instances of Joseph reading the minds of his confreres, reminding them of small infractions they had committed and forgotten. Also, Joseph, like others in this tradition, was said to know *à distance* whenever a pope or other VIP expired. For example, in a report that combines telepathy and foreknowledge:

> One morning, after having celebrated Mass, Joseph rushed into the cell of the Father General, who happened to be in Assisi for a visit, and in his presence, told Fr. Roberto Nuti (the first biographer of Joseph) that he wanted to confide a secret. Nuti promised to keep the secret; Joseph told him that the Pope had died. He knew this because—while saying Mass that morning—he had not found the Pope's name in the record of the living.
>
> He added that on Sunday this news would be known throughout the city. And so indeed on Friday morning, July 29, 1644, Pope Urbano VIII died in Rome. On the following Sunday, Marino Nati, secretary of Cardinal Barberini, brought the news of the death to Assisi—which validated in all particulars the Saint's prediction.[10]

At this time, information was not conveyed instantaneously by technology; all communication was person to person, so it's hard to imagine any leaks between Rome and Assisi to explain Joseph's knowing the "secret." The records prove that he knew of the pope's death before news of it arrived from Rome.

People often asked Joseph to pray for someone in distress, and he would say:

> "I plant the seed, but the gift is up to God." If they told him the name of the person, Padre Giuseppe would describe that person with precision—naming the relatives, what work they did, even the street where they lived. He spoke

as though he were reading about them in some book of genealogy, things that stunned all who heard because everyone knew that Padre Giuseppe had never before passed through Osimo or known anyone from Osimo; in fact he had never even heard of the town until he left Fossombrone to come to the Convent of the Conventuals.[11]

All these apparent *ad hoc* extensions of cognition occurred in the thick of everyday life. The following excerpt illustrates Joseph the healer at work:

Andriella Gravini, a gentlewoman from the city of Salice, testified in the processi: When I was a little girl, my left eye and my mouth were contorted toward my ear and my mother, terrified, didn't know what to do. A man from Copertino arrived at that time and told my parents to take me to Padre Giuseppe, said to be a saint. The morning after we heard this, we all—me, my parents and one of my brothers—went to the Church of the Grotella in Copertino where we found Padre Giuseppe saying the Mass. We entered the sacristy and my father approached him. When he came toward me he called me by name and told me not to worry because my affliction was nothing. He made the sign of the cross on my eye and my mouth and I was immediately healed. Padre Giuseppe then told me to recite the Our Father and Hail Mary every day. He wanted the little cross that I had on my Rosary, exchanged it for a medallion, which I was to bring with me to devotions.

Afterward, we returned to Salice. I said the Our Father and the Ave Maria maybe once every eight days and lost the medallion. After a few years, my father gave me away in marriage. One morning after the marriage, while I was getting dressed, I felt so dizzy that I fell to the ground and almost died: I could not see, I could not move—everyone at home was terrified. My parents and two aunts and brother were with me when this happened, but before we could get to Copertino, I got even sicker to the point that it seemed I was going to die.

When we arrived at the Grottella, they carried me inside and placed me at the altar while Padre Giuseppe was saying the Mass. I still couldn't see a thing. When the friar saw me, he told me not to worry; he took off his priestly vestments and came to me. Stand up, he said, and so I did, much to the amazement of everyone. Then he made me climb up on the altar and put something on my head, I'm not sure what. I suddenly felt quite happy and Padre Giuseppe told me to get down by myself, which I did, and I began to walk, again to the amazement of everyone.

Then he brought me to an altar and told me that I had not done as I was told—had not said either the Our Father or the Hail Mary every day, but only once every eight days. He told me I had lost the medallion he gave me. He said I had married badly because I was too young, and that for this I was afflicted. He hit me over the head a few times and pulled my hair—yes, I was stupid, they told me the groom was old and his mother was strange—this was all true. Padre Giuseppe knew all these things that no one knew except me. Then he told me that my husband would from here on treat me like a lady. And in fact, my husband did treat me like a lady, as long as he lived. The Padre gave me a relic to wear, as I do to this day. We were all so happy when we left him and grateful that my health had been restored.[12]

The next example could be described as a coincidence; even so, the effect was unnerving:

Returning from L'Aquila, Padre Giuseppe and his companion, Antonio Pecorella, brought a little cardinal that had been given to Giuseppe. Brother Antonio was ruminating silently over who might have given the cardinal to Giuseppe, thinking of one possibility after another. Walking on, Giuseppe turned to him, "Nobody I can think of gave me that little bird. I want to set it free. Open the cage and let it go!" Antonio was filled with sacred terror, seeing himself with a person who could read his mind.[13]

The following proves how annoying it could be to have someone like Joseph around:

A novitiate, while reciting in the choir, was daydreaming about going to the orchard to eat figs. Padre Giuseppe, after the Office, rebuked him for not having concentrated on the Hours. The novitiate claimed to follow the Hours closely. Padre Giuseppe said, "What if I climb that fig tree and count how many you have eaten?"
    And then he told him every single thought that he had entertained during the Office. The same novitiate, whose name was Francesco de Angelis, went to kiss Padre Giuseppe's hand after choir, and Giuseppe said to him, smiling, "And by the way, when we say the Matins, I don't want you to be sleeping."[14]

One more example, itself typical, of similar cases found with the Curé of Ars and Padre Pio, often in the confessional booth: the sense of having one's personality scanned, reaching back into the past and sometimes toward the future. Brother Francesco, from the Convent of the Chiesa Nuova in Assisi, testified:

I know from experience that Padre Giuseppe had a gift from God to know the inner workings of souls. In fact, when I first went to speak with him, without ever having met me, he told me point by point everything about my life, both things of the present and things of the past, but especially things he had seen within my soul. Such things could not possibly be known by anyone except God himself. And everything that he told me was true; and he told me other things that would happen in the future and that indeed did happen.[15]

Bernini distinguished precognition from telepathy (without using those terms). In discussing Joseph's foreknowledge, he states that he knew of "22 cases of precise predictions of death" in the recorded trials. It should be noted that these numbers are by no means final or definitive, but only reflect records available to Bernini before 1722. Bernini gives several examples of apparent precognition, one very concise like this: "A woman requested for her sons, destined to study at the university in Rome, to be blessed by Padre Giuseppe. The Padre replied that they wouldn't go to Rome but to Heaven. Both sons were killed during the journey to Rome."[16]

On a brighter note, an organist, Signor Della Porta, had not heard from his brother, who was away in Bergamo, and was bemoaning what he believed to be his death to Joseph, who replied: "No, he is not dead, he's alive, and on Monday you'll receive a letter from your brother."[17] As foretold by Joseph, Della Porta in fact received a letter from his brother, who was alive and well.

This is typical of many ESP stories from Joseph; the narratives often combine telepathy and foreknowledge. Another example of foreknowledge is one in which Joseph had to fend off an outburst of rage. The Baron of Lequille, Don Horatio Saluzzo, was using small-town Grottella for a tryst with his lover. Joseph divined the baron's secret and was pestering him to go to confession and terminate the illicit affair.

One day Joseph, who was loitering near the church, noticed the baron passing, and he looked at and walked toward him. They were about to meet when the baron whipped out his dagger and lunged at the friar, making the motion to stab him. Joseph deflected the blow with his arm and cried out, "Repent, my son, because from this moment on you must render an account of your misdeeds to the Lord." A few days later the baron took ill, and before long his body was covered with festering sores. When the afflicted man passed by in his carriage, Joseph grimly observed, "Here today, tomorrow the grave," and by September 11, 1634, after a hasty confession, the baron was dead.[18]

Passing over some convoluted death predictions, consider this different kind of story, a case of conversion by embarrassment:

> Dianora di Nardo, a vain prostitute, was passing through Copertino. Padre Giuseppe saw her enter the church and said to all present: "Here's Mary Magdalene!" And then, turning to her, he said: "When? When? God wants you! Leave behind those vain gowns and love God, Magdalene!" The moment Dianora heard herself called "Magdalena," she stopped wearing her flashy gowns, and wore instead a dress of rough wool—repenting everything, thanks to Padre Giuseppe, who laughed with joy from this admirable change, which he saw coming by his prescience.[19]

Joseph was using a bit of imagination therapy here, suggesting to the woman she was in another time and setting and about to meet Jesus in the flesh. Joseph, in turn, played the part of Jesus so effectively that Dianora was inspired to model her behavior after Magdalene.

INFUSED WISDOM

Can people be "infused" with wisdom from a source beyond themselves? It was claimed that Joseph displayed such infused wisdom. To look at this question, a parallel to mediumship may help. Although the vast majority of mediumistic or channeled literary production is of a low quality, there are exceptions, in which a person of modest mental and educational equipment becomes entranced and seems suddenly to acquire heightened mental powers. In the case of "Patience Worth," the vehicle for infusion was wit, sacred history, pithy rhymes, wise saws, and prodigious memory feats.[20]

When the American medium Pearl Curran became possessed by "Patience Worth" she could (a) improvise on the spot in the various styles of her previous literary productions; (b) simultaneously compose something with one hand while dictating orally another composition, producing two coherent streams of words without overlap or confusion; (c) produce dialogues or narratives switching from one style to another, sometimes deliberately mixing them up in the same composition.

In these high-speed performances, the author never blotted a line. The material seemed almost preformed, and she could instantly switch from one line of composition to another, as if she were drawing on hidden storehouses packed with ready-mades. The entranced Pearl Curran performed at a level beyond anything one would guess of an untutored Midwestern housewife.

"In some way the dissociation has resulted in the formation of a self of greatly increased caliber," wrote Morton Prince,[21] adding two pages later that the medium's genius consisted of being "released from the inhibitions that clog and check the normal consciousness. She ('Patience') is a dissociated self, and as such freed from the burdens and concerns of life, from all the claims that split the will and bind her fancy." Prince concluded his study of "Patience Worth" with this striking assertion: "Either our concept of what we call the subconscious must be radically altered, so as to include potencies of which we hitherto have had no knowledge, or else some cause operating through but not originating in the subconscious of Mrs. Curran must be acknowledged."[22]

In the case of the medium "Mrs. Willett," it appeared to competent observers like the philosopher C. D. Broad that in her entranced state, she was able to discuss abstract ideas in a style and at a level of competence beyond her normal capacities. Mrs. Willett had little interest in abstract philosophy and psychology. But entranced, she articulated ideas of a caliber on a par with the deceased Frederic Myers and Henry Sidgwick (see chapter 9) and Gurney. Broad wrote: "Surely it *is* very surprising indeed that anything of this kind should come from a lady so completely uninterested in and ignorant of philosophy as Mrs. Willett was, and that it should be couched in language so characteristic of the persons ostensibly communicating."[23]

The best explanation of Mrs. Willett's performance may in fact be that the excarnate intelligence of Myers "infused" the medium with *his* knowledge.

How does this compare with Joseph? Recall that he was academically challenged and as ignorant of theology and the rites of exorcism as Mrs. Willett was of philosophy and psychical research. Joseph never spent time with books or was interested in theological abstractions. Bernini recounts the claims of many learned religious who swore that Joseph displayed spiritual, even theological, wisdom beyond his education.

What was the source of this wisdom? "Infused" from what? As Joseph grew in fame and met various distinguished people—Spanish admirals and German dukes, the king of Poland and the princess of Savoy, and countless others who were awed by him and valued his conversation—he must have acquired some practical wisdom. In his relentless struggle to master himself, he must also have learned a great deal about the byways of the inner life.

Many were hypnotized by his awe-inspiring powers. He made graphically real for spectators the concrete possibility of Jesus walking on water and ascending to heaven—"arguments" that might shock the most acute intellect into submissive credulity. For witnesses of Joseph, the entire fantastic supernatural apparatus of Christian belief would acquire what seemed like overwhelming, tangible reality, as indeed we know from the reports of people said to run away, pass out, or thrill with sacred terror upon hearing him scream and watching him rapt in ecstasy. The sheer authority of such a bewildering personality must have contributed to the impression that he was infused not only with higher powers but also with higher theological wisdom.

But I doubt that his case was comparable either to Pearl Curran's or to Mrs. Willett's. My guess is that Joseph wowed his theology-stuffed superiors with amazing candor and startling good sense. Michael di Monte Albotto, a Capuchin who documented Padre Giuseppe's inability to study, wrote the following:

> Padre Giuseppe was quite gifted with an ability to understand in a way that was superior to the kind of understanding acquired in school. He responded to some theological doubts I proposed to him in a profound way, using simple language and modest examples. The subjects were: Predestination, the Holy Trinity, the efficacy of Grace, Free Will, and such things.[24]

Nothing more specific is given. We need more details from these exchanges to judge whether Joseph really knew things incommensurate with the limits of his known training and intellectual skills. None of the testimonials of his alleged wisdom seem to prove anything as surprising as what Patience Worth or Mrs. Willett could do.

The reason Joseph gave an impression of unexplained "infused knowledge" may have something to do with his use of "symbolic" thinking. Giacomo Roncagli deposed that Joseph had the gift of wisdom because "he always spoke by means of symbols even though he had never studied and barely knew how to read." He communicated his ideas by gesture and symbol with such skill that educated individuals went on record affirming that he possessed something they called "infused" wisdom. In my opinion, the friar cut through abstractions and got to the living heart of meaning, and by means of his symbolic imagination, communicated with people in a natural way.

For an infusion of Joseph's wisdom, let's look at his raplike couplets on the less than pure motives that sometimes prompt people to "do good." Each couplet begins, *Chi fa ben sol,* or "he who does good only." For example, *Chi fa ben sol per paura / non fa niente and poco dura.* "He who does good only from fear / does nothing that will endure." *Chi fa ben sol per usanza / se non perde poco avanza.* "He who does good only from habit / will gain little and advance less."

Each couplet focuses on some inner motivation that is less than pure and that in fact undermines the value of the alleged good. One might, according to Joseph, do good by force, by luck, by putting on a show, from vainglory, from avarice, from neglect, or solely from the desire to save oneself. In Joseph's view, the only valid criterion for "doing good" is love. Without love, all that we do is suspect. The couplets form a subtle psychology of mystical love, but the insights are compatible with Joseph's mental endowments, infused, if you like, by his own experience and honestly garnered self-knowledge.

HEALINGS

Among the claimed charisms of Joseph, the healings were no doubt experienced with awe but also with relief and gratitude. Accounts of "miraculous" healings are scattered throughout the records of his life. This saint, mostly a figure in a local community, served as health department factotum and chief emergency respondent on call for everybody and anybody in desperate straits. And with all that responsibility, he did the job *pro bono publico.* And to add miracle to miracle, his healing powers were said to *increase* after he died. It was ardently assumed their saint would respond more effectively from the unobstructed heights of heaven; so soon after he died, many called on him for help with particularly high expectations.

Are there criteria for "miraculous" healing? According to Lambertini (later, Pope Benedict XIV[25]), the sick person must not have responded to other medical interventions; the seriousness of the condition must be established; and the healing must occur immediately and be permanent and without relapse. Stringent. Lambertini specified these criteria in his classic study of beatification and canonization, and had before him the depositions on Joseph's healings.[26] Most striking were the reported rapidity and permanence of the friar's alleged healings.

Lambertini relied on two reports of healing to support the Cause for Joseph's beatification. The process was complicated and drawn out. Three bishops of Nardo, Assisi, and Osimo introduced the Cause; under Clement XII in 1735, an inquiry was launched and brought to a favorable conclusion. On the feast day of the Assumption of Our Lady, a solemn public decree affirmed Joseph's heroic virtue. The first step accomplished, discussion of the miracles began. The congregation devoted three meetings to this, which terminated in October 1752. Lambertini, now Pope Benedict XIV, published the decree approving two healing miracles.

For six years Victor Mattei of Osimo (where Joseph had just died in 1663 and whose body lay in state at the sacristy) had a swelling "as large as a loaf of bread and very hard" on his right knee. Incapacitated, intense pain tortured him. The surgeon saw no way to treat the growth, so Victor gave up on human help and tried—he could scarcely walk—to approach Joseph's body. He obtained permission to visit Joseph's room.

He entered and came to the private chapel where the saint had said Holy Mass. There he made an act of lively faith and pressed his knee against the step of the altar, which was worn down by the knees of the saint during his long protracted prayers. On touching the step, all pain and the swelling disappeared at once, so that no trace of the infirmity remained. The knee was perfectly healed and could be moved like the other, which had never been affected.[27]

So was this wrought by the intercession of the dead saint or by the sick man's faith? All we can say for sure: *If* the facts are as reported—the duration of the affliction, size of the growth, and immediacy of healing—we have evidence for unexplained healing power.

The second case that Lambertini affirmed as miraculous involved the son, Stephen, of the previous miracle recipient, also occurring in the year Joseph died. Accidentally struck by a stone, the boy's eye was crushed and scrunched inside the socket. The doctors said that Stephen's vision would never be restored; his mother, hopeful because of what she believed Joseph did for her husband, brought the afflicted boy to Joseph's tomb. After repeated prayers, "the boy then pressed his blind eye to the stone that covered the saint's grave and instantly recovered his sight."[28] Even if the boy were not really made blind by a blow from a stone, again, the reported speed of the healing upon contact with Joseph's remains would still need to be explained.

In 2009, Jacalyn Duffin, a Canadian physician-historian, published an overview of medical miracles and Catholic saints based on a study of documents in the Vatican Archives. She reviewed four centuries worth of testimony of "medical miracles." She had been invited by Church authorities to examine the medical records of a patient in remission from acute leukemia and later discovered the patient's story was related to canonizing the first Canadian-born saint, Marie-Marguerite d'Youville.

Duffin's book focuses on unexplained saint-caused *miracle* claims.[29] The historical records indicate a phenomenon worthy of study, she concludes; her fourteen hundred cases, dating from 1588 to 1999, included people of forty-eight countries, from Australia to Uruguay. To qualify as a "miracle," the healing must be "complete, durable, and instantaneous."[30] Extraordinary speed of recovery was frequently encountered, according to Duffin, the sort that would prompt the physician to remark, "I can't explain this."

The most impressive conclusion of this study was the stability of extraordinary healings reported through the last four centuries. Despite the advances of modern science and the use of medical examiners not necessarily Catholic or believers in "miracles," Duffin found that carefully documented healings continue to occur in present times. This rebounds to some degree upon the plausibility of the healing stories that swirled around Joseph.

We can also say that healings arising from prayer have been observed and systematically studied. R. Gardner published a paper comparing modern experimental prayer studies in the *British Medical Journal*.[31] Gardner reviewed seven cases involving group prayers occurring between 1951 and 1982. In six of them were rapid healings of individuals suffering from various grave illnesses. Another notable study published in an alternative (albeit peer-reviewed) journal reports on "10 cases of rapid and complete healing of serious and long-standing illnesses, including rheumatoid arthritis, multiple sclerosis, various kinds of cancer (bone, brain, and kidney) and other debilitating and life-threatening diseases that had not been, or could not be, cured by conventional medical treatment."[32]

The facts suggest that rapidly effective mental healing occurs today as it was said to have occurred with Joseph in Bernini's 1722 biography. In Morton Kelsey's history of healing and Christianity,[33] he notes that healing stories, physical and mental, take up roughly a fifth of the gospel texts. Kelsey thinks this emphasis on the body is uniquely Christian (even calls it "materialistic"); there is a deep concern with the health of body and soul. Jesus appears as a healer, an exorcist, and a prophet. The healings were introduced as signs that the kingdom of God was at hand. After a healing encounter in the Gospels (e.g., Matt. 9:22), "Jesus turned and saw her. 'Take heart, daughter,' he said, 'Your faith has healed you.' And the woman was healed that moment."[34]

Do people in general really possess such a potential for self-healing? The question seems important, but the emphasis in the Church has turned from healing toward morality and dogma. In Thomas Matthews's study of early Christian art, Christ was at first portrayed as carrying a wand, a symbol of the magician. During the first three centuries, most artworks memorialize miracle stories, with Christ portrayed as the great healer. The Protestant Reformation traded miracles for economic rationalism, otherworld longings for the paradise of capitalism.[35] The healing arts were entrusted to modern science and industry. The primitive Christian philosophy of spiritual healing would fade into medical materialism.

John Dowling, a general practitioner, wrote a short but pointed piece on the cures at a modern-day healing shrine, Lourdes, and how they are medically assessed. Today there is an international committee of medical experts that decides whether a given case fits Lambertini's criteria. As Duffin's book reminds us, there remains a persistent flow of cases that baffle physicians, but reluctance to admit the unexplained persists. Dowling calls attention to the problems of some doctors: "It's very hard for many doctors to accept a cure as scientifically inexplicable, let alone miraculous, and some have reacted to the unexpected cure of their patient by declaring the original diagnosis false, even when it was well supported by full investigations."[36]

Not all trained physicians resist new and unexplained phenomena. Take, for example, the French surgeon Alexis Carrel, who visited Lourdes in 1903. Recently out of medical school and skeptical of miracles, he decided to spend some time with seriously ill patients at the famous shrine. One of them, Marie Ferrand, was in the last stages of tubercular peritonitis and was thought to be very close to death. Barely able to speak, she insisted, however, that she wanted to bathe in the pool. Carrel at first refused to allow this because he thought any movement would kill her. He considered her case hopeless. The young woman kept pleading, so they carried her to the grotto and immersed her frail dying body in the pools.

It was three o'clock in the afternoon. Much to Carrel's amazement—at first he thought he was going mad—her gray sunken face immediately began to change, and her pulse slowed (it had been racing at 130). The crowd didn't even notice what was happening, but within an hour Marie Ferrand, except for weakness and lingering pallor, had regained her health.

Carrel and others observed it happen, a continuous transformation, right before their eyes: "The blanket which covered Marie Ferrand's abdomen was gradually flattening out." Within a few hours, Carrel and other physicians examined and palpated the woman's abdomen and found her completely rid of any swelling. Carrel wrote his eyewitness account in the third person: "There could be no doubt whatever that the girl was cured. It was, of course, the most momentous thing he had ever seen. It was both frightening and wonderful to see life come pouring back into an organism almost totally destroyed by years of illness."[37]

Claims of healing miracles continue to be made in modern times all over the world, despite rarely hearing much about them. The two volumes by Craig Keener I cited in the introduction cover a wide range of reportage. Keener is more concerned to prove the ongoing reality of miracle claims than justify the validity of the claims, although he attempts to do so whenever possible.

Massive numbers of people are claiming healings and other dramatic miracles throughout the world, including in the West. Those scholars who still write as if all such claims in antiquity must be legendary write as if in a social vacuum, oblivious to overwhelming testimony against their assumptions.[38]

This needs to be clarified. What the contemporary claims prove is that the ancient claims may have been based on real healing or apparent healing experiences; but they say nothing about the cause of the healings, whether paranormal by modern standards or psychosomatic. And they say nothing about the supernatural status of the claims.

There are indeed credible reports of unexplained healings—modern scientific studies designed to prove the effectiveness of prayer and mental healing. In chapter 2, we cited the effects of placebo and nocebo, the case of the man who kept cancer at bay as long as he believed in a useless drug called Krebiozen. We have no clear understanding of why a belief can bring about the temporary or permanent healing of cancer. The critical variable, as far as the actual evidence, seems more to be faith in the supernatural than the supernatural itself (whatever that is).

The people who cried out to Joseph in prayer or went to his tomb for healing did so in good faith. There is also a method in Joseph's experience in stories of Jesus, and other traditions, which relies on physical contact with the healer. Jesus (John 9:6) "spit on the ground, made some mud from the saliva, and put it on the man's eyes" who was said to be blind from birth, and restored his vision. In Luke 8: 43–44, we read: "Now there was a woman suffering from a haemorrhage for the past twelve years whom no one had been able to cure. She came up behind him and touched the fringe of his cloak; the haemorrhage stopped at that very moment."[39] Contact with Jesus's body is what heals; objects, moist from the sweat or blood of Joseph, applied to afflicted parts, were said to result in healing. The belief that one is touching, seeing, or smelling divine power is what seems to spark the healing prodigies.

A UNIQUE APPROACH TO EXORCISM

Joseph was sometimes called upon to heal—or rather, exorcise—souls said to be demonically possessed. Exorcising demoniacs was a major practice in early Christianity and was widespread during sixteenth- and seventeenth-century Europe. In Bernini's narrative, talk of demons comes up almost casually. Belief in invisible agents intent on causing havoc was assumed without much question. Bernini published four books on the history of heresies and presumably took the demonic seriously.

As a priest, Joseph was supposed to be able to deal with victims of possession, but he was not facile with the formal rites of exorcism. Nevertheless, he was sometimes called upon to treat those thought to be possessed. Joseph would never disobey his superiors, so he had to devise his own method of "exorcism," his own original procedure for de-possessing somebody of a "demon."

Remembering, perhaps, a saying of Jesus—"resist not evil"—Joseph made it a point not to impose himself or take an antagonistic or even superior view of the presumed demonic entity. The secret of his treatment was to be completely disarming. He would say there was nothing at all personal about his arrival and that he was merely acting under holy obedience, so the demon might just as well calm down and quit making a fuss. There was nothing confrontational about Joseph's approach to the demoniac.

By refusing to directly confront and, in effect, certify the demon as a demon, there was no need for the afflicted person to behave *like* a demoniac. Joseph is said to have obtained positive results using his method of no method. Rather than *de-*possess he seems to have helped the victim *re-*possess himself. His method consisted of not resisting, even (paradoxically) affirming the "demonic" element. This was his philosophy of exorcism, an acting out of the principle of nonresistance to evil. He took the wind out of the demoniac's sails by the power of nonresistance. By not naming or treating the supposed demon as a demon, he deprived the negative entity of its combative *raison d'etre*.

"MIRACLES" PRODUCED AFTER DEATH

Candidates for canonization must produce miracles after their death. Bernini begins the relevant chapter like this:

> Now let us finally consider the miracles that went on after Padre Giuseppe's death, things that happened by invoking him or his name, or by touching one of his relics, or by kissing an image of his face. In the processi, 50 miracles

are recorded from his lifetime; 80 are recorded in the 59 years since his death. I mean miracles that have been exhibited through formal testimony.[40]

These were mostly healing "miracles." For example, a pope attested this:

> During the time when his illness was at its worst and it seemed doubtful that he would live, Alessandro VII not only invoked the help of Padre Giuseppe but with extreme devotion put on a night shirt that had belonged to the Padre. No sooner had he donned the garment than the healing began to work. The pope's pain stopped instantly and he was able to urinate. He did not die and, thanks to the intercession of Padre Giuseppe, lived for another five years and became Pope.

What today one might call a meaningful coincidence—a placebo or autohypnotic effect—was construed in Alessandro's world as proceeding from the miraculous intervention of a deceased holy man. Another example:

> Padre Antonio, Franciscan at the Convent in Osimo, came down with an illness that left him speechless and paralyzed to the point that he seemed near death. A lay brother whose job was to assist the sick remembered that the dying man had been so devoted to Giuseppe that he prayed before his sepulcher every day. The brother brought a blanket that once belonged to Padre Giuseppe. Covering him with it, he said out loud: "Antonio, pray to Padre Giuseppe!" At the sound of the Padre's name, Antonio's voice boomed like thunder: "I'm praying to him!"
>
> He opened his eyes and moved his legs and arms; color returned to his face and, realizing that he was well, raised himself to sit on the bed, utterly happy, even laughing. Then, seeing a little table near the bed on which there was a vase of holy oil, with the voice and movements of a healthy person asked what the vase was doing there. The layman told him they had been ready to perform the rites of extreme unction.[41]

The story provides more details purporting to show that the healing was permanent. In almost every healing, results are said to be sudden and complete. Is Bernini exaggerating, fabricating? Lambertini, who defined the criteria for supernatural healing, chose "sudden" and "complete" as essential descriptors. Perhaps it was Joseph's healings that contributed to Lambertini's selection of criteria. Bernini puts it like this:

> What characterizes Padre Giuseppe's miracles consists in their being immediate, instantaneous, bringing increasing renown and credibility to Padre Giuseppe and more amazement to those present. The noble Graziano Benigni of Assisi, very sick and near death, invoked the Saint and touched his Rosary and improved right away and later was cured. Giovanni Martelli of Assisi, languishing near death because of a horrible stomach pain, prayed to Padre

Giuseppe and the pain stopped. Cornelio Saccalossi was cured immediately of a malignant fever through the slightest of contact with a beret that belonged to Padre Giuseppe. Several people received similar graces and the processi attest to miracle healings carried out "right away, in that instant, on the spot, on the same day" at only the invocation of his name or after mere contact with his rosary, his gown, his cord, his beret, or even a morsel of candied fruit that his lips had touched.[42]

One could say there must have been thousands of callings on the dead Padre that bore no results; in a percentage of cases the ailing person may get well coincidentally or as the result of a placebo response or any number of possible unknown, even unknowable, causes. But for many, if not for most people of Joseph's time, especially in the time soon after his death when his remains were still visible and his presence vividly felt, divine intervention apparently was the most probable cause.

Joseph kept a safe distance from women in life, but from his alleged station in the next world, he seems to have overcome his shyness. "Padre Giuseppe saved countless women from dying in childbirth," notes Bernini. Childbirth in seventeenth-century Italy was a dangerous enterprise, dangerous to the newborn and to the mother. Joseph himself knew only one of five of his siblings, the rest having died very young.

Bernini plays up the figure of Joseph as helper of women. One example will have to do, in which a strange treatment was administered. The Perugian Angelica di Costanzo miscarried a baby girl and barely survived herself. So intense was her pain and suffering, she begged for death. She appeared to be hanging by a thread and those attending her were impatient to begin the last rites:

> In these torturous moments, compassionate Anastasia di Bastiano took some crumbs of bread Padre Giuseppe scattered in the dining hall, which she saved in a little linen sack soaked in his blood. She put the crumbs in a spoonful of broth and made the dying woman swallow the mixture. Then she put the linen sack on the woman's stomach and begged for Padre Giuseppe's help. As soon as she swallowed the broth and the sack was on her stomach, a second dead fetus was disgorged from her womb. Freed of this fetus, the woman's life was saved.[43]

The woman's belief in and physical contact with Joseph's corporeal remains seems here to have helped her disgorge a dead fetus, which otherwise would have killed her.

There are stories of young boys and girls, even infants, being mysteriously healed or saved in perilous circumstances. The reports prove that in the minds of many, the dead friar was still ranging about and capable of exerting saving influences. The community believed that after death he was an active healing agency. I met a woman in Assisi in 2010, a native of Copertino, who said that she was in debt to Joseph for graces he had bestowed on her. I was struck by the warm conviction she had of being helped by a saint who died four centuries ago.

Chapter 29 in Parisciani (GP) is cheerfully titled "The Glorious Sepulcher." It covers what happened around the tomb of Joseph shortly after his death, beginning with an account of the autopsy. The physicians were amazed to find the heart had been completely dried out and looked like "toast" (*abbrustolito*). They felt they had witnessed something supernatural, "proceeding from the heat of Divine Love that boiled in his heart."[44] If Joseph really did generate all that physical heat, it does help us understand the mystical figure of speech, *incendium amoris* ("fire of love"), as containing more than metaphoric reality.

People visit the tombs of saints and prophets hoping for grace, inspiration, or a miracle of healing. Once Joseph's body was prepared and presented for exhibition, the padres started hearing one word, *aiuta* (help). In the chapter on the glories at his tomb, we find page after page of sworn testimony as to how the calls for help produced results. Stories range from accounts of long, grinding headaches suddenly vanishing to people who were receiving extreme unction being snatched from the brink of death and restored to health and well-being.

Sometimes the reply came in the form of an apparition of the dead friar, typically with an upbeat message, followed by the ill's prompt riddance. Healing events usually involved a relic of the saint and the belief it had been in contact with his body. Perception of contact is crucial to the healing effect. Anything he brushed against or handled could work: a shred of tunic, a blood-stained rag, a bit of written script.

Contact with postmortem Joseph sometimes involved his ghostly appearance. Domenica Cenneo was mortally ill in Copertino; a young woman of good family, the doctors could only shrug, raise their eyes, and point to heaven. The woman, however, prayed fervently to Padre Giuseppe and soon after saw an apparition of the holy man with his disciple, Fra Antonio Pecorella.

"Don't doubt, you will be well," Joseph said, sounding like his old live self and touching her on the head. The ghost of Joseph kneeled beside the young woman's bed, and recited the litany, which was repeated by the ghost of Pecorella. Joseph placed his hand once more on her head, and the apparition vanished. At that moment, according to the depositions, the healing occurred.[45]

Healing transactions were mediated by relics, mementos, personal effects—anything linking the person coming for help directly, tangibly, to the saint's vividly imagined power and presence. Mr. Evangelisti's unhappily born seven-year-old daughter, Antonia Vittoria, was crippled and mute; her two hands, near paralyzed, trembled; and one of her legs, without feeling, dragged along. As residents of Osimo, the family obtained pieces of cloth touched by Joseph and a few patches of one of his old tunics.

Fiora, the mother of the sick child, took the relics and wove them into a wreath she placed around Vittoria's neck. Soon after, we are told, "Vittoria began to walk, and the paralysis was gone; she was able to raise her arms without tremor, and her tongue uttered the first words of her life."[46] With stories like this floating around, the belief arose that Joseph could be called upon to rescue people from pain, sickness, and mortal danger, even after his death.

So much then for a picture of Joseph's impressive outer deeds and the impact he had on the world around him. But let us now switch to a different perspective on the man and try to peer inside and see what was driving him. The extraordinary phenomena were all public effects of something private and invisible; they were by-products, actings out of his fiercely focused mystical life. We need now to say something about what kind of mystic Joseph was.

NOTES

1. Butler, III, p. 588.
2. Ruffin, 1982, pp. 56–57, 262–65.
3. DB, p. 198.
4. DB, p. 196.
5. DB, p. 197.
6. DB, p. 199.
7. DB, p. 198.
8. Hillman, 1975.
9. Moore, 1996, p. 159.
10. DB, p. 63.
11. DB, p. 126.
12. DB, p. 168.
13. DB, p. 170.
14. Ibid.
15. DB, p. 171.
16. DB, p. 177.
17. GP3, p. 16.
18. GP3, p. 16; GP3, p. 20.
19. DB, p. 179.
20. See Prince, 1927/1964, passim.
21. P. 431.
22. Ibid. p. 509.
23. Broad, 1962, p. 313.

24. DB, p. 75.
25. Three valuable volumes from the Latin classic by Benedict XIV have been translated into English. See references.
26. See Lambertini, 1740–1758.
27. Pastrovicchi, 1980, p. 123.
28. Ibid., p. 124.
29. Duffin, 2009.
30. Ibid., p. 140.
31. See Gardner, 1983.
32. Kelly and Kelly, 2007, *Irreducible Mind*, p. 135.
33. Kelsey, 1973.
34. See also Luke 7:50 and 18:42.
35. Weber, 2009.
36. Dowling, 1984.
37. Carrel, 1950, pp. 36–37.
38. Keener, 2011, vol. 1, p. 506.
39. Interestingly, Jesus then says: "Somebody touched me; I felt power had gone out of me." Is this another example of Crookes's claim about an unknown force associated with organically evolved living agents?
40. DB, p. 213.
41. DB, p. 214.
42. DB, p. 218.
43. Ibid., p. 217.
44. See GP, pp. 937–38.
45. GP, p. 946.
46. GP, p. 949.

Chapter 5

The Mystic

> This is what happens in ecstasy—the soul becomes unified (*l'anima si congiunge*) and enters the great sea of the high God and beholds that which cannot be said or recounted.[1]
>
> —Joseph of Copertino

We have reviewed the main events of Joseph's life and discussed reports of his controversial powers: *charisms* ("gifts") in the language of Catholic theology, *siddhis* ("attainments") in Patanjali's yoga, *paranormal* or *psi* in some scientific circles. But we have yet to touch on the heart of Joseph, what *to him* was most important—his mystical life.

His fame is due more to his outer manifestations, which tend to overshadow the less obvious question of his inner life. He was not an articulate mystic like Meister Eckhart or Teresa of Avila, and because of his outer manifestations his superiors discouraged him from writing letters or talking too much of his experiences. So we have only a small number of letters, his "strophes" or raplike poems and wisdom rhymes, and the sayings written down by diarist, biographer, and inquisitor.

His inner life must be inferred from his behavior as well as from statements he made. In a chapter on Joseph's raptures, Bernini refers to the negative or apophatic mysticism of Dionysius the Areopagite. This unknown fifth-century writer greatly influenced the Christian Neoplatonism of Renaissance thinkers. He identified *eros* with *agape*, reading eros as "yearning." An image stands out of the whole cosmos yearning to revert back to its divine origins: an erotic homesickness for something out of this world shaped Joseph's mystical quest.

Chapter 5

MYSTICAL EXPERIENCE

Mysticism is from the Greek root *mueo*—in the passive voice, "to be initiated," by implication, into a secret. The mystery rites of the ancient world were initiations into the secrets of the god. In the mystical sense, the supreme godlike state of consciousness is nameless and ineffable. A unique state of consciousness, like no other in impact or profundity, it may be thought of as part of religion, but also occurs spontaneously in nonreligious settings.

Scholars disagree about what counts as authentic mystical experience. There is division over whether the experience is universal and self-generating or constructed from acquired cultural materials. A second big issue: Are certain types of the experience better, higher, more authentic than others? Are there clear markers of the real thing?

On the first question, mystical experiences are always colored, framed, and to a degree interpreted in light of their time, place, language, and culture; but that does not prevent them from *also* having certain core features, or from being rooted in a common cause. Different cultures name and construct the meaning of the experience of the sun differently; but the sun gives light, warms, and supports life for all people, times, and cultures.

Radical constructivists emphasize the differences and underplay the commonalities, disputing the idea of a perennial mystical experience.[2] For a critique of constructivism, see Robert Forman (1990) and other scholars who stress the role of "pure consciousness" as the common core of mystical experience. With Forman, I should say I am drawn to the idea of pure consciousness lying behind all the differences.

Here is a puzzle for the constructivist. On a boat once sailing from Brindisi I met a Welshman who was traveling around the world on a wisdom quest. One day, he said, he experienced out of the blue a light that filled him with incomparable bliss and deep intuitions into the nature of reality. The experience came unbidden and nothing in his early life could account for it. Amazed and disoriented, he left his home and family on a quest to understand what had happened to him. Everything else in his life by comparison now paled in significance. It seems to me that something outside his cultural history radically changed him.

Edward Robinson's book *The Original Vision* (1977) documents children's mystical experiences. The idea that children's mystical experiences are constructed from their culture seems implausible; it seems that children are too young, having lived not long enough to absorb what is needed for such a profound experience. Mysticism, I believe, is more than cultural construction; but it can displace or transform the cultural conditioning. Mystics are interesting just because they break through personal, tribal, and culture-bound limitations. They often clash with their native belief-systems, as did

Meister Eckhart with Christianity, who was censured, and Hallaj with Islam, who was beheaded for his worldview in AD 922. The Hebrew prophets were critics, deconstructors of the mainline cultural and political powers. Mystics, who may also be prophets, may transcend their constructed cultures, but not without paying a price.

As for the second question: Is there a hierarchy of mystical experiences, a scale of mystical virtues? R. C. Zaehner believed that Christian mysticism was more authentic than mescaline-induced mysticism.[3] For Walter Stace, the experience of radically introvertive "undifferentiated unity" was the benchmark of the supreme form of the experience; exemplars would be the Buddha, Meister Eckhart, and Samkhya yogis.

Stace, an analytic philosopher, distinguished between introvertive and extrovertive mysticism: in the first, one is withdrawn into oneself, rapt in the blissful unity of pure consciousness; in the second, the unity experience includes and embraces the external world—a rapturous sunrise, a transporting piece of art or music, the ecstatic touch of one's lover, and so on. Stace believed that introvertive states are the purest specimens of the phenomenon. He disapproved of (what he deemed) Teresa of Avila's inferior intellectual skills and ecstatic emotionalism; by these criteria Stace might not regard Joseph as a mystic at all, whose emotionalism was so intense and who was no intellectual.

Is the introvertive path the higher, more perfect way to experience the oneness of being? It's hard to see why. In his many books, Paul Marshall (2005) has emphasized the importance, variety, and lively presence of extrovertive mysticism. Many experiences of union arise not from cool detachment but from passionate contact with the world. Richard Jefferies, AE (the pseudonym by which George Russell went by),[4] and Walt Whitman were ecstatic in and through the world; they were not solitary birds winging it "alone to the alone."

With Marshall, whose writings are grounded in experience, I think that *extrovertive* mysticism is the most complete type of the experience—transforming our living perception of the earth, healing the wounded world around us, going further than individual bliss toward collective enlightenment. Catherine of Genoa worked effectively nursing the sick and dying while inwardly being ecstatic, as Von Hugel describes in detail.[5] Catherine of Siena, ecstatically withdrawn yet at the forefront of papal politics, sought to make peace and unify the world even as *she* was inwardly unified.[6] The Buddhist *bodhisattva* is dedicated to freeing humanity from *dukka* or discontent; inward enlightenment spills over, extrovertively, into the task of world enlightenment.

Stace and Zaehner are not alone among scholars who want to narrow the range of mystical authenticity. Some Protestant theologians reject the entire phenomenon of mysticism as "essentially world-negating and solipsistic."[7] Meanwhile the Catholic scholar E. C. Butler (1858–1934) had no sympathy for the negative theology of the Areopagite nor for anything visionary or rapture-oriented—indeed, for anything extreme or histrionic. (All strikes against Joseph.) The learned Butler was not interested in the physical phenomena of mysticism. The Anglo-Catholic W. R. Inge recoiled from the erotic side of Christian mysticism. Interest in the paranormal, he protested, was symptomatic of "debased supernaturalism."[8] Similar attitudes are fairly widespread among scholars.

It seems a puzzling attitude. To demean the erotic, the esthetic, and the supernormal seems unnecessarily to impoverish human experience, no less the scope of mystical experience. Why not embrace all the fruits and flowers (so sadly needed) that are rooted in good mystical soil? Something else is worth noting. These debased outlaws—levitation, healings, scrutiny of hearts, odor of sanctity, and so forth—offer a definite, factual basis for Butler, Inge, and the like to entertain a "supernatural" or transcendent worldview. To dismiss whole realms of experience as "debased supernaturalism" seems unchristian toward those who gain solace or inspiration from their experience and unscientific by virtue of its stolid incuriosity.

HIGH-STRUNG SPIRITUALITY

Although wary of calling too much attention to Joseph, his superiors were curious about his inner life. How could they fail to be? Here was a brother who could fly! Roberto Nuti and Arcangelo Rosmi recorded their impressions, so we have a fair collection of impromptu statements about his inner life. Also, the intense way he practiced the Franciscan virtues and the strange phenomena reveal things about his inner life.

As for the distinction between introvertive and extrovertive mysticism, Joseph straddled both without much difficulty. Clearly, his ecstasies were introverted, cold to the touch, dead to the world; but he also went into ecstasy at the sight of a leaf. He was enraptured when a brother proclaimed the beauty of the blue sky. He was unable to complete a rarely permitted lunch with his adoring acolyte, the Princess of Savoy; at the third bite she reminded him of the Madonna, which rendered him senseless and cataleptic. Saying Mass Joseph fell into trances, attended by strange bodily movements. Specific moments in the rite (like when he raised the host for the consecration) triggered these states. These were all extrovertive expressions of his mystical life.

Joseph was akin to the nature mystic in his way with animal life. As a Franciscan friar, he inherited the creation-friendly mysticism of Francis of

Assisi. Modern Italian literature began with the latter's "Canticle of Creation" where sun and moon are personified as "brother" and "sister." Francis sermonizing the birds and taming the wolf of Gubbio iconically illustrate an ethos of amity with animal nature.

Chapter 5 of Parisciani's magnum opus is titled "San Francesco in Terra," which explains how Joseph modeled himself after St. Francis.[9] At points the comparison is strained. Joseph conformed to the Church's dictates, however arbitrary. Francis, the bolder, more independent spirit, unleashed an energy that inspired the Spiritualist movement and its revolt against the excesses of Church authority.[10] Joseph, stuck in the craw of the Catholic Reformation, was driven inward, his extrovertive side flaring up only occasionally.

But Joseph's mystical drift was bifocal, introvertive *and* expansive, although his political circumstances were so oppressive as to keep driving him inward. One story I can mention sounds a pioneering note for animal liberation. It describes at length how the friar saved a hare from a certain marquis and other landlords who were convinced they had the right to hunt and kill any creature on their land. Joseph intervened in the midst of a hectic chase—he stood firmly, stroking the hare under his robe, and lectured the miffed but flummoxed landowners. The creature was under the protection of the Madonna, the friar announced, which cancelled their hunting privileges!

Other stories, if accurate, would illustrate an ability to direct the behavior of birds, such as the case of a little warbling cardillo he asked to visit a group of nuns at a specified time each morning, exactly when the group chant was to start. Several nuns swore under oath that the cardillo behaved as if it were following Joseph's instructions.[11]

All the extrovertive stories, including his visible levitations, leave hidden his most intimate inner life. He began as an introvert, his childhood sickness and progressively confined mode of life driving him deeply within himself from the beginning. For Joseph the "other world" had become *his* real world, a place he pursued relentlessly. He was explicit about not forming attachments to anybody or anything; which sounds like Meister Eckhart, for whom detachment was the spiritual virtue *par excellence*.[12]

As Joseph understood it, the only way it was possible to be filled with the immensity of God was to empty oneself completely: the *via negativa* of Thomas Aquinas and the marriage to Lady Poverty imagined by Francis of Assisi. The last six years of his life he lived mostly alone in a confined area, a room without sunlight half the year, not a place conducive to extroverted transports or nature mysticism.

Bernini begins his discussion of rapture with a reference to Dionysius the Areopagite. From the *Mystical Theology*, these words would have made sense to Joseph, and consoled him, ensconced in the tomblike desolation of his living quarters:

In the diligent exercise of mystical contemplation, leave behind the senses and the operations of the intellect, and all things sensible and intellectual, and all things in the world of being and nonbeing, that you may arise by unknowing towards the union, as far as is attainable. . . . For by the unceasing and absolute renunciation of yourself and of all things you may be borne on high, through pure and entire self-abnegation, into the superessential Radiance of the Divine Darkness.[13]

We may imagine Joseph in Osimo living out these instructions and creating from the depths of his own consciousness what he called his "forest paradise."

The extroverted mystic was more in play earlier in his career. Bernini tells a story of Joseph meeting some brothers. In a high-spirited mood, he seizes one of them by his arm and whirls the (rather large) man around as if he were a paper doll. Or recall the fantastic Christmas scene of Joseph dancing to the sound of shepherd pipes, ecstatically rising and jigging in the air above the nave of the church. I can hardly imagine a more extroverted mystical manifestation.

In the lore of mysticism, there is a dark night of the soul.[14] In 1645, after two such "dark" and arid years in Assisi, the ecstatic flights came back in full force. When questioned about the dry times, he was evasive, saying they were "an evil that he suffered" and regarded them as signs of "his infirmity and imperfection."[15] He also hinted that his levitations, when his spirit was up, were the result of his fasting and his frailness. He also spoke of how often he prayed *not* to have such violent ecstasies, especially when in the glare of the public eye.

After his involuntary upliftings in space—so inward and yet so public—he would cover his head with his hood and retreat to his cell. His strangeness deprived him of human company. The rapturous flights became his wound (*ferito*) and sore spot (*piagho*). Casual talk of ecstasy frightened him; just hearing the word *paradise* could render him senseless.

He feared ecstasy because of its consequences; not far from his mind were thoughts of the Inquisition. There may also have been moments of fear of the ecstasy itself, the dizzying erasure of self it brought on, the mortifying loss of control, and too often accompanied by pains of perverse self-doubt. What we know is that Joseph could *get out of his ordinary self* with stunning frequency. Unlike those transient and discreet mystical experiences William James thought were normative, Joseph is an icon of mysticism on the rampage, a mysticism that must be contained and monitored for its dangerous excesses.

Nuti writes: "On many occasions, to bring him back they would drag him on the ground, pinch him, twist his fingers, put candles in his mouth, and the like, none of which he ever resented." Once the friar remarked rather light-heartedly: "*Paesano*, you know what the brothers do to me, when those dazed states come upon me?—they twist my hands, and practically break my fingers!"—he pointed to a cut finger and one that was swollen—. "look at what they do to me!" Then he smiled.[16]

In Assisi he gradually overcame his reticence and sometimes spoke about his experiences, mostly in the third person:

> Whoever enters ecstasy is like someone thrown into the sea and swimming. He sees things that are in the depths of the sea, in complete oblivion to the earth. But the others, who are present, see only the movements of a body in water, but are unable to see what he sees in the vast sea. This is what happens in ecstasy, because the soul becomes unified (*l'anima si congiunge*) and enters the great sea of the high God and beholds that which cannot be said or recounted.[17]

Friedrich von Hugel, in his study of St. Catherine of Genoa, paints a similar model of the soul. The psychological functions—thinking, sensing, feeling, intuiting—become "unified": all complementary and mutually enhancing.

Von Hugel describes an ongoing self-unification occurring in Catherine, a movement toward *psychosynthesis*.[18] Catherine fasts, sees visions, and evolves toward the perfect unity of her inner forces. Every action she performs exemplifies a unification of idea, goal, and energy. The oneness of the mystical experience is out of time and in time, cosmic and psychological, changeless and dynamic, a creative welding of disparate elements, an ongoing self-unification.

Some master of the Collegio Universitario wanted to know from Joseph in what manner the soul unites with God in ecstasy. The friar responded by telling a story about the soul. The soul is *una regina*, "a queen"; the way the queen (soul) unites with the king (God) is to completely bring the senses under control, without cognitive distraction. For the soul to unite with the One, the general chaotic motions of thought and life itself have to be channeled, focused, and stilled. The mystical state, Joseph says, is what happens "when the soul unites with God and one appears foolish and beside (*fuori*) oneself, while being aware of one's *viltà*—wretched creatureliness." So even in the midst of ecstasy, he saw himself as "appearing foolish" and tainted with creaturely "vileness." The perfection of the mystical state seems to escape Joseph.

The friar liked to underscore his gnatlike status before the divine whirlwind; no tyro of the *via negativa*, he meditated deeply on his nothingness. He said it was the sole way to become receptive to the fullness of the divine, using one of his favorite words, becoming *nulla*. Joseph was struck by the idea of smells being invisible to the naked eye; you could experience something, but not see what caused it, so he compared his ecstatic experience to an invisible fragrance and sometimes to a taste: "So it happens in ecstasy. One feels an inexplicable consolation, without seeing the object it arrives from. Ecstasy is like a taste (*assaggio*) of the true glory of paradise."[19]

His inner life was intensely emotional. If there are "hot" and "cool" styles of mysticism, Joseph was undoubtedly hot. Mystics of "cool" persuasion would be Plotinus, Meister Eckhart, and of course the master of cool, the Buddha. The term *nirvana* refers to the "extinction of fire" while for "hot" mystics there is the honorific term *incendium amoris,* "fire of love." Akin to hot Catholic mysticism are Shaivism, Sufism, and Kundalini Yoga, whose methods, like Joseph's, cultivate "mental excess" to fuel the mystical fire.

Proneness to the fiery side of spirituality may be caused by illness and may appear pathological. Consider the case of Gemma Galgani (1878–1903) and her very hot mysticism of suffering. Father Germanus, Gemma's spiritual director, writes of her: "The thirst to suffer torments of every kind seemed to consume and rend her whole being."[20] Gemma writes of her own experience:

> For the last eight days I have felt something mysterious in the region of my heart that I cannot understand. The first days I disregarded it because it gave me little or no trouble. But today is the third day that this fire has increased. Oh, so much as to be unbearable. I should need ice to put it out, and it hinders my sleeping and eating. It is a mysterious fire that comes from within to the outside. It is however a fire that does not torment me; rather it delights me, but it exhausts and consumes me.[21]

Hot mystics taste the divine in fire, pain; they blend with the anguish of the crucifixion. Joseph, as we saw him performing at Mass, powerfully identified with the crucified god. Contrast an early Buddhist text whose symbol is *sunyata,* "emptiness." In the "cool" style of mysticism, "seeing the world as empty is the key to bringing about the fading away of desire, hatred, and delusion."[22] Among the cool mystics, the world of affect is devalorized: one says farewell to the fire of love, the aim is to dry out, bring to a halt the driven consciousness.

Joseph and St. Teresa of Avila, baroque Catholics of the Counter-Reformation, differed in several ways. Joseph was known chiefly for his spectacular charisms; Teresa was an author and spiritual educator, engaged as reformer with the world; they were similar in their high mystical temperature, the vehemence of their ecstasies and wildness of their levitations. They both prayed to soften the psychic forces that battered them. In states of union, she said, one has "secret intuitions often too strong to be misunderstood" and as a result one "cannot refrain from amorous exclamations."[23] High-temperature mysticism is erotic; for example, consider the image of Angela of Foligno caught up in ecstasy before a portrait of Jesus in church as she slowly disrobes herself.[24] Teresa's visionary encounter with an angel holding a spear was the subject of a sculpture by Gian Lorenzo Bernini; the orgasmic look on the tilted face of the saint caused a sensation in Rome. Bernini materialized in marble the image conveyed by Teresa in her writings:

> I saw in his hand a long spear of gold, and at the iron's point there seemed to be a little fire. He appeared to me to be thrusting it at times into my heart, and to pierce my very entrails; when he drew it out, he seemed to draw them out also, and to leave me all on fire with a great love of God. The pain was so great that it made me moan and yet so surpassing was the sweetness of this excessive pain that I could not wish to be rid of it.[25]

> The Jesuit Poulain writes of this type of mystical experience. "For God," we are told: wishes to be the fragrant air that we breathe, the wine that will inebriate us, the life of our life, the impassioned Lover of our souls. He will vouchsafe to us the "kiss of His mouth" and will receive ours in return. He will not be content until He is merged into, almost identified with the beloved soul that has given herself to Him. He desires an intimate and mutual penetration.[26]

In chapter 20 of her *Autobiography*, Teresa of Avila discusses the nature of mystical union and rapture, or "elevation or what they call flight of the spirit, or transport—it is all one." The umbrella term is *ecstasy*: "The Lord gathers up the soul just as we might say as the clouds gather up the vapors from the earth, and raise it up until it is quite out of itself . . . and the cloud rises to Heaven and takes the soul with it, and begins to reveal to it things concerning the Kingdom."

During the rapture the body becomes cold and insensible yet in "the consciousness of the greatest sweetness and delight." The cold exterior belies the interior *incendium amoris*. Once the force that triggers the rapture is unleashed, there is no way to resist it: "I was being lifted up by a force beneath my feet so powerful that I know nothing to which I can compare it, for it came with a much greater vehemence than any other spiritual experience and I felt as if I were being ground to powder." At first this rapturous force frightened Teresa. It also left her with feelings of "strange detachment" and "a new estrangement from things on earth." This led to sensations of uneasiness and "distress."

Once she was exposed to sensations of divine reality, the return to ordinary life was more difficult to bear. She now longs for "the Good, which contains all that is good within Itself." The experience was physically painful, as though her "bones had been wrenched askew." Agony is mingled with joy in the longed for reunion. At the same time, the pain and distress leave her feeling physically lighter. This may last for hours, during which "the faculties are lost through being closely united with God."[27] The supreme union, in which all the faculties are suspended, is brief. This is part of the rapture that Joseph calls *stordimento*—being dazed and trying to comprehend what one is seeing.

The deathlike façade of the body conceals a busy, complex scene of internal activity. One may get into a state, says Teresa, "with the body unable to move for hours on end and the understanding and the memory sometimes wandering." She remarks on the healing effects of rapture: "Often a person who was previously quite ill and troubled with severe pain finds himself in good health again and even stronger than before. Moreover, if the rapture is deep, it may take two or three days to recover one's faculties."

She comments on the origins of her rapturous experience. The soul "while enraptured, is mistress of everything, and in a single hour, or in less, acquires such freedom that it cannot recognize itself. *It sees clearly that this state is in no way due to itself*" (italics added). The state seems to her to be an influx of something *other*, and, until actually experienced, entirely unknown.

In the prayer of quiet, you lower the volume of the supraliminal mind, reasonings, and sense-based emotional chatter; in the prayer of union, you appear to be more than yourself, expanded or extended, one might say. Perceiving this induces a new sense of freedom in Teresa; she reminds the reader how difficult the prayer of quiet is. She looks around at the mad, bad world and remarks, "How friendly we should all be with one another if nobody were interested in money and honor! I really believe this would be a remedy for everything." After her experiences, she says, money and honor no longer appeared important.

VIRTUES OF THE MYSTIC WAY

Joseph made himself a mystic through the monastic virtues he practiced: his will to quell every unruly biological impulse; the ascetic-athletic capacity to stay riveted on his central goal; and perhaps the most important, love, his master value. The forces propelling him began early:

> Giuseppe began to experience the ecstasies when he was a boy of just eight years, surprised by them at a time when he could not understand what they were. Whether he was hearing sounds or songs, or seeing sacred images, or helping with the Mass, he would freeze and lose himself in ecstatic admiration, which would provoke teasing from his friends.[28]

Joseph is recorded as saying:

> As I ate I thought about the saints and often cried, not caring where I was or what I was doing; I stood for a moment outside myself, and returned to see the world through changed eyes, distancing myself from my fellows and conversations with them. I took all the linens off the table and stretched out on it to sleep. I was constantly seeing the Virgin of the Grottella who pulled me toward her and transported my soul, and even my body.[29]

The airborne effects apparently sprang from an image of the Madonna he loved to meditate on. Dwelling on stories of the saints could launch him on ecstatic excursions, and the frequent changes of state altered his perceptions. He sought to detach himself from people as he learned to "see the world through changed eyes," which, he explains, came from the experience of "standing outside himself." He had a gift for creative dissociation,[30] a carryover from his bedridden days when he was forced to cope with intense bodily discomfort.

Joseph explained his ecstatic experience by a metaphor of images in a mirror. He was fascinated and intimidated by Naples and its museums. In answering a question about ecstasy, Joseph refers to a museum. What he said was recorded by Cardinal Brancati; it would have intrigued Leibniz. "If in a museum there was a great mirror and images of everything were reflected in it, looking then one might discover in that mirror with a single gaze all the paintings (*dipinti*). This is how ecstatics comport themselves when God shows them the divine secrets."[31]

This describes the experience of simultaneity the mystics often refer to in their writings. Leibniz used mirror imagery to describe his theory of mind. Discussing his own extrovertive philosophy of mysticism, Paul Marshall quotes Leibniz: "Every monad is a mirror that is alive or endowed with inner activity and is representative of the universe from its point of view."[32] This is Joseph's "great mirror" that "with a single gaze" can take in all the *dipinti*. Leibniz's monad, like the *purusha* of Samkhya yoga, is uncreated, indestructible, and from its perspective reflects or underlies the totality of being. The monad of a mystic like Joseph gains access to its subliminal "representation" of the universe; and attains knowledge of the oneness of being.

Seeing all with a "single gaze" echoes Boethius's *totum simul*, a state of simultaneity that transforms the experience of time. One "sees at once, in a single glance, all things that are, that were, or are to come." The mirror reflects nothing in particular but everything potentially, a symbol perhaps of pure consciousness. In the intuition of Boethius: "Eternity is the whole, perfect, and simultaneous possession of endless life."[33]

Joseph's method of gaining glimpses of this mirror of eternal consciousness was not by philosophical speculation or dialectic. It was by practicing the common virtues of a friar's life, and doing so in a uniquely intense and persistent way. For example, the mystical and esoteric sense of poverty was celebrated in the *Laude* of the Umbrian mystic Jacopone da Todi (1228–1306):

> Poverty is to have nothing and so to want nothing;
> But to possess all things in the spirit of freedom.[34]

This is not *poverty* as understood in everyday economics, and its philosophy won't fly on Wall Street. Joseph avoided talking abstractly about mystical experience. He conveyed his views by actions and gestures, often quite histrionic, occasionally verging on the hysterical:

> One time a few people invited him to their home with the intention of offering money to improve his lot, but on realizing that he would not take what they offered, they managed to secretly put a coin of little value in the pocket of his cape. As soon as Padre Giuseppe found the coin, he began to sweat and scream, as though he had a great weight around his neck, and those who had tricked him had enough compassion to realize that he simply couldn't take it.[35]

The revulsion from the coin harks back to the special loathing St. Francis felt for money. Francis, in fact, was well known for his chivalrous love of Lady Poverty. In twelfth century Umbria, bartering had ceased to be the chief means of trade, and as a result money acquired a newly seductive status. One could now accumulate money, hoard and use it to make more money, an idea so enchanting that in the end the Church's disapproval of usury would lose all moral cachet. Francis saw the new interest in money as a growing evil, and took every opportunity to act out his antipathy toward it. Thomas Celano reported this piece of performance art:

> That friend of God despised very greatly all the things of this world, but he cursed money more than all other things. . . . A certain secular person entered the church of St. Mary of the Portiuncula to pray, and he left some money near the cross as an offering. When he had gone, one of the brothers simply touched it with his hand and threw it on the window sill. The saint heard what the brother had done . . . and rebuked him and upbraided him most severely because he had touched the money. He commanded him to lift the money from the window sill with his mouth and to place it with his mouth on the ass's dung outside the place.[36]

Equating money with excrement was a Franciscan trope, cursing it as the chief obstacle to love of God, nature, and humanity. Liberation theologian Leonardo Boff wrote a twentieth-century biography of St. Francis that treats this theme of poverty from a different but complementary perspective. Boff puts Francis second only to Jesus in offering "a model for human liberation." He says that Francis's animus toward money was based on the rise of the acquisitive bourgeoisie from the feudal system:

> The development of the world of the artisans creating the market system gave rise to a new meaning for being: the desire for wealth, for goods, for power. Together with this, a new ethos was developed, that is, a new way of life with different relationships to nature, to others, to religion, and to God. Science and technology did not arise as pure and free responses to reason but rather

as answers demanded by the rise of production, of the marketplace, and of consumerism. . . . Because of production, the rationality that was developed to its utmost was analytic-instrumental reason, to the detriment of other forms of reason (dialectic, wisdom, etc.)[37]

Reason, according to Boff, turned into an instrument of domination that trumped the value of love and corroded social relations. The Franciscan spirit of Joseph was at odds with what would come to pervade the ethos of present-day global capitalism. How far we have descended toward the antimystical was made clear in 2013 by Pope Francis, a Jesuit by training but, like Joseph, a Franciscan in his critique of the idolatry of money:

A new tyranny is thus born, invisible and often virtual, which unilaterally and relentlessly imposes its own laws and rules. . . . To sustain a lifestyle which excludes others, or to sustain enthusiasm for that selfish ideal, a globalization of indifference has developed. Almost without being aware of it, we end up being incapable of feeling compassion at the outcry of the poor, weeping for other people's pain, and feeling a need to help them, as though all this were someone else's responsibility and not our own. The culture of prosperity deadens us; we are thrilled if the market offers us something new to purchase. In the meantime all those lives stunted for lack of opportunity seem a mere spectacle; they fail to move us.[38]

Bernini's *Vita* dwells on Joseph's poverty, his surly refusal to accept gifts, his dread of anything resembling money, his irritation when presented with a pillow to make him comfortable. Stripping himself of possessions was part of mortifying his attachment to material objects; poverty was a key virtue he practiced to break the spell of his bondage to ordinary consciousness. The same was true for another monkish virtue he practiced.

For enlightened liberals, Kantians, and anarchists, lauding "obedience" must be suspect, and for good reasons. But with Joseph the mystic, it was an instrument for honing the focus and intensity of his consciousness. He practiced holy obedience, like poverty, as a mystical virtue, as part of the training one has to undergo to graduate from all attachments, gross and subtle, that keep us in bondage. Joseph was relentless in the way he practiced obedience. It was also a way of keeping his distance from the world:

He was always reluctant to deal with women or lay people. . . . He was reluctant to eat meat or to leave his cell, even in summer to walk through the convent orchard. He would, however, do anything any time the superior commanded him. He would obey not only his superiors, but even his cell companion and laypeople in the convent. He would not open or close a window without an explicit order or consent, because he never wanted to act out of his own needs but always in the spirit of obedience. If anyone asked for his cord, he would refuse, unless they could say right away that the Guardian had given permission for them to have it. If the Guardian did not give him reason, he would not budge an inch from where he was standing until a new order pushed him to do so.[39]

The phrase here that should stop us cold is: "... *he never wanted to act out of his own needs.*" That may sound inhuman or just stupid, but for Joseph the mystic, again, it was part of the discipline of self-conquest. It would be glib to interpret the idea of "holy obedience" as a trick of the Church to enforce a general submissiveness in the populace. It might very well serve to enforce mindless cohesion, but that was not the case with Joseph. Joseph's exaggerated display of holy obedience was personal, not political; it was governed by the need to maintain the intensity of his conscious focus, to model his thought and behavior in accord with the mystical archetypes he strove to imitate.

In my view, his extreme asceticism was used to achieve an existential lightness of being and to acquire as unfiltered a perception of reality as possible. That is mysticism, not masochism. One "crucifies" the ego as part of a radical experiment; one strives to quell the merely mechanical will to exist. A comrade from the high country of consciousness, Rumi the Sufi poet, wrote: "Pour out wine till I become a wanderer from myself; for in selfhood and existence I feel only fatigue."[40] Rather than "pour out wine," Joseph fasted and practiced his all-year-round Lenten diet.

Chastity, of course, was another virtue, another technique deployed to frustrate the almighty imperative to survive, the natural instinct to replicate and reproduce oneself. Detachment from the automatisms of all natural urges was his overriding psychospiritual goal, part of his method of raising to breaking-point psychical tension, which might catapult him into "dazed" rapture.

The mystical quest for Joseph is also the story of a survivor. At first we see him abandoned, traumatized, physically immobilized. Slowly he learns to dissociate from a grossly oppressive environment, including his own body. He does this with the help of techniques of prayer and meditation learned from the local culture. He doggedly uses the spiritual tools at hand to serve his needs, his dawning quest for a repaired sense of a severely wounded identity. He had a talent for practice, for staying on track, and managed to mutate from the dish-breaking klutz of Martina Franca to an original mystic and a bona fide thaumaturge. I want now to connect Joseph's story with a modern counterpart from a different tradition.

A COMPARISON WITH BENGALI ECSTATICS

Ecstatic practices like Joseph's are found today among modern Bengali mystics: *siddhas*, "perfected ones," for whom the pursuit of ecstasy is the essence of religious practice.[41] The similarity to Joseph is evident with *bhakta siddhas*, or devotional saints, where intense emotions, love, and the erotic are means of creating *bhava* "ecstasy" and its notable effects.

June McDaniel recorded an interview with Yogesvari, a married woman with a reputation for miracles during states of possession; in her trances, she is said to have materialized food and cured people of various ailments. Similar to Joseph, when she was a child she played in temples, stared into the sky, and saw visions of Kali, the female deity she worshipped. Yogesvari was unable to maintain normal relations with her family when she went into *bhava*. Like Joseph to his monastery, she was drawn to ashram life, where McDaniel was able to interview her.

It was finding a linga and images of Shiva and Kali—purely symbolic structures like crucifixes or images of the virgin—that propelled her siddha career. Sometimes in the course of helping someone, an amulet might appear out of nowhere. "I don't know where these things come from," she said, like Joseph, adding, "I don't do anything for myself."[42] The important thing is *bhava*—a term whose meaning McDaniel finds hard to define precisely. In essence, it's being *ek-static*—dissociated, divinely elsewhere. Says Yogeswari Deva: "When I was in Khardaha, my disciples saw me playing with snakes, and a little girl used to come out of me and play with me. My disciples have seen this, but I did not feel anything at the time. I was under the influence of *bhava*."[43]

It's easy to think of Joseph (and other Catholic saints) when reading the words of the married *siddha*:

> I do not experience possession whenever I sit, but I desire it very much. It comes according to Bhagavan's wishes. I have seen God in many forms. In Khardaha when I had *bhava*, I spoke in Sanskrit. But I don't know Sanskrit. People used to surround me. They also said that they smelled the scent of flowers and incense sticks in my presence. . . . Before experiencing trance, my heart fills with tremendous joy, and I can see a bright light, I don't feel then like talking to others. When I used to experience possession, a man once came and touched a hot iron to my body, but I did not feel anything. Many people came to examine me.[44]

Save for the xenoglossy, there's hardly an item here that one couldn't find in Joseph's repertoire.

McDaniel describes two groups of Bauls, a term referring to closeness to God, applied to Sufis and to Hindus. Baul signifies someone freed from obligation, a wanderer who is mad for love of God. Bauls play down doctrinaire differences between Muslim and Hindu, mosque and temple. This Sufi form of the ecstatic quest, in which Muslim and Hindu live comfortably together, shows how the mystical state transcends the cultural distinctions constructionists emphasize. Joseph, compared to the Bauls, was unable to rise above the partisan ethos of the Counter-Reformation. Had he been under the sway of the older Renaissance vision of Pico della Mirandola and Marsilio Ficino, he might have been flexible enough to match the catholicity of the Bengali mystics.

Another, more famous Bengali mystic was Anandamayi Ma, who had interesting opinions about the nature of *bhava*, which she identified as a cosmic life force, akin to Bergson's *élan vital*, restless and creative. This she inferred from her own experience. The following quote echoes in a general way Joseph's foray into theory when he likened his screaming raptures to an explosion of gunpowder. Anandamayi Ma points out that *bhava* builds up pressure and must be expressed: "When something is boiled in a closed vessel, there comes a stage when the vapor will push up the lid . . . (when) a wave of ecstatic emotion surges up from within, it becomes difficult to check it."[45]

With Anandamayi Ma, *bhava* took two forms, trance and possession. Entranced, she would fall on the ground, cold and apparently dead, as ants crawled over her eyes (with Joseph it was flies). When possessed, she would dance and sing and move about in highly expressive ways, as was true of her Italian counterpart. During chanting God's name at Kirtan her body underwent transformations:

> There were occasions when her body would stretch and become much taller than usual; or again it would shrink into an inconceivably small size. At times it would become rolled up like a round mass of flesh, as if there were no bones. Sometimes the entire body would so throb and thrill with strong emotions surging through it, that it would get swollen and red, with every single hair standing on end. She would sometimes shed tears or laugh and become stiff as in a stupor.[46]

Although the body is transformed, there is no mention of levitation. The main point of intersection with Joseph is the *bhava,* or ecstasy, and the extraordinary effects said to emanate from that state. There seems a common human potential shared by Joseph and Anandamayi Ma, based on the way mind is related to matter, which leads to my last comment.

From an early age Joseph was disposed to dissociate from his body and from his everyday mind, a tendency magnified during five years of bedridden illness. This by itself did not make him a mystic. He might have made choices or leaned toward becoming an artist or perhaps a bandit, but immersed in his Catholic milieu, he exploited his tendencies to pursue religion, which for him with his temperament could mean only one thing, the mystical life. As Stace noted about Christian mysticism, Joseph's practice was marked by intense emotionalism: "A mutual love between God and man . . . is especially characteristic of Christian mysticism to such an extent that this alone is sufficient to distinguish it from all other mysticism."[47]

The emotionalism of Christian mysticism peaked among the female mystics of the thirteenth century, and in a way Joseph was part of a renaissance of this early period, which Bernard Mcginn describes as the "flowering" of a "new mysticism." The novelty involved an *excessus mentis*, objectively manifest in *prolonged* ecstasy, rapture (levitation), visions, inedia, and other extreme manifestations.

Today, these unusual capacities are often dismissed by scholars as impossible, dangerous, or otherwise objectionable. Undaunted, we should underscore the empirical link between mysticism and psychophysical anomalies. The case of Joseph exemplifies that linkage to a striking degree and should leave us with this thought: profound alterations of consciousness are possible with some human beings that point to the potential metamorphosis of physical reality. The world that we apprehend with our normal, everyday consciousness may well be a façade that conceals other, much greater realities.

NOTES

1. GP, p. 439.
2. See Katz, 1978.
3. Zaehner 1978.
4. AE, 1955.
5. Von Hugel, vol. 1, 142, writes of her "double life." "This devoted work of Catherine, this serving of the sick 'with the most fervent affection, and immense solicitude,' had also the remarkable circumstance about it that, notwithstanding all her attentive, outward-looking care, she never was without the consciousness of her tender Love." Her inner state never caused her to fail in her external performance as nurse.
6. Gardner, 2009.
7. See McGinn, p. 275.
8. Ibid., p. 276.
9. Despite his devotion to the spirit of Francis, Pope Alexander declared that one Saint Francis was enough for Assisi and sent Joseph to a remote hermitage in Fossombrone, forcing him once more to be on the move and detached from outer circumstances.
10. See Coulton, 1906. "In Dante's lifetime, not a century after St. Francis's death, friars were burned alive by their brother friars for no worse fault than obstinate devotion to the strict rule of St. Francis" (p. 2).
11. See the chapter "San Francesco in Terra" in GP for details.
12. See McGinn, 1981, pp. 285–94.
13. Luibheid, 1987.

14. Note the classic by St. John of the Cross, esp. chapter 10, pp. 69–72.
15. GP, p. 437.
16. GP, p. 437.
17. GP, p. 439.
18. See the book *Psychosynthesis* by Roberto Assagioli, 1971.
19. GP, p. 440.
20. Germanus, 1933, p.190.
21. Germanus, 1933, p. 241.
22. Choong, 1999, p. 16.
23. Poulain, 1912, p. 293.
24. See Poulain, 1912 (passim), for images of her mystical eroticism, but it should be noted that "stripping oneself bare" is her metaphor describing an inner process.
25. Peers, 1960, p. 114.
26. Poulain, 1912, p. 96.
27. Peers, 1970.
28. DB, p. 24.
29. DB, p. 20.
30. Grosso, 1997, pp. 181–98.
31. GP, p. 440.
32. Marshall, 1992, p. 228.
33. Boethius, 1962, p. 115.
34. Underhill, 1919, p. 167.
35. DB, p. 208.
36. Celano, 1963, pp. 192–93.
37. Boff, 1984, p. 6.
38. *Evangelii Gaudium*, p. 47.
39. DB, p. 209.
40. Nicholson, 1973, p. 81.
41. See McDaniel, 1989.
42. Ibid., p. 224.
43. Ibid., p. 226.
44. Ibid., p. 225.
45. Ibid., p. 200.
46. Ibid., p. 195.
47. Stace, 1960, p. 131.

Part II

STEPS TOWARD UNDERSTANDING

Chapter 6

Reconnoitering Explanations

> As we think, we live. This is why the assemblage of philosophic ideas is more than a specialist study. It moulds our type of civilization.
>
> —Alfred North Whitehead, *Modes of Thought*

Joseph's story is not easily explained by standard materialism; the friar's performances soar beyond the prevailing outlook. To make sense of Joseph the mystic and thaumaturge, we need to expand the prevailing concept of mind.[1]

AN ALTERNATIVE MODEL

Let's begin with a basic question. Are minds *emergent* properties of brains? Is all that stuff inside us—moods, feelings, memories, images, dreams, and the like—made of, derived from, (in some nonobvious way) nerve tissue, chemicals, electricity, and nothing else? With an assumption like that, the furniture of Joseph's worldview would be broken to bits. Nothing transcendent (extraphysical or spiritual) would remain, and his most cherished ideas would be reduced to nada.

If minds are mere shadowy by-products of living brains, belief in an afterlife, for example, becomes instantly incredible. Joseph had a reputation for being a healer, but mind as shadow of matter seems an unlikely candidate for explaining the instantaneous healings that have been documented. Clearly, an extended concept of mind is required, a causally more potent concept, if we hope to make sense of the queer phenomena that cluster around Joseph's story.

But is emergence from matter the only possible conception? It may seem like the only option in the prevailing popular scientific milieu. But science is clueless as to *how* consciousness (or any of our higher mental functions) could conceivably emerge from a nonconscious physical substrate. Neuroscience can describe the correlations between mental events and brain events, but correlation is not reduction, nor does it imply emergence. Harping on the correlations creates the illusion that we know more than we actually do.

Should we be more patient? Is it reasonable to expect we will ever show how mind "emerged" from matter? A philosopher brain scientist from Berkeley, Alvin Noë, put it like this: "After decades of concerted effort on the part of neuroscientists, psychologists, and philosophers, only one proposition about how the brain makes us conscious—how it gives rise to sensation, feeling, subjectivity—has emerged unchallenged: we don't have a clue."[2]

Add this statement from the philosopher Jerry Fodor: "Nobody has the slightest idea how anything material could be conscious. Nobody even knows what it would be like to have the slightest idea about how anything material could be conscious. So much for the philosophy of consciousness."[3]

The complete lack of progress toward explaining the emergence of consciousness from brain matter suggests it is time to put the idea out to pasture. There is, after all, a logical alternative to emergence: nonemergence. We may, in short, assume that consciousness (whatever it ultimately is) does not emerge from the brain at all, but enjoys an entirely independent existence of its own. Mind and consciousness each would be their own thing, logical primitives. Still, how shall we describe the relationship between brain and consciousness, if not emergence? We may think of the brain as an organ that detects, diverts, transmits, shrinks, expands, filters, dilutes, registers, or expresses an *already existent consciousness*. It doesn't make the stuff—partly because, as William James said, consciousness is not any kind of *stuff*—not a thing, or as Jean-Paul Sartre put it, it is a kind of *nothingness*.[4] It is more like a function, a vehicle for expression, a potentiality to become something actual.

Various metaphors are possible, more or less useful, for describing the relationship between brains that are locatable in familiar space and minds that are not. Whatever the relational verb or figure of speech, the main job of the alternative view is to underscore that consciousness is not *in itself* physical. It is a mysterious stranger in the physical world, an observer and a performer, a presence and an epiphany. And it is also the great "nothing." It is also the most obvious thing in the world to all of us.

In 1898, William James invoked the idea of nonemergent, irreducible mind in a famous lecture on immortality. Consciousness is a function of the brain, he agreed, but the word *function* has more than one sense. The brain could *produce* consciousness (emergent view) or it could *transmit* consciousness (nonemergent view). Consciousness, or the mental capacity for consciousness, is latent in the deep structure of nature: before brain, mind was.

The nonemergent view, he said, is consistent with a whole spectrum of important kinds of experience (psychic, mystical), which otherwise we would think is impossible. The nonemergent view saves the phenomena, the emergent view makes them automatically dubious.

There is a further logical advantage to nonemergence: If mind is *not* brain-produced, brain death would not necessarily imply consciousness death. Revise our view of mind-brain from productive to transmissive, and the idea that we survive death gains a new lease on life.

Over a hundred years have passed since James said all this, and we have come no closer to explaining the origin of consciousness. There is nothing to prevent us from thinking of the brain as an organ that "transmits"—rather than manufactures—our mental life. In the history of thought, this idea has an interesting pedigree. You can trace it from James and Bergson to Myers, Emerson, Schopenhauer, Kant, back to the Renaissance Neoplatonists and to Plotinus and Plato. The belief in the primacy of mind is found among the seers, mystics, and thinkers of the so-called Axial Age (800–200 BCE).[5] This model reflects a perennial human intuition at odds with the more recent scientific belief that the material sciences are the sole keys to unlocking the mysteries of mind, life, and human destiny.

The friar from Copertino relied heavily on earthy metaphors, but his metaphors resonate with the James-Bergson model. Joseph's "model" is revealed in his instruction to people who came to him for help. He would have them say: "Lord, you are the spirit (wind) and I the trumpet; without your breath nothing will resound." The trumpet doesn't create the breath but allows it to resonate, just as the brain doesn't create the mind but allows it to manifest in the context of human life.

A second metaphor of Joseph's is more complex but carries the same message: "The things of this world all have their contraries. And as the elements resist one another, thus can the celestial influences be impeded. And man, who has the use of reason and free will can resist and impede every baleful event with prudence and much more with divine grace."[6] So, because we have bodies, the "celestial influences" can be impeded. However, we *can* resist the flood of contingencies that crowd out the celestial from our mundane consciousness; we can shape our experience so as to maximize receptivity to the higher mental forces.

The idea of a standing impediment James borrowed from Fechner's notion of a mobile psychophysical threshold.[7] This can be verified by self-observation. We experience that threshold drop as we "fall" asleep, followed by the rush of "hypnogogic" imagery, as if from nowhere, usually in rapid succession. In my own experience, it is possible to prolong the hypnogogic interim and learn to control the imagery and thus explore so-called *lucid* dreaming, an elusive but interesting state that begins to bridge the gulf between the conscious and the subliminal self.

Consider the scene of Joseph dying, his consciousness opening to glimpses of "Heaven"—Fechner's threshold dropping rapidly. The surgeon who presided over Joseph's passing testified:

> While I was in the room of the friar a few days before he died, Baccelliere Bonfini of this city of Osimo, one of the Conventuals, performed a beautiful rendition of the hymn Ave Maria Stella. Padre Giuseppe fell into ecstasy, remaining in the position already described and stayed there for about half an hour until Baccelliere finished his singing. He was then given the order of holy obedience to return to himself and the friar recovered all his senses right away and came out of it, showing great humility and even giving us a smile. But the sickness and raptures sent Giuseppe closer and closer to heaven until the moment of the last rites and his passage to heaven. When one asked him how he was, placidly he would say: "As pleases God, as God wants."[8]

For someone so familiar with being ecstatically dislodged from his body, dying seems to have been an effortless, smooth transition. As Bernini described it: "But the sickness and raptures sent Giuseppe closer and closer to heaven until the moment of the last rites. . . ." The practiced withdrawal of attention from external reality might well explain Joseph's smooth manner of dying, which appears here to be nothing less than a veil lifting onto a new stage of existence. If consciousness is outside the brain, death would be a clarification of that fact, a revelation, perhaps similar to accounts of modern near-death experience. Death, if this view is correct, would entail a sudden shift of perspective from brain-filtered to mind-unfiltered consciousness, like stepping from one shaded room to another lit up by the sun.

Fechner's mind-brain threshold is mobile; from moment to moment our attention is more or less tightly gripped by the spell of life. But fatigue, hunger, drugs, monotony, inspiration, danger, music, erotic enchantment, near-death, ascetic ecstasy, and so on, all are ways of tinkering with the threshold, contracting and dilating the floodgates of consciousness.

Theorizing psychic phenomena faces severe problems. The effects we would like to understand are in a class radically different from anything in the physical sciences. What kind of science could capture the likes of Joseph in its conceptual apparatus? In addition to the spontaneous freedom of his will and the volatile cultural variables acting on him, the phenomena seem to operate outside the common constraints of physical reality. There are intelligible patterns but it's impossible to predict how they play out in experience.

Another complication is that the *source* of "psi" phenomena is often obscure. The so-called "experimenter effect"[9] makes it unclear in any group situation who is the author of the effects, or if there is a single author rather than a network of subliminal coauthors. How is science possible when the causal agency is so elusive? This mix of complexity, indetermination (free will), experimenter effect, and sheer extra-physicality make the hope of acquiring a "normal" scientific understanding of Joseph's phenomena extremely difficult.

And to further confound the hope for a scientific explanation of these outlaws of nature, many students of parapsychology believe there is something systematically elusive about the phenomena, something evasive that makes mastering or harnessing them impossible.[10]

Still, the point remains: mainline materialism cannot comprehend Joseph's extraordinary phenomena. An expanded view of mind is absolutely essential. We have in the first place to assume that mind and consciousness are irreducible facts of nature and possess fundamental causal powers. In plain language, our minds are real in their own right and have the power to do things—things we can only learn about through experience. To reduce our minds to anything derivative and "less real" is to bump our heads against mountains of brute fact.

Our brains usefully keep us mentally oriented to the struggles of earthly existence; but at the same time they also work as the default obstruction to possible enlightenment. Joseph revolted against the normal dictates of his brain and sought to free himself from the distractions of "the world."

He used different methods, all of them extreme, which he practiced relentlessly. He pushed everything to super-rational—*un*worldly—extremes. Intent on detaching himself from his biologically evolved nervous system, his goal was to break into another sphere of being and unite with another reality. The ascetic practices are exacting; the indifference frustrates normal brain use. "I'm good for nothing," he often said, *wanting* to be "good for nothing." Every hint of worldly gain or advantage must instantly be repelled; it is the extreme route to escape the prison of his brain.

SEXUAL TENSION AND ECSTATIC LEVITATION

Assuming the "transmission" mind-brain model, can it help make sense of some of Joseph's unusual phenomena? Perhaps indirectly, by means of intensified psychical tension. It was part of his vow of chastity to go against his most powerful instincts, in particular, sexuality. According to a famous myth in Plato's *Phaedrus*,[11] the sight of bodily beauty awakens the erotic *daimon*—the "wings" of the psyche—thus enabling it to ascend to the realm of the gods. Sexuality oriented around the lure of physical beauty is the secret engine of Platonic ecstasy; it is the road of psychic ascent to the gods.

Ecstatic eros, however, competes with pandemic eros, the attraction to beauty that ends in copulation instead of levitation. So there is a tension between daimonic eros and pandemic eros, one aspiring to the rarefied heights, the other caught in the shoals of biological reproduction. (Sexist Plato identifies pandemic eros with heteroeroticism and daimonic eros with homoeroticism.) The main point is this: Tension is crucial to ascent; without tension, the imaginal levitation of the psyche is not possible. Without tension, the enormous energy of pandemic, reproductive eros cannot be utilized for the ascent to the gods.

Platonic eros is the daimon that raises or "levitates" the mortal to the immortal, human to divine consciousness. The energy of Platonic eros is uplifting; one is "carried away" in the ecstasy of love. Bernini offers an interesting psychological view. Sexual arousal, sexual temptation, sustained erotic tension: this, according to proto-psychoanalyst Bernini, is the matrix of Joseph's mystical raptures:

> Stimulation of the senses and diabolic suggestions surely afflicted him and he waged war against temptation. But we also want to refer to the cause of his ecstasies and raptures, which was the same cause that manifested in St. Paul: namely, the compensatory relationship between heavenly flights and the depths of strong temptations. He suffered such powerful temptation around the time he experienced his ecstasies and raptures, during which his soul was swept up to heaven. It was as if heaven would raise him up high only when he was most tempted.[12]

This is a psychodynamic interpretation of the levitations, the strength of which Bernini equates with the strength of the temptation resisted. He infers this from the fact that the ecstasies and raptures correlate with the "depths of strong temptations."

So the more Joseph is tempted to yield to his erotic temptations, the greater the tension and the more powerful the rapture or levitation. Bernini's gloss is that the heavenly forces pull Joseph up only when he is about to sink into the abyss. He has to push his yearning toward the edge, he has to be driven by his *excesses of mind*. Bernini alludes to the baroque conceit of *the divine game*. God likes to bring his best servants to the edge of the abyss to test their mettle and draw them out to the limits of their performance. The "divine game" is a figure of speech that seems to work very well for certain erotically over-charged servants of God.

Was there a sharp boundary between erotic temptation and the more broadly affective side of Joseph's feeling life? My impression is that in the friar's case, psychical tension resulted from the clash of his mystical vocation with *all* his affective tendencies. This was obvious in his relationship to Maria of Savoy where he struggled to master even his purely affectionate attachment to her. In the end, he called a total halt to her attempts to be a part of his life in any concrete way. "God wishes that I be detached from *every* affection other than his divine will," he once remarked—such sweeping demands could only heighten psychical tension.

For Joseph, levitation meant escape from the unbearable tension of just being in the world. It was an all or nothing game he chose to play. Forced by his superiors to lead a tomblike existence, unable to establish any kind of normal emotional outlet, all that remained was to practice his spiritual arts and constant inward retreat. The increased psychosexual tension played into the dynamics, the explosives, of his levitations.

Unconsciously, it seems, Joseph deployed his sexual energies to propel his ecstatic flights. Other traditions are more direct, more reflexive about the erotic induction of mystical consciousness, for example, the Platonic and the Tantric. Unlike the Catholic antipathy to sexuality Joseph had to deal with, Alain Danielou's *Gods of Love and Ecstasy* tells us that "it is the principle of Shaivism that nothing exists which is not part of the divine body and which cannot be a way of reaching the divine"[13]

In Joseph's Counter-Reformation world, the erotic had to be repressed, played with perhaps as part of a "divine game," or, more safely, banished completely from mind. Yet Danielou could be painting a portrait of Joseph when he writes: "Certain ritual techniques allow us to operate on the latent energies present in the human being and thus to transform him into a vehicle for the transmission of certain powers, raising him to a higher level in the hierarchy of beings and making him into a sort of demigod or superman, and thus closer to the world of spirits."[14]

In Arthur Avalon's description of kundalini yoga, we find a Joseph-like description of the adept's body, being cold and deathlike in ecstasy: "During inhalation . . . he should consider that a new celestial body is being formed."[15] Joseph's "ritual techniques" of fasting, poverty, humility, and chastity made him a "vehicle for the transmission of certain powers."

We come back to the idea that when the brain is deflected from its routine tasks, *whatever* facilitates the extraordinary effects seems to come into play more readily. Joseph, I conjecture, drew upon repressed, powerful sexual energies to accelerate his extraordinary flights, though consciously he associated sexuality with diabolic temptation. This conflicted, hyperintense state seems to have served as a potent driver of the force that made the levitations possible.

Outside the Catholic tradition, we find a more conscious use of sexual energies for magical or spiritual purposes. Hindu, Chinese, and Tibetan cultures deploy methods of heightening psychosexual tension, a common strategy that worked by mobilizing, but checking rather than repressing, sexual energy. More broadly, the Vajrayana methods of Mahayana Buddhism aim to mobilize all forces, good and evil, so that whatever "defilements, desires and appetites cannot be quickly discarded must be skillfully utilized. . . . Ennobling means transferring the force of the desire to an object identified with the goal of Liberation."[16] This seems to describe Joseph when he transferred the energies of his sexual temptations toward images of heavenly union.[17]

A movement in nineteenth-century America was based on the use of erotic energies in service to spiritual enlightenment. A feminist obstetrician, gynecologist, and vocal enemy of the corset, Alice Bunker Stockham (1833–1912) was an American votary of Karezza, a term she coined from the Italian *carezza* or "caress." Stockham wrote about the practice of Karezza, a technique of *coitus reservatus*, in which partners sought to remain aroused short of achieving climax; the aim of the exercise was to increase psychical tension and induce purer states of consciousness.

Stockham thought this was the best way to keep couples faithful to each other; matrimony would triumph by using the energies of sex to raise each other's consciousness toward higher and higher peaks of ecstasy. She claimed that many blessings arose from these sexual practices: "A sense of lightness was communicated to the body and also a sense of levitation, giving one a feeling of hovering in the air. . . . Finally there was the reward of mystical experience, a feeling of supreme exaltation and ecstasy, with the promise of reaching in time the greatest heights in the spiritual planes."[18]

Along with this grand vision of erotic human potential, Stockham promoted gender equality and believed that proper use of Karezza on the part of both genders could spiritualize marriage, provide birth control, and beat back the oppressive patriarchy. But in 1873, a wealthy and powerful man, Anthony Comstack (1844–1915), created the New York Society for the Suppression of Vice, which put America under strict moral surveillance. Comstack decided it was perversely criminal not to have orgasms and attacked Alice Stockham. He also forced John Humphrey Noyes, a social reformer and promoter of Edenic sexuality in nineteenth-century upstate New York, to flee to Canada.[19] Comstack drove Ida Craddock to commit suicide after repeatedly jailing her for peddling pornography when she had merely published an anatomy book with pictures of naked bodies.

Modern Catholic ideas on sex and the sacred are more reflexive than their Counter-Reformation counterparts. Jeffrey Kripal addresses the topic in several of his books. He suggests that asceticism cannot escape the erotic but is itself "a form of unacknowledged eroticism."[20] Discussing "male Catholic asceticism" and a former Jesuit, Don Hanlon Johnson, Kripal writes that the dynamics of monastic discipline are "not so much about repressing and eliminating sexual energies as they are about *exaggerating*, disciplining, analyzing, and sublimating them into more and more intense (homo) erotic forms." To be clear, Kripal does not equate homoeroticism with homosexuality.[21]

Johnson is cited as recalling meditating in seminary on an image of the barely clad Jesus hanging from a cross and being "deliciously aroused."[22] Here then is a way that sex might be used to ignite mystical states of consciousness, based on an attitude of affirmation, not on recoil or repression of the erotic, and not therefore liable to give rise to levitation.

Joseph may be compared to a more recent ecstatic extremist, the Bengali mystic and devotee of Kali, Ramakrishna. Joseph and Ramakrishna were alike with regard to their "mental excesses." For one thing, the excesses forced them into embarrassing situations in their spiritual communities. "These visions and ecstatic states eventually reached such proportions that it became impossible for Ramakrishna to carry out his priestly duties," observes Kripal, who has written about the erotic mysticism of Ramakrishna.[23]

Like Joseph, Ramakrishna was intensely and involuntarily immersed in inner life, and was often oblivious to the world around him. The sexual dialectic secretly operative in the multiple lives of Ramakrishna suggests some parallels to Joseph's case.

Joseph from the start proved ill-suited to normal human service. Take, for example, his priestly duties. When Joseph did say Mass or appear in a public ceremony or procession, major disturbances often resulted. A casual reference to some aspect of the sacred, and he would collapse to the ground senseless or float into space, and remain in these states until summoned back by his superiors. Kripal's remarks on Ramakrishna describe Joseph: "Ramakrishna might be described as hyper-associative. Almost anything he saw or heard could awaken powerful forces that often overwhelmed him. When one is in love, he explained, 'even the littlest thing can ecstatically remind one' [of the beloved]" (p. 66).

Joseph got carried away by *anything* suggesting the sacred, and in particular went wild on sight of paintings of the Madonna or relics of Francis of Assisi. Associations reported that led to ecstasy were with a single word, a song, a sacred time, the blue sky, a green leaf, a veil, a pair of shoes, a grey leveret, a sea urchin, a sash.

Ramakrishna and Joseph were similar in the intensely sublimated way they engaged with their respective feminine principles, Kali and the Madonna. Their first ecstasies were both stimulated by sacred feminine figures. Both holy men had difficulties descending from their feminine archetypes—so different in style—into the world of incarnate female particulars.

Ramakrishna was recognized by his community as emotionally somewhat off-balance from his long unrelieved continence; sex with women was therapeutically suggested but rejected. He was not sexually responsive to women, and seemed to have been more attuned to men. This gender preference and the way he showed it clashed with the heterosexual biases of his culture.

Joseph was in flight from women and most likely his sexual temptations revolved around women, although it is not inconceivable they too were also homoerotic. As far as I can see, it's not the gender but the intensity of desire that correlates with levitation, although guilt over homoeroticism might intensify the repression and hence the psychic charge. Hindu and Catholic ecstatics have roughly similar phenomenologies of siddhis and charisms; the Hindus appear less prone to levitation than the overwrought Catholic saints do, but there is not really enough data to tell. Some very good evidential cases come from the Catholic Counter-Reformation that was in repressive high gear. Europe was swarming with skeptics, reformers, and subverters of Church authority.

However secret his homoerotic compulsions, Ramakrishna was not isolated or forced into a mindset that cherished absolute chastity as the preferred highway to enlightenment. Joseph's sustained sexual repression tipped the psychic balance, reached a critical point, and jolted ecstasy into levitation. Joseph seems always poised to be swept into ecstasy, a readiness Bernini refers to as "mental excesses."

One of William Blake's "Proverbs of Hell" reads: "The road of excess leads to the palace of wisdom."[24] Combine Joseph's volcanic disposition and Counter-Reformation restrictions and inhibitions, and the excess of sexual tension might be the road to the palace of wisdom. Using Joseph's own metaphor, the psychosexual "gunpowder" built up to a point, then exploded into the visible *moti*. Is there room for such outliers in our thought world?

WOMEN IN THE FRIAR'S LIFE

Joseph's experience with women was problematic, a powerful prompter of inner conflict and therefore psychic tension. Psychoanalyst Karl Stern's *Flight from Women* is a shrewd dissection of Descartes, Schopenhauer, Sartre, Ibsen, and other male culture stars and their disturbed attitudes toward women. From all appearances, we must add Joseph of Copertino to the roster of notable men in flight from women.

However gauche and fearful of women in the flesh, Joseph became ecstatic at the mere mention of the Madonna, whom he apparently related to on familiar visionary terms. The Madonna was for Joseph the anti-type of his affectless mother, the impoverished Francheschina. The Madonna was a creature of his mind, images of which appeared in paintings he meditated on. He reacted intensely to painted or sculpted images of the Madonna, embracing and kissing them. His biological mother was just his "nurse," he often said, the Madonna was his "true mother." The one wiped and spanked his behind; the other inspired ecstasy and rapture.

To break the spell of "the world" meant release from procreative sex and bondage to family life. Mystical union was an all-consuming enterprise, and he relied on the Madonna for inspiration. But as far as real women were concerned, Joseph's instincts were always *to take flight*. The incident in Assisi proves this: To avoid talking with the "vehement" Spanish ambassador's wife, he went into ecstasy and flew over her head, causing her to faint.

Walking in the cathedral at Assisi, he was seized by the idea that the Virgin in a painting by Cimabue was staring at him. His diarist noticed him gazing at the painted image, looking uplifted and transfigured. Joseph clapped his hands and smiled, and all he could say was, *"Dom Arcangelo, amore! amore!"*

Thanks to his spectacular raptures, Joseph became a celebrity, and when he did venture into a public venue, he met real women who grabbed and swiped at him, begged for his prayers and blessings, and tried to negotiate a memento of his body or a piece of his clothing.

He wasn't happy with women who approached him out of curiosity, as this report shows:

> Things did not go so well for the other women, badly advised, who out of feminine curiosity, wanted to see high and inscrutable secrets of heaven with their own eyes. The Marchessa Artemisia de' Medici, sister of the Duke of Corgna, made an agreement with another woman of Perugia to go to Assisi for the purpose of experiencing the rapture of Padre Giuseppe. The plan involved their presenting themselves in Church, first the one woman and then, last to enter, the Marchessa. With appropriate words, they would invoke the names of Jesus and Mary, so that all present would witness Padre Giuseppe's ecstasies in response to the names, as usually happened. The plan was approved with applause and they followed it as was agreed.
>
> But as soon as the Marchesa entered the Church, Padre Giuseppe, with holy indignation, turned to them and said: "Ah. You've come here out of curiosity, have you? Don't you know, Marchesa, that God can make miracles out of even this piece of wood? Go away, all of you!" The Marchesa later deposed that she was mortified by these remarks, and quickly saw that Giuseppe was able to penetrate the secrets of her heart.[25]

There was a woman the friar had a heartfelt relationship with. Let's hear it from Bernini:

> The person who loved Padre Giuseppe the most during this time, with a tender affection, was the Infanta, Maria Savoia, a princess of great piety and intuition, huge of heart, daughter of Carol Emanuele and Catherine of Austria. The great Lady, a Third Order Franciscan and devout pilgrim of royal lineage, after having

seen all the sanctuaries of Italy, arrived in Assisi longing to see both the body of St. Francis and its living "copy"—Padre Giuseppe.

So the Infanta paid homage to St. Francis in the Church and homage to Padre Giuseppe in the Sacrestia. For many of the days that followed, she was situated in Rivotorto, close enough to Assisi to visit Giuseppe several times a week. She revealed to him with the utmost purity of intention all the secrets of her soul. Sweet conversations would ensue and last entire days, and would not end without some miracle happening. The Infanta was deaf and could not hear words without the help of a silver ear horn.[26]

Joseph had a difficult time with the infanta's ear horn. To be heard by the princess he had to speak directly into her ear horn, and that meant getting very close to a real breathing woman. The trepidation he endured during these close encounters with the infanta's ear horn was an occasion of amusement for the brothers. Here now is the story of a very short breakfast date.

One morning, the Custodian granted her (the Infanta) permission to have breakfast with Padre Giuseppe in the Sacrestia of the Church of St. Francis. Giuseppe, who emerged from his cell saying he was offered breakfast by a lady pilgrim, after his third bite, fell on his knees in ecstasy and, arms spread open and eyes fixed on the face of the serene Infanta, he saw the stupendous beauty of the Queen of Heaven. Called back to himself by the Custodian's command, he went quietly toward his cell. That night a frate from the convent teased the Padre, marveling at the holiness of the princess. The Most Serene Infanta ultimately left Assisi, having been advised to do so by Giuseppe, completely full of God and holy love for Padre Giuseppe, with whom she left her heart.

Joseph must have felt drawn to the infanta and decided it was wise to ask her to leave Assisi. He was unable to handle her ardent willingness to serve and be near him. The picture given by Bernini is perhaps unique: after the third bite of their only dining experience together, he falls on his knees in ecstasy but sees the infanta *as the Queen of Heaven.* In a way, it was unfortunate not to be able to relate to an actual woman in a purely human way.

The infanta tried to stay in touch and repeatedly begged for permission to see him, but to no avail. In a letter, she expressed her desire to provide for Padre Giuseppe's needs. Giuseppe's response—For the love of Christ!—Leave me alone with Lady Poverty!

The princess made a new undershirt for him to wear under his tunic and asked the Father General to exchange it for the old one he wore. Commanding him under holy obedience, the Custodian insisted he accept the new undershirt. The response was annoyance and—completely out of his persona—he *disobeyed* the order. Furious, he tore off his clothing and said: "Command me! Off with my tunic! Done! Off with my undershirt! Done! How about—off with my flesh and skin!" Was this an act, a temper tantrum, or just a burst of boorishness? Eventually, the scorned gift ended up in the reliquary of the infanta of Savoy.

Perhaps there was a reason Joseph was reluctant to accept the infanta's gift. The undershirt, which she surely touched and perhaps tenderly fondled, would be something he would wear against his own naked body. With his acute sensibility and violent imagination, he might have been wary of temptation; for him it might have been like having the infanta's hands wrapped around him, caressing him all night. No, Joseph reserved his deepest affections for images, icons, signs. The Madonna of his mind was all he needed and all he ultimately desired.

Whatever the forces that were roused by Joseph's mental Madonna, it's hard to dissociate them from the friar's levitations. Would they have occurred at all if Joseph was sexually more integrated with the earthy feminine side of himself? Would his ecstasies have had the same locomotive power? Perhaps only a person violently at odds with his sexuality but also exquisitely attuned to his mental Madonna could produce the bizarre coincidence of opposites that describes levitation.

DIABOLIC INTENSITIES

But now, in a darker register, consider that fear and suspicion are also ways of intensifying psychic tension. They too might facilitate breakthrough, stimulate sudden expansions of consciousness. The erotic is not the only way psychic tension is increased; other, perhaps less savory, emotions can also be very effective. And indeed uncanny things went on with Joseph and his *fratelli* in their living quarters. Encounters with the diabolic were apparently commonplace and sometimes got physical:

> Because of the sound of screams and chains, some religious bolted their doors with a crossbar, another fled through the dormitory, and still others fainted or fell into deliria. It sometimes happened that Padre Giuseppe was interrogated about the cause of the strange noises. Not able to deny the fact and not wanting to lie, Padre Giuseppe would put on a serious face and calmly say it had all been a joke. Then he would fall silent. He was good at turning the ire of hell against him into a kind of game.
>
> He was asked: "In your solitude, has the Devil ever tempted you?" He replied: "He appears before me holding long horns." He gestured to show how long the horns were. "I was not intimidated because I'm always with God; I am withdrawn from the world."

That God and the Devil like to play games with us was a baroque conceit. Joking about the Devil, as in the "long horns" passage, is walking a thin line;

the joke might evolve into the laughter of rejection, recalling what was a comic cliché in Boccaccio's plague-ridden world. It was harder to joke about the Devil during the Counter-Reformation. Joseph's internal environment was dogged by fear of heresy, fear of the Inquisition, and, indeed, fear of the Devil. Keith Thomas wrote: "When all the forces of organized religion had been deployed for centuries in formulating the notion of a personal Satan, he had a reality and immediacy which could not fail to grip the strongest mind."[27] Educated people today wonder how folks could be so naïve and superstitious. But without protective modern notions of impersonal law and natural causation, the temptation to personify evil and be wary about dark forces would be much stronger. For Joseph, fear of the Devil was real and most likely heightened his vigilance and expectant mood, stirring up and enflaming his transcendent imaginings.

Joseph projected the images that gripped his mind on innocent bystanders. He seemed to half-pretend, half-project seeing or otherwise engaging with his favorites—Francis, Catherine, Anthony, Philip, the Madonna—not that much of Jesus, come to think of it—but enough. His subjectivity seemed constantly poised to proclaim and project itself outwardly. He projects the image of Mary Magdalene on a local street lady. He was convinced that he saw Saint Anthony watching over him while the Inquisitors were grilling him (the effect was to compose his mood).

Joseph's imaginative life was so intense as to mold the shape and even the substance of his perceptions. He was not alone in this field of imaginal quasi-psychokinesis. For example, there is the permanent hallucination of a ring of espousal that Saint Catherine of Siena claimed to "see" continuously on her finger, after consummating her mystical marriage with Christ.[28]

In Joseph's psychic world the boundary between fact and imagination was porous. One night, it was reported, invisible hands took him by the throat, gripping him until he was numb, leaving bruises on the neck, which Dr. Fagiani examined the next day and attested to.[29] Another night Joseph was reportedly attacked by a bandit attired in black; he screamed and fought back, his hands seen flailing and gripping at air.

Yet on another occasion Francesco Ugolini, who was curious about Joseph's doings in the wee hours, spied on him. He observed (and formally deposed that) two black dogs with huge paws accosted the friar in the basilica, pulling at him from two sides and clawing at his neck. In a panic, Joseph cried out for Jesus and St. Francis; at once rows of tall candles erupted with luminous flame. Besides Ugolino's eyewitness testimony, there were marks on Joseph's neck from the black dogs' paws, which his physician duly treated.[30]

About those devilish dogs, Joseph's confessor reports the victim as saying: *Malatasca mi voleva strozzare questa notte!* "Evil-Pocket tried to choke me that night!"[31] Something came out of Joseph's "pocket"—a metaphor of the subliminal mind?—something that wanted to choke him! The examples show a continuum in which something is trying to express itself externally: from projecting an image on another person to a public hallucination that leaves visible marks on his body.

The encounters with Malatasca appear to involve a succession of degrees of materialization: from seeing something "as if" it were the devil to encountering an objective phantom, the black dogs that Ugolino said he witnessed. Since PK may assume many forms, we may conjecture that some of Joseph's hallucinations occasionally attained transient degrees of tangible presence, even perhaps transient degrees of personal identity. For documented examples of such transient materializations, there is the extraordinary case of Marthe Beraud, aka "Eva C."[32]

Again, in Joseph's experience there was no sharp boundary between the real and the unreal. From the totally subjective to the ambiguous and quasi-real, from hallucination to partial or transient materialization, patterns of putative fact suggest an ontologically wobbly picture of reality, in spirit more like quantum mechanics than solid Newtonian physics. If we hope to mentally grasp these experiences, a more elastic concept of mind and body seems necessary.

For the dark domain that made up part of Joseph's lived world, one may consult historian Brian Levack's *The Devil Within*.[33] Levack found that a concentration of cases of diabolic possession occurred in the 1600s, contemporaneous with the life of Joseph. What Levack says confirms the reality of the darkly rich texture of Joseph's world:

> But references to possessions in the records of witchcraft prosecutions, published narratives of possessions and exorcisms, demonological treatises by theologians and inquisitors, and records of exorcisms performed at shrines and other locations support the claim that the number of possessions in the early modern period was exceptionally large and probably greater than at any time before or since.[34]

What then were the "symptoms" (Levack's term) that led people to infer that a person was a *demoniac*, that is, possessed by the Devil?

Here's the list: convulsions, physical pain, rigidity of limbs, muscular flexibility and contortions, preternatural strength, levitation, swelling, vomiting, loss of bodily function, prolonged fasting (more associated with saintly figures), the ability to speak in languages previously unknown, drastic changes of voice, trance experiences and visions, clairvoyance, blasphemy, and immoral gestures and actions (i.e., possessed women liked to raise their skirts).

Among these "symptoms," nine are found in reports of mystics, mediums, and shamans, and are associated with ecstasy and possession. Some of the symptoms of the possessed are exceedingly strange and incredible. Levack is careful to point out the reasons why such reports might not be reliable, but at no point does he dismiss *in toto* the reality of any of them:

Yet even if we accept the likelihood that all narratives of possession have been filtered through the lenses of observers who were predisposed to see and hear certain things, we cannot dismiss such reports as entirely fictional. . . . accounts of possessions that were witnessed by large numbers of people, sometimes in public venues, must be granted at least a measure of credibility, especially when observers who disagreed on the causes of the demoniacs' behavior did not deny that they had witnessed it.[35]

So especially in Joseph's time and world, belief in and fear of the Devil was pervasive, and so were many publically witnessed behaviors associated with diabolical possession. It sometimes appears that objective reality itself can be shaped by cultural belief, even to the point of supposing that if enough people believe in the existence of devils, tangible "devils" may in some inexplicable way now and then manifest and interact with a fully awake public.

Joseph had to contend with a second, related problem, undoubtedly real, and more terrifying than the Devil himself: I mean the lawyers, theologians, inquisitors—word-spinners, rule-jugglers, and spiritual bureaucrats; in short, all the guardians, superiors, and enforcers of the Church. Any person *excessive* in thought or deed was liable to rouse suspicion, particularly if he or she attracted too much attention.

We discussed Joseph's dealings with his Inquisitors in chapter 1. What I wish to stress now is that belief in the Devil and fear of the Inquisition intensified points of his interior environment; psychically, we could call them fault-lines and pressure points. They put him on edge, drove him further toward breaking, toward the next leap beyond which he always seemed poised to take. During his last six years in Osimo, his mobility was *most* restricted and the raptures were correspondingly more intense. The atmosphere of suspicion and diabolic threat increased the psychic tension, always priming him to escape to another world.

JOSEPH'S ECSTASY AND THE NEAR-DEATH STATE

The near-death experience (NDE), so well reported, often involves mystical, life-transforming effects.[36] In some cases, "near death" may be figurative. Profound depression or the conviction that death is imminent may trigger an experience similar to the ones caused by physical trauma such as cardiac arrest.

With heroic asceticism and mental discipline, a minority of human beings seem able to achieve a near-death breakthrough. In the age-old quest for enlightenment, there are many styles, methods, and schools of thought. Thanks to modern resuscitation technology, a new tradition of mysticism has evolved from spontaneous near-death experiencers and the researchers who study them.

Joseph and the NDE? It appears that the aim of his spiritual practice was, *in effect*, to induce in himself a state resembling certain key features of the NDE. Joseph's experience was shaped by his own spiritual beliefs, symbols, and practices, and in the thick of his own culture, which as a matter of historical fact, was going through a kind of collective NDE.

My first observation is that Joseph is often reported to appear like someone who is near death. Bernini often refers to him as looking like a "cadaver," worn from lack of sleep, lean from fasting, lacerated from bouts of self-flagellation. Again, the likeness to death: during ecstasy his body became cold, insensible, respiration barely detectable, sometimes cataleptic—outwardly, bodily, *as if dead.*

But what happens during a modern NDE? As Ed Kelly writes in this description of cardiac arrest:

> Cardiac arrest . . . is a physiologically brutal event. Cerebral functioning shuts down within a few seconds. Whether the heart actually stops beating entirely or goes into ventricular fibrillation, the result is essentially instantaneous circulatory arrest, with blood flow and oxygen uptake in the brain plunging swiftly to near-zero levels. EEG signs of cerebral ischemia, typical with global slowing and loss of fast activity, are visually detectable within 6–10 seconds, and progress to flat-line EEGs within 10–20 seconds of the onset of arrest. In sum, full arrest leads rapidly to establishment of three major clinical signs of death—absence of cardiac output, absence of respiration, and absence of brainstem reflexes—and provides the best model we have of the dying process.[37]

Persons who undergo cardiac arrest enter a physical state that, according to the scientific consensus, should prevent the occurrence of *any* form of consciousness. But numerous medically documented cases of cardiac arrest, in which people have conscious experiences, have been collected. These experiences are more vivid and intense than ordinary life and they are often deeply transformative.

Due to oxygen deprivation in the brain, the neurophysical structures in what is called the "global workspace" are *not* working. Contrary to mainstream expectations, patients experience *heightened* consciousness, situated in stunningly real and deeply meaningful internal environments (*not* like dreams). They meet and converse with deceased persons; they find themselves in the presence of a mysterious, all-embracing light, and the aftereffects are often life-enhancing and long-lasting.

One striking account is of Joseph McMoneagle, whose NDE apparently left him with increased psychic powers, "remote viewing"[38] in particular; as a result, he was employed by the Cognitive Sciences Lab of SRI-International.[39] McMoneagle describes his experience of a voice and light being whose splendor he speaks of with words he says are totally inadequate.

His experience, he states, infinitely dwarfed the most rapturous of sexual orgasms. "There is no comparable place in physical reality to experience such total awareness."

McMoneagle's statement calls to mind something Socrates said in the *Phaedo*:[40] As long as we, our souls, are "nailed" to our bodies, we will never know the bliss of supreme reality. Again we are at odds with the mainstream, but NDEs give reason for entertaining such an idea. The NDE suggests that, freed from our bodies, consciousness expands; being in our bodies, it is normally contracted.

McMoneagle's report explains an item in Joseph's religious psychology. I was suspicious of Joseph harping on himself all the time as "the greatest sinner." It sounded like pious hypocrisy. How could a friar with perfect humility, ever congenial with his brethren, a recognized guide and inspiration of the people—why would such a man see himself (allowing for some irony) as shameful, imperfect, a terrible sinner?

In the presence of the ineffable near-death light being, McMoneagle claims he saw himself very clearly; and the sight of his failings caused him pain. "It was a horrible feeling, just seeing how I matched up against the Light."[41] In the encounter with the Light, he became hypersensitive to all the shady spots in himself. Joseph's meetings with the Light were a regular occurrence. As such would he not also be acutely aware of every "shady spot" in himself? Would he not be sensitive to concerns that might seem slight to others but that to him appeared like huge fallings off from the infinite prize?

The mystic and the near-death experiencer may be having insights into the same but normally hidden reality. The Dutch cardiologist Pim van Lommel (2001) published a paper in the British medical journal *The Lancet*, a study of NDEs and cardiac arrest. The paper caused a sensation, appearing on the front pages of newspapers around the world. Such stories make an impact because they suggest that science has given its stamp of approval to the afterlife hypothesis. For those who have the experience more is involved than mere belief. Van Lommel closely analyzed the phenomenon, and claims to see something he calls "eternity" and "endless consciousness."[42] In line with the model sketched in this chapter, in an NDE one encounters consciousness defiltering itself from the brain: witnessing, for example, the panoramic memory, contact with discarnates, the numinous light, and so on.

The near-death state is one in which the usual cognitive "filter" is removed and one is flooded by extraordinary states of consciousness. If the brain works like a filter, expansion of consciousness makes sense in the NDE; near death disengages the filter and the floodgates are opened. I think it fair to say that the mystical core of the NDE seems like what yogis and meditators achieve slowly and gradually, if at all: supreme felicity and enlarged psychic powers. If we view Joseph's ecstatic life through the NDE lens, his spiritual practice was analogous in aim to what happens by accident in these remarkable experiences. With practice and deliberation, he broke down the filter and overcame resistance to the subliminal influx.

Psychiatrist and near-death researcher Bruce Greyson organized the phenomenology of NDEs into four branches, each displaying subtypes. The figure of Joseph matches Greyson's grid of the main elements: cognitive, affective, paranormal, and transcendental or mystical. Joseph's experience (cultural inflections aside) appears made of the same elements of the near-death prototype. Consider the enhanced cognitive features listed by Greyson: alteration of the sense of time, quickening thought processes, and the experience of the life-review.

All the foregoing were common fare for Joseph, who seemed to have the total arc of his life present to his mind's eye. He frequently stated what was coming: news of the death of friends and dignitaries (popes, in particular); inquisitors who were coming to arrest him; news about events at a distance (the revolution of Mansaniello in Naples); the time and place of his own death; and so on. He seemed always to have major changes, good or bad news, at his psychic fingertips, so to speak. As fame grew, crowds harassed him, but Church officials intervened and whisked him away incognito. Perceived as proficient in previewing the lives of others, the *processi* contain firsthand reports supporting his cognitive outreach in time and space. Joseph qualifies for Greyson's first criterion.

A second near-death criterion is a heightened affective world: experiences of unconditional love, bliss, ecstatic union. A fullness of love is described in many near-death narratives. As we learn from Joseph's life, such heights of consciousness were reached, and fairly often. Extravagant affect was the hallmark of his personality. As diarist Rosmi noted, he was sometimes reduced to repeating one word, *l'amore*. Joseph was on familiar terms with the near-death world by virtue of his expanded cognitions and his highly developed affective states.

The paranormal was Greyson's third marker of NDEs. We have looked at some reports that Joseph had direct access to other people's minds, to events in the future, and events at a distance. Under the rubric of the paranormal, we may mention his unexplained upliftings in space, his curious talent for leaving mysterious fragrances in his wake, and the many healings ascribed to him. In the realm of the NDE, Joseph was no stranger to the regions of the paranormal.

Fourth on Greyson's list are the "transcendental" features of NDEs: a mysterious border, discarnate souls, visionary domains, mystical light beings, and an atmosphere of vast impartial love. As with the paranormal criterion, these especially powerful and life-transforming features of the

NDE go to the love core of Joseph's mystical world: the essence of his desire, which was to unite his whole being with the supreme love object. Unlike the average person who has an NDE once, however, Joseph apparently spent a good deal of his time periodically immersed in this psychically expanded environment.

Needless to say, his methods of inducing the experience were highly specific. Fasting, obedience, prayer, meditation, detachment from everything were used to impede normal brain function, disconnect attention from the objective world, and lower the threshold of Fechner's mind-brain barrier. In mystical and NDE, the sensory-motor function is disrupted, followed by subliminal bursts of consciousness into supraliminal view. A peculiar type of dissociation, through spiritual practice or accidental cardiac arrest, make the experience possible. The near-death and Joseph's mystical state fit the present model; the brain is rendered quiescent allowing the gates of consciousness to open.

EXPANDING MIND

The first step toward coming to grips with Joseph's wild talents, then, is to question the dominant concept of mind. Otherwise, his story will strike you as beyond belief. We must stipulate an expanded concept of mind. The stumbling block is the assumption that minds are emergent brain products, and nothing more. Karl Popper called this "promissory materialism,"[43] the faith that some day neuroscience will demystify consciousness. But there are no signs of that actually happening.

There is nothing to prevent us then from starting from a different premise: mind and consciousness do not emerge from brains and are not second-class citizens of the cosmos; they are irreducibly real factors of nature, autonomous and powerful realities. Joseph's anomaly-ridden case starts to make sense in light of the premise of an expanded, preexistent mind and consciousness. Stick to the mainline reductive view and his mystical and paranormal phenomena cease to be intelligible. The mystical becomes regression or insanity, the paranormal illusory or fraudulent, and spiritual practice a symptom of failure to adapt to a vibrant consumer society. Remove the straight-jacket of materialism, make room for Van Lommel's "endless" and Dossey's "nonlocal" mental existence, and we have the premise for a radically different story. One thing I am prepared to predict: people will continue to have all manner of extraordinary experiences that call for more accommodating theories. The need to break out of the black box of unscientific materialism will remain and is likely to grow.

NOTES

1. There is of course a long philosophical history to the fortunes and misadventures of mind, in the modern period ranging from Descartes to Gilbert Ryle's *The Concept of Mind* (1949), and on to the present. The restoration of mind to its proper place in nature has been on a crooked, halting path; a few citations will have to suffice. H. D. Lewis's *The Elusive Mind* (1969) is a sustained defense of mind against the various reductionists of the time, and for more recent examples, several anthologies may be cited: Koons and Bealer, eds., *The Waning of Materialism* (2010); Baker and Goetz, eds., *The Soul Hypothesis* (2011); and Nagel, *Mind, Life, and* Cosmos (2012).

2. Noë, A. xi.
3. Fodor, 1992, pp. 5–7.
4. Sartre, 1958/1989. *Being and Nothingness: An Essay on Phenomenological Ontology*. London: Routledge.
5. Grosso, 2015.
6. GP, p. 306.
7. See James on Fechner, footnote in Ingersoll Lecture.
8. DB, p. 135.
9. Experimenter effect, defined in Wolman, 1977, see p. 925: "Term used to refer to the finding that experimenters working under the same objective conditions and with subjects from the same population may get different or conflicting results which conform to their own expectations."
10. See Hanson, 2001; Kennedy, 2003. Hanson makes use of the trickster archetype as ingeniously undermining every effort of the human mind to master "psi." The expression "rebellious reality" (in this connection) I first heard from Dr. Emilio Dido, a physician of Padre Pio, when I interviewed him with Karlis Osis in New York City in the early 1980s.
11. *Phaedrus*, see Josef Pieper, 1964.
12. DB, p. 191.
13. Danielou, 1982.
14. Ibid., p. 183.
15. Avalon, 1964.
16. Blofeld, pp. 74–75.
17. See Walker, 1970; Bharati, 1970, pp. 68–79; Blofeld, 1970.
18. Walker, 1970.
19. See Grosso, 1995, pp. 141–44.
20. A personal communication.
21. For extensive discussion of sexual energy and mysticism, see Kripal's *Roads of Excess, Palaces of Wisdom: Eroticism and Reflexivity in the Study of Mysticism* (2001). This book explores a new genre, the mysticism of scholars of mysticism. It also expands scholarship by daring to incorporate the author's erotic and mystical experiences as part of his intellectual project.
22. Kripal, 2007, pp. 224–25.
23. Kripal, 1998.
24. Keynes, 1972, p. 150.

25. DB, p. 90.
26. DB, p. 88.
27. Thomas, 1971, p. 470.
28. Thurston, 1952, p. 130.
29. SG, p. 169.
30. DB, ibid.
31. Ibid.
32. See Somer, 2009, on Schrenck-Notzing, pp. 299–322.
33. Levack, 2013.
34. Ibid., p. 3.
35. Ibid., pp. 4–5.
36. See discussion of this connection in Grosso, 2014, "Plato's *Phaedo* and the Near-Death Experience," in *Death and Dying*, ed. S. Kakar, pp. 44–69. London: Penguin.
37. IM, p. 418.
38. The expression "remote viewing" is a more recent synonym for *clairvoyance*, extrasensory awareness of the physical environment.
39. McMoneagle, 1993.
40. Plato, 1966, see pp. 223–31.
41. McMoneagle, 1993, p. 32.
42. See Van Lommel, 2010.
43. Popper and Eccles, 1997, pp. 96–97.

Chapter 7

Joseph as Performance Artist

However original and outlandish a personality Joseph was, he sprang from a specific social and cultural setting. Phenomena are reported in all cultures and times and are shaped and interpreted accordingly. Reports of rapid, unexplained flowerings in vineyards occurred during the ancient rites of Dionysos—the god of the vine.[1] Tibetan monks in the cold fastness of the Himalayas get proficient in tummo yoga, the psychic genesis of bodily heat.[2] A harsh, cold environment might inspire one to discover tummo yoga; central heating and warm clothing would not.

Aboriginal "clever men" of the Australian outback are talented in long-distance clairvoyance (Elkin, 1977) while reports are widely recorded of the Norwegian *vaerdoger* (astral double) said to be seen before a traveler reaches his destination. Nineteenth-century spiritualists produced apports, table-tilting, mediumistic "controls," and heartwarming messages from supposed dead revenants. In modern technological society, there are reports of phone calls from the dead and the use of diodes, computers, TVs, and smart phones—used for transmitting messages, usually clipped and obscure—from the dead.[3]

Given the crucifixion of Christ and belief in mystical marriage, Catholic mystics produce stigmata and female mystics create "rings of espousal," ring-shaped formations on the espoused fingers' skin. And with the Christian belief in the resurrection of the dead, it is interesting to find such detailed reports of bodily incorruption. Catholics exhume the bodies of their saintly dead, and the hagiographies report surrealistic tales about the bodily remains of the holy.[4]

Further, levitation seems to be somewhat of a specialty during certain periods of Catholic Christianity, possibly linked, as touched on in the last chapter, to extreme sexual repression. The capacities assume forms that fit the needs and symbolic accoutrements of the prevailing culture. Hard to imagine a rash of stigmata or levitations breaking out in Kansas today, a place so unlike seventeenth-century southern Italy.

On the other hand, these groupings and trends are by no means absolute; see, for example, Ian Wilson (1989) on contemporary English cases of stigmata, where the culture differs sharply from medieval or seventeenth-century Catholic Christianity. Also, the odor of sanctity is reported of some purely secular mediums in the nineteenth century (as well as saints from other traditions), and in fact there are good accounts of levitation *extra ecclesia.*

In the case of Joseph, his "creative illness"—five bedridden years—drove him inward, and forced him to rely on intangible ideas, images, and symbols for consolation. Before he got sick he was in family crisis and in very bad economic straits. Want and crisis pervaded his circumscribed life. His culture was also in crisis, shaken by the tectonic strains of the Protestant Reformation and the scientific revolution.

The "mental excesses" that Bernini wrote about Joseph parallel the excesses of baroque artists like Caravaggio and Gian Lorenzo Bernini[5] (father of Joseph's biographer). A movement of art was known as tenebrism, a seventeenth-century style of painting in dark tones and shadows. Tenebrism was in tune with the darkly mystical side of the culture. The word *baroque* refers to something askew, an "irregular pearl"; Joseph was definitely an irregular pearl of the highly irregular seventeenth century.

A CHURCH IN TURMOIL: THE PSYCHIC INTENSITY OF THE AGE

The Church was the main cultural force in Joseph's life. His mother was steeped in saintly lore and strong on Catholic morals. His early social network was very small: mother; older sister, Livia; and two busy uncles, ordained clerics in the Church. Remember, he was perceived as odd right from the start, and his moniker was "Gapingmouth." Joseph's sole human resource was a powerful, sixteen-hundred-year-old religious organization, of late operating in emergency mode during a long Thirty Years War (1618–1648) and challenged by creators of new science and by revolutionary, skeptical thinkers.[6]

Conflict unfolded on the battlefields of Europe and on the inner battlefields of dogma and heresy. Leading the fray for the conquest of wayward minds was the Society of Jesus, founded by Ignatius of Loyola (1591–1656). And for those recklessly enamored of the will to "choose" (i.e., the *heretics*), there was the Holy Inquisition, designed to demonstrate the advantages of agreeable orthodoxy over inflammatory heresy.

In his study of a contemporary of Joseph, the painter Caravaggio, Peter Robb wrote :

> The counter reformation put Italian culture on a war footing—asserted the catholic church's claim to total control of Italian minds and bodies. . . . Coercion and persuasion were its twin prongs. The inquisition was the stick, a vast repressive machinery that worked through informants and secret courts to meet ideological deviance with humiliation, prison, torture and burning alive.[7]

It is hard to read the above and not see in Joseph's aerial performances the motif of escape writ large. The reaction of the Church was to try to bring him down. The Holy Office attacked his integrity by subjecting him to inquisitions based on false charges, moved him arbitrarily from one convent to another, driving him bit by bit toward solitary confinement in Osimo. And yet imprisonment freed him to pursue his mystical explorations with greater concentration and intensity, but without any human comforts.

Profound spiritual crisis informed the cultural background of Joseph's life. Historians remark on the great fear, melancholy, and anxiety that pervaded the hearts and minds of those intensely uneasy days. John Donne captured the disorientation when he wrote "An Anatomie of the World," which laments the untimely death of a lady endowed with the sacred charm of a goddess. Her death was a symbol of "the frailty and decay of the whole world." Wrestling with the specter of death, and smarting from the shock of the new cosmology, it reminds him of the frailty and decay of a beautiful woman.

"Shee, shee is dead; shee's dead: when thou knowest this, thou knowest how poor a trifling thing man is." A new picture of the universe began to emerge and was perceived in novel ways; for Giordano Bruno, the expansion was intoxicating; for John Donne, as for Pascal, it was disturbing, a source of anxiety. Donne, in 1611 (Joseph was eight years old), expressed the metaphysical malaise that pervaded those fast-moving times:

And new Philosophy calls all in doubt,
The Element of fire is quite put out;
The Sun is lost, and th'earth, and no man's wit
Can well direct him where to looke for it . . .
'Tis all in pieces, all cohaerence gone.

Effects of the de-centered cosmology reverberate in the social world: "Prince, Subject, Father, Sonne, are things forgot." The social plane suddenly seemed ruled by anarchic self-interest, and Donne bemoans the lack of the cohesive, tempering spirit of the feminine divine. Much in a spirit akin to Joseph, he adores the Madonna (or an English surrogate) as his guide to the region of being he calls "Heaven." Donne puts it like this:

This is the world's condition now, and now
She that should all arts to reunion bow,
She that had all Magnetique force alone,
To draw, and fasten sundered parts in one.[8]

The intimation of looming catastrophe, the sense of being lost in the cosmos—for Joseph Desa and John Donne—stirred nostalgic yearnings for the "magnetic" enchantment of the feminine, the figure of the goddess. Henry Adams and more recently Carl Jung also took exception to religious *man's* co-option of the divine. In Henry Adams's account of the cult of Mary, the European Middle Ages drew deeply upon the mercy and inspiration of the feminine principle. Adams tells us that Francis of Assisi was the sworn enemy of the syllogism and therefore of philosophy, scholastic disputation, and the intellectualizing spirit that would come to reign in the modern world, repressing if not obliterating the goddess-constellated imagination and its cohesive powers.

Beyond the syllogism, the medieval *soul* was drawn to the cult of Mary. Joseph prayed to the Madonna for help in his theological test for the priesthood. The mystical madonna promises to transcend syllogistic theology and thus get rid of the blinders that veil living contact with real spiritual nourishment.

The counterreformers of the Church mobilized the powerful symbols and dogmas in the repertoire, using the very things the reformers most despised: saints, miracles, and the splendor of the senses in art, music, pageantry, and architecture. No pains or cash were spared to enthrall the pious imagination; one was to see, hear, smell, and breathe the virtues, the dogmas, and the sacred narratives. For Joseph's coiled energy and doggedness, all manner of provocation lay at hand. By all indications, he was sensitive to every cue that prompted or beckoned him to take flight, first in his imagination—and then more literally.

The Council of Trent, ongoing from 1545 to 1563, chose to employ the arts to illustrate and promote the dogmas of the Church, actively financing the best artists. Deviations from the rules might get you summoned to the Inquisition, as happened to Paolo Veronese over some trifle. There were objections to polyphonic music until Palestrina proved that a decorous polyphonic music of the Mass was possible.

According to Canon 8, September 10, 1562, the meaning of the Mass must be clear "so that the words may be comprehensible to all; and thus may the hearts of the listeners be caught up into the desire for celestial harmonies and contemplation of the joys of the blessed." Pius, now music critic, wrote of the Missa Papae Marcelli, that "of such nature must have been the harmonies of the new song heard by John the Apostle in the heavenly Jerusalem."[9] In short, within its carefully constructed boundaries, the Church encouraged a musical art dedicated to inducing the ecstasy of "celestial harmonies."

Emphasis on the clarity of words and the need to be "comprehensible to all" from the Council of Trent is notable because of the entirely different point that Nietzsche made in *The Birth of Tragedy* about Palestrina. Nietzsche pits Dionysian ecstasy and music against the life-corroding rationalism he thought was coming to define "modern man."

Commenting on the origins of modern music and wishing to revive the Dionysian spirit, Nietzsche takes opera to task, which he blames for being *too Socratic*, too attached to rationality and concerned with definition, and *therefore* the enemy of the gods of life and ecstasy. Nietzsche was critical of opera, but spoke highly of Palestrina's music: "Is it credible that this thoroughly externalized devotional operatic music could be received and cherished with enthusiastic favor, as a rebirth, as it were, of all true music, by the very age in which had appeared the ineffably sublime and sacred music of Palestrina?"[10]

Nietzsche was surprised that both types of music arose at the same time, referring to opera as "this passion for a half-musical mode of speech . . . alongside the vaulted structure of Palestrina harmonies, which all medieval Christendom had been building up." What disturbed the young German thinker was that a rationalizing tendency was taking over the mentality of the Western world—something completely at odds with the Dionysian ecstasy he perceived as a touchstone of a more authentic life. That Palestrina was akin in spirit to Dionysos is as surprising an idea as opera being akin in spirit to Socrates. But the comparisons do make sense: Palestrina and Dionysos offer ecstasy; Socrates and opera are engrossed in the dramatic world of talk, ideas, and politics—generally, most would agree—the opposite of ecstasy.

For Palestrina, music served the community of believers: to instill church dogma and induce sensations of the "heavenly Jerusalem." A series of motets published in 1650 were "enough to satisfy the impatience of thousands who desired to feed upon the nectar of their sweetness."[11] Filippo Neri—one of Joseph's heroes and also reportedly a levitator—was Palestrina's spiritual director. A chain of interlocked personalities sustained the ecstatic disposition of individuals with a range of temperaments similar in spirit to Joseph's during this period.

The council, reacting to Protestant critiques, spoke to the purpose of images in painting. Clarity of meaning was again stressed; so was the need for drama and emotional color. Merely profane and sensuous allusions and obscurities were to be avoided. Instead, "through the saints the miracles of God and salutary examples are set before the eyes of the faithful, so that they . . . may fashion their own life and conduct in imitation of the saints and be moved to adore and love God and cultivate piety."[12]

The task of the artist was to induce a consciousness of heavenly states and to create models for people to "fashion their own life." Architecture was designed to provide church visitors with feelings and moods of transcendence, luring the gaze upward into domes painted with forms and figures soaring in heavenly spaces. A rightly disposed subject might very well react with a powerful spiritual experience.

The dome served as a type of machine for inducing metaphysical vertigo. Artists and architects played visual games with the sense of infinity. Others played on the ambiguity of new ideas of space and used them to hint of other worlds. The new art of perspective suggested feelings of the infinite, all things coming together at the vanishing point of the composition. Piranesi was a master at inducing sensations of metaphysical vertigo, especially in his mind-spinning *Invenzioni Capric di Carceri*.[13]

SENSE AND PSYCHOPHYSICS

The seventeenth-century religious imagination was charged with imagery of the Crucifixion, the Ascension, the Martyrs, the Saints, the Miracles: all represented in words, chants, prayers, litanies, oratorios, paintings, etchings, sculptures, just about everywhere in public space. It was extremely *theatrical*. The Church made itself into a theater of spiritual glorification and the arts were used to memorialize the great icons of belief while also, if possible, creating vivid sensations of spiritual uplift and conviction. In principle, all the arts—architecture, sculpture, painting—were about lifting the imagination into another reality.

Joseph everywhere was greeted by words and images suggesting supernatural events, powers, and realities. Relics, images, and the presence of symbols were there for the susceptible; images of one or another miracle or martyr were always nearby.[14] Joseph told his diarist Arcangelo Rosmi that his first flight into the air occurred while contemplating a painting of the Madonna and Child in Grottella. The first time he saw Cimabue's painting of the Virgin in Assisi he took leave of his senses and flew into the air.[15] Eyewitnesses deposed descriptions of his ecstatic response to their singing. Music becomes a stepping-stone to another reality. A statue representing the Immaculate Conception had a very powerful effect on the highly responsive Joseph.

For some predisposed individuals, works of art generated highly expressive reactions and sometimes triggered events that we generally think impossible. Francis of Assisi heard a voice speak out of a crucifix in the church of St. Damiano, repeating three times, "Francis, go and repair my house." The event launched the saint's career. Padre Pio was staring at a statue of the crucified Christ when his stigmata appeared. As a consequence, his life was never the same again. This was a period of Western history when the link between art and religion (or magic) was still strong.

THE LIGHT AND THE DARK

Other artistic devices were charged with psychic significance; artists, for example, experimented with light and shadow. Gian Lorenzo Bernini's sacred art combined architecture, sculpture, and natural light funneled through hidden architectural openings, prompting viewers to sense the light as if it were coming from heaven, from some secret, hidden, and decidedly higher source. In the Netherlands, Rembrandt was using daubs of glazed white paint to manifest the soul of light against the dark backdrop and mystery of being. Caravaggio also used with great effect the theatrical technique of chiaroscuro—"clear obscurity." It is a state of mind that suggests entry into a liminal, hypnogogic space, the twilight world between dreaming and waking.

Light and color can profoundly affect people. The mystic cobbler Jacob Boehme's great inner illumination was sparked by a chance perception of sunlight on a burnished pewter dish.[16] Seventeenth-century writers were fascinated by the mystical properties of light. Athanasius Kircher, in his *Ars Magna Luci et Umbrae* (1646), said there were two kinds of light, the light of the sun and the light of consciousness: "Just as in this corporeal world there is a light by means of which whatever things exist continue to be preserved, so also in the archetype, that invisible and super-celestial world, there is a light from which . . . all things proceed . . . and of which this material light is, so to speak, but a symbol."[17]

Chiaroscuro, a paradoxical expression, recalls Kircher's theory of a hidden, supernatural light poised to break in upon us from the surrounding darkness. Chiaroscuro, not just an artistic technique, suggests a state of mind, an image of consciousness dawning in the night of the unconscious.

The technique goes back to Leonardo, who used the term *sfumato*, from the verb *sfumare*, "to tone down" or "to evaporate like smoke." Employed in drawing or painting, it specialized in subtle gradations and transitions between forms. In the hands of Leonardo or Giorgione, it was used to drape a portrait or landscape with a film of dreamlike enchantment.

Caravaggio's tenebrism spread across Europe during the first half of the seventeenth century. From the word *tenebroso*, meaning dark or gloomy, it represents a sensibility as well as a style. Its aura of dramatic illumination was apparent in the art of El Greco, Rembrandt, Artemisia Gentileschi, and others from the period. A dazzling example of tenebrism is Jusepe de Riberas's

Martyrdom of St. Andrew, painted in 1628, the year that Joseph was ordained a priest.

With an extremism parallel to Joseph's, Caravaggio's life was marked by a kind of chiaroscuro, a dangerous dialectic between shadow and illumination, a violent mystery presaging bold explorations of thought, modern visual perception, and the mysteries of the subliminal mind. In the art of the masters of tenebrism, human lives are portrayed as living in fitful patches of spotlight, flickering moments of conscious intensity flanked by impenetrable shade. Shade of what?

The drift of baroque sensibility was to deconstruct the finite, the static, the contoured objective world; there was a need to experience light as free, disentangled from objectivity; and to depict life in the extremes of restless mobility. The etchings of Rembrandt portray light hovering precariously, vibrantly over the tangible forms they illuminate, almost as if the forms were props to reveal the light. The Dutch master's etchings and paintings were adept at evoking this mystical light. Two quietly but deeply suggestive examples illustrating this are his 1642 etchings of *St. Jerome in a Dark Chamber* and *Student at Table by Candlelight*.[18]

The idea of a theater of mystical light harks back to medieval Gothic architecture. Abbot Suger had the task of rebuilding the Abbey of St. Denis; the perception of light, he reports, reflected on gold woke up his mystical sense:

> The loveliness of the many-colored gems has called me away from external cares . . . (and) induced me to reflect, transferring that which is material to that which is immaterial . . . then it seems to me that I see myself dwelling, as it were, in some strange region of the universe which neither exists entirely in the slime of the earth nor entirely in the purity of Heaven; and that, by the grace of God, I can be transported from this inferior world to that higher world in an anagogical manner.[19]

The contemplation of light reflected in gold triggers an otherworldly experience of mystical light, which brings him to "some strange region of the universe," a fantasy familiar to the ancients.

Precious stones figure in the Myth of the True Earth in Plato's *Phaedo* where they appear as symbols of enlightened consciousness, according to which our familiar earth is a mist-covered portion of the "true earth" where everything is "more transparent and more lovely in colour." "In fact," Socrates says, "our highly prized stones, sards and jaspers, and emeralds, and other gems, are fragments of those there, but there everything is like these or still more beautiful."[20] Our heightened esthetic perceptions are not just pleasant blurrings of daily reality, according to this neglected Platonic myth; they reflect a more enlightened vision latent within us—a vision of the "True Earth."

The handling of light by baroque painters reflects the mystic aim of detaching the light of consciousness from objects that reflect, color, and confine it, and experience it in its original, unfettered purity. Light and shade usually serve to define an object with precision and clarity, but in the baroque mind-world, "light has acquired that life of its own which withdraws the plastic form from the domain of immediate tangibility," wrote the art critic Robert Hughes.[21] Detaching consciousness from the bounded and the tangible—experiencing its purity and isolation; this is the essence of introverted mystical practice. It must have struck chords with Joseph's passionate need to travel *beyond*.

SPACE

Around this time the Church was having difficulties with revolutionary ideas about space. Bruno, Galileo, and Joseph of Copertino each in their own way caused major disruptions. Joseph's problematic levitations were preceded and accompanied by philosophical and astronomical breakthroughs in the conception of space—for example, by Giordano Bruno (1548–1600), the prophet of infinite *acentric* space. As Bruno immodestly announced: "If Copernicus is the dawn, then I am the sun of the New Era."[22]

His arguments and speculations were meant explicitly to open the mind to a *boundless* cosmology. The story is told in Alexandre Koyre's *From the Closed World to the Infinite Universe* (1957), which portrays Bruno as martyr to the "infinite universe." Before the judges of the Inquisition he said: "I believe in an infinite universe, the effect of the infinite divine potency, because it has seemed to me unworthy of the divine goodness and power to create a finite world."[23] Later, of course, Galileo's experiments and telescopic observations would lead to an entirely new cosmology, moving us with a new precision toward Bruno's vast, postbiblical cosmology.

Amid the ferment of scientific thought, artists and architects of early Europe were busy pictorially recreating space. Leon Battista Alberti[24] developed the mathematics of terrestrial perspective, which was a form of conquest of three-dimensional space; the baroque artists went beyond that, managing to open the viewer's imagination of space, inventing a kind of pictorial geometry of the otherworldly. They created a plastic form of space that fused dream and reality, heaven and earth, in a kind of baroque surrealism.

Artists introduced novel changes in the perception of movement, with a far-reaching shift from the tactile to the painterly. Heinrich Woelfflin calls this "the most decisive revolution which art history knows."[25] In contrast to classical art, which aims at creating boundaries, "the baroque negates the outline ... the figure evades consolidation within a definite silhouette. It cannot be tied down to a particular view."[26] This could be a description of Cubism. The revolution that Woelfflin alludes to implies there are no privileged viewpoints; anywhere might become a scene for artistic breakthrough or for mystical revelation.

The world is dematerialized in baroque sculpture; for example, in Gian Lorenzo Bernini's statue of Saint Teresa in ecstasy, "the surfaces and folds are not only of their very nature restless, but are fundamentally envisaged with an eye to the plastically indeterminate."[27] Everything down to the slightest detail evokes the sense of uneasy mobility, with erotic overtones and undertows.

Artists of this period dissolved the partition between profane and divine space. The dome above was offered as a sensory cue aiming to lure the viewer into a simulated heavenly journey. The baroque artist "sought to transcend the natural world with the aid of artifices, dramatic and extroverted pathos and illusionism on the one hand and extreme close-up, internalization, alienation and distortion of reality on the other."[28] The effect might unnerve and disorient, as Joseph's aerial displays unnerved and disoriented witnesses.

Artworks in churches and chapels around Europe fed the collective psyche with images suggesting mystical flight. Baroque art, mobile and fluctuating, deserted terrestrial geometry, orienting the psychology of viewers heavenward. The diagonal conspicuously enters the composition, and the artwork ceases to be an esthetic enclosure, but a launching pad for spiritual levitation.

Kant (1951) would later define the autonomy of the artwork for modernism, as an object one could isolate from practical life and contemplate in a disinterested fashion. The baroque theater of the divine would have rejected this; the artwork was a psychic conduit to transcendence. The diagonal was the baroque symbol of transcendence, an arrow of intrusion from higher passageways, a pointer to hidden exits and entrances, calling forth feelings of motion, precipitous falls, sudden ascents.

Against partition and equilibrium, the particle gives way to the wave, and the contour of the object "at all points leads the eye beyond the edge."[29] The baroque style anticipates the quantum dematerialization of matter. Bernini the sculptor shapes dead stone into images of tremulous life, the artwork an analogue of ecstasy, orgasm, and resurrection. He was the dominant artist of the European Counter-Reformation; after his death his reputation sank. Today it has been restored; according to Robert Hughes, Bernini was the inventor of "the last great universal language of spirituality."[30]

SACRED ILLUSIONISM

Baroque artists created illusions of floating to orchestrate sensations of heavenly heights; we could think of it as a kind of false feedback. All available craft was deployed to make the idea of heaven credible to the viewer, which was in tune with St. Ignatius Loyola who encouraged the use of sense and imagination to meditate upon the higher matters.[31]

"The principle of illusionism," write Bauer and Prater,[32] involves "creating a sense of spatial expansion in which monumental ceiling and mural painting transcend the bounds of real architecture into illusory celestial realms." Staring up at the dome of the Cappella della Santissima Sindone in Turin creates the feeling of being drawn out of one's body up into a heavenly system of gyrating lines that converge on a central point of light. Constructed by Guarini in 1667, it looks like a carefully crafted mandala designed to pull one's consciousness out of body.

Illusionism works differently in a ceiling fresco by Fra Andrea Pozzo at St. Ignazio's in Rome called Allegory of the Missionary Work of the Jesuits. It took three years to execute (1691–1694). Here architecture and painting unite seamlessly; you are standing inside the painting because the painting is also the ceiling of the room. You look up at a vast rectangle crowded with swirling figures, and from all sides feel the sharp acclivity of towers and vistas; your eyes are fixed on the hovering form of Ignatius, who blends with the light; figures are clambering upward, hanging on the sides of buildings, floating dreamlike in space. Clinging to rocky ledges, they seem about to fall into the abyss or hurtle upward into the light. Given to dissociation and absorbed in this scene, one could be prompted to have an out-of-body experience.

When Joseph was called to Rome with his companion Lodovico, he noticed the splendor of St. Peter's nave but refused to look around at any of the sights. When asked why, he replied that he knew that he would be swept up in ecstasy, if his attention fixed on some sacred image. Clearly, this would not be a good place to make a spectacle of himself, so he kept looking down and moved on, afraid of being carried away by ecstasy.

Imagery on church walls everywhere suggested that movement into celestial space was possible, imagery that served as psychical prompters, energizers of the disposed spiritual imagination. With Joseph—as so much testimony clearly states—a flight of imagination might turn into a bout of levitation.

Baroque painting and architecture, in addition to their many obvious functions, were about building mental space ships, machines for psychically propelling one beyond one's customary sense of possible reality. Bernini, observed Rudolf Wittkower, sought to eliminate all barriers separating the experiencer from the artwork, "to release him from the bondage of his normal existence, to replace reality by a different, dreamlike reality."

Particularly in the Cornaro Chapel, which contained perhaps his most famous statue of Saint Teresa in ecstasy, Bernini "created a supra-real world in which the transitions seem obliterated between real and imaginary space, past and present, phenomenal and actual existence, life and death." The object was to induce "the beholder to forget his everyday existence and to participate in the pictorial reality before his eyes . . . and transport the individual into another reality."[33]

The Altieri Chapel is a good example of this high spiritual theater. Eight years after Joseph died, Ludovica Albertoni was beatified; Bernini (the sculptor) was commissioned to memorialize her life and death, and produced a work that was placed in the family chapel in San Francesco a Ripa in Rome. The statue is the chapel's visual focus, with light flowing in from a hidden source. Like Joseph, Ludovica was an ecstatic, observed to levitate, but was known more for giving her wealth away and helping the poor.

The statue portrays the moment of her death, which was also the moment of her supreme ecstasy:

> Infused with light, the white marble sculpture of Ludovica is the climactic element in the chapel. The statue depicts the *beata* in a semi-recumbent pose, her head thrown back on a lace-bordered pillow, her eyes rolled back, and her mouth open. Lying in bed with her knees bent and slightly apart, the agitated garments flowing over her body as if animated by an unseen force, Ludovica grasps her bosom and waist. Her private, intimate communion is undisturbed by the intrusion of the observer, who feels compelled to tiptoe before her.[34]

As Shelley Karen Perlove describes the sculpture, we are meant to feel it drawing us into an orbit of "unseen force" that is agitating the drapery: "Ludovica's garments, whose movements and disposition may not be explained by the laws of nature, impart a visionary quality to the sculpture. The colored drapery beneath the statue is most irrational in its arrangement, the masses of folds rather mysteriously repeating the configuration of the *beata's* body."

Bernini has portrayed Ludovica's death as an ecstatic swooning and embrace with Christ. The intent of this artwork—the artistry is peerless—is to draw the viewer into the scene as witness of an ideal death. According to Bernini's vision, Ludovica experiences death as ecstatic release. Painting, sculpture, architecture, the recessed space, and mysterious lighting of the Altieri Chapel combine to "suggest a supernatural presence in the space inhabited by the *beata*."

The arts were supposed to promote Church dogma while simulating *and* stimulating powerful spiritual experiences. The spiritual theater of churches, liturgies, processions, as well as opera, painting, and sculpture created an atmosphere that favored the occurrence of altered mental states: an environment designed to trigger the kinds of experience mystics like Joseph had. Cues and incentives were everywhere available: in the arts and crafts, in a belief system advertising miracles, and in suggestive images of a beckoning heaven. Joseph, immersed in this aggressive Baroque theatricality, actively assumed and performed his roles with great, often spectacular, success.

JOSEPH AS PERFORMANCE ARTIST

In telling the story of Joseph, names like John Donne, Caravaggio, and Rembrandt have come up; placing him in the company of artists seems as easy as the saints who were the masters he consciously imitated.

In one way, Joseph was a conventional artist. He wrote and liked to sing and even dance his rhyming "strophes." All that he wrote was religious, most of it pious platitude.[35] But his real artistry was of a less recognizable type. In 1635, when Joseph was thirty-two years old, the Spanish poet Calderon de la Barca's play *El Grand Theatro del Mondo* was first performed. The world is the stage where we perform the drama of salvation or damnation before the audience of God; it was a popular conceit of the time. "All the world's a stage" we know from Shakespeare in Jacques's speech from *As You Like It* (Act 2, Scene 7).

In light of this theatrical metaphor of life, I want to look at Joseph as a performance artist,[36] which, apart from being descriptive, I believe may shed light on his extraordinary phenomena. It is not that he faked anything or that he was conscious of himself *as* a performer.

To begin with, just being a priest involves public performance. Saying Mass is a mystery rite and a kind of theatrical event; the priest wears vestments and handles various "props"—altar, pyx, chalice, paten, chrism, Eucharistic wafer. He follows a specific choreography, the elevation, the consecration, much kneeling and bowing, and so on. He sticks to a plot line with prescribed utterances; sings, gestures, may be accompanied by music, all amounting to a kind of theatrical performance. More than esthetic diversion, the aim is to commune with the divine.

Joseph's priestly performances were *especially* theatrical; his ecstasies on occasion were so intense that he appeared to rise off the ground, producing a dramatic effect Aristotle would classify as *spectacular*.[37] There is an element of tragic irony in Joseph's career as priestly performer; his feelings and gestures were so expressive, and he was so absorbed in the role he played, he lost control of his body. Under the sway of involuntary forces, the Mass fell apart. His performances were so extraordinary they destroyed his career as a priest.

Belief is known to liberate psychic powers. Joseph began to levitate in public only after he became a priest. Becoming a priest, it seems, intensified his belief that he was now properly licensed to commune with the supernatural. He could now fully surrender to his vocation and play the part with complete confidence, a factor that researchers repeatedly say is essential in producing "psi."[38]

Joseph's mystical style was very dramatic. He would scream before being carried away by ecstasy, attracting the attention of the Inquisition precisely because of his histrionic and therefore suspect behavior. Charged with being "affectedly" pious, he was accused of carrying on *as if* he were a *messiah*. So, in spite of his efforts at humility, he was accused of being an actor—and, to make matters worse, of appropriating the role of the leading man (so to speak) in the great drama of salvation. Savvy realistic people perceived his powers as possibly threatening Church authority. Unfortunately, the fame that Joseph won for his star performance as miracle man ruined his chances for anything resembling a normal religious life. His spectacular acts made him a theatrical curiosity, something he neither desired nor in any way needed.

In spite of himself, his public acting out played on the emotionally charged symbols shared by believers from all over Europe. His most inspired performances were often sudden improvisations. People fainted, some fled. Most saw him as a not-to-be-missed exhibition of divine power; others feared more sinister influences. Whatever the audience interpretation, it was gripping theater; and his fan base never ceased to swell and threaten disorder whenever he was spotted in a public venue.

He was most effective in the eyes of his audience at Mass. The show was irresistible, hovering in the air, his toes barely grazing the ground, the aerial riffs backward and forward, the heavy-metal screams of the manic ecstasy. His public celebrations drew such crowds that Church officials insisted he say Mass alone, which was only partly successful.

All the peculiar ascetic oddities he practiced and exhibited were inherently theatrical, effects that ranged from the bizarre and inspiring to the terrifying. His one-year tour of Apulia under the patronage of Antonio of San Mauro was a big success, although in the end it led to his troubles with the Inquisition. It must have been riveting to witness the friar's upliftings, his immunity to fire,[39] his impassivity to pain, his indifference to hunger—his detachment from *reality itself!* The composed effect of his robe during the *voli* must have been seen as part of a pose, a theatrical gesture, a frame that heightened the supernatural focus.

Nor did he lack in basic training in the art form he practiced. His mother, Frances, fed him with images and stories of saintly heroics. He absorbed the visual arts, verbal icons, and codified religious instructions he was exposed to. He studied models of saintly perfection that he re-created in himself. Given his genius for dissociation and his pliable sense of identity, he was highly successful at his spiritual art; indeed, he was known in his lifetime as the "new St. Francis." It was normal for him to *imitate* Christ and other saints; he was by profession ready to renounce his natural persona and assume new ones. The adoption of a new name in the priesthood formalized his new role in life, a role in which his task was to perform in a divine drama.

Practicing his monastic virtues—obedience, poverty, chastity—was the training he undertook and put to use in his spiritual art form. Joseph carried his predilection for performance into every facet of his life. When he was accosted by arresting officers—which happened several times—he prostrated himself on the ground, shaping his body into a cross—a brilliant theatrical gesture. The arresting officers were stunned by the superemphatic display of nonresistance. He knew all the moves and was playing the part of saint to perfection; but, uncynically, I think he was mainly playing to the audience of the One he inwardly communed with.

His absolute rejection of money or material gifts was a constant performance that defined his way of life. His refusal to have anything to do with material amenities was so pronounced it annoyed his family and his religious brothers. Joseph's artistry also took the extraverted form of ecstatic adoration. There was nothing retiring or low-key about his enthusiasms. He was indiscreet in the way he expressed his adoration of the Madonna. He would scream and dance and sing, and reportedly, he bullied his brethren into joining his Madonna raves.[40] The mysterious fragrances were a novel part of his ensemble, clinging, incredibly, to the persons of his audience, lingering on their bodies and belongings, long after the "show" was over.

One feature of his life is not unusual for theatrical careers: he became a victim of his fame. Fans—fanatics—pursued him; women tore at his tunics for some relic of his person; jealous superiors watched him like hawks and made trouble for him with the Inquisition. Even dying, at the time and place he predicted, was part of his stupendous act. The brothers stood by and observed, participated, and recorded every word and gesture of his grand finale.

He requested to hear a favorite chant; his death became a performance set to music. Joseph's last actions on earth, his stately yet histrionic death, were a moving display, and a comedy in the sense that he "played" his death as if it were a triumph, a homecoming, an event of great if solemn joy.[41]

The friar was born into a culture that offered him a role to play, a set of scripts, archetypal imagery, a wealth of historical precedent, all, I believe, aids that helped him produce the astonishing effects reported throughout his career. If you have a script and models to imitate, a great story to act out, and a lively, eager audience, it can bolster the full expression of your artistic-spiritual potentials. Joseph was in the right milieu to develop and amplify his very peculiar talents. In his baroque world, his life makes perfect sense as mystic performance artist *par excellence.*

The cultural milieu offers, at best, part of the explanation. Other things need to be addressed, such as the physics of levitation, which is far more difficult to talk about, especially for a nonphysicist such as myself. In the next chapter, undaunted, we will dive into some deep waters and speculate on some strange possibilities.

NOTES

1. See Otto, 1965, pp. 96–99.
2. David-Neel, 1971.
3. Rogo, 1986, pp. 107–19; Ellis, 1978.
4. Thurston, 1952, pp. 233–82; Summers, 1950, pp. 75–77.
5. See, also by Domenico Bernini, *The Life of Gian Lorenzo Bernini* (2011) Pennsylvania State University, translation and critical edition by Franco Mormando.
6. Owen, 1908/1970.
7. Robb, 1998, pp. 2–3.
8. Donne, 1946, pp. 171–72.
9. Symonds, 1886, p. 334.
10. Nietzsche, 1927, p. 1051.
11. Symonds, 1886, p. 334.
12. Ibid.
13. Piranesi did an extraordinary series of etchings called *Capricious Inventions of Prisons*, which somehow combine tenebrism, chiaroscuro, and twentieth-century futurism; see Penny, 1988, pp. 56–57.
14. Mathews, 1993, p. 59.
15. See for details chapter 3.
16. Underhill, 1956, p. 58.
17. Roob, 1997, p. 263.
18. See Hind, 1912, vol. 2.
19. Hughes, 1968, p. 118.
20. *Phaedo*, 109b–114c.
21. Hughes, 1968, p. 118.
22. Mendoza, 1995, p. xxi.
23. See McIntyre, 1903, p. 76. Following Bruno's intuitions, Galileo's telescope opened the stellar universe to scientific inspection. Ever since, science has witnessed a steady expansion and complication of the idea of space. Today, modern telescopes like the Hubble have revealed the unimaginable vastness of our expanding universe. The artistic imagination today is nowhere near catching up to the microspace of quantum mechanics or to the accelerating expansion of the macro-spaced universe.
24. Alberti, 2011.
25. Woelfflin, 1932, p. 21.
26. Ibid., p. 54.
27. Ibid., p. 57.
28. Bauer and Prater, 2001, p. 9.
29. Woelfflin, 1932, p. 57.
30. Hughes, 2011, p. 279.
31. See Mottola, 1964.
32. Bauer and Prater, 2001, p. 7.
33. Wittkower, 1955, pp. 27–28.
34. Perlove, 1990, p. 15.

35. See Lucio Maiorano's *San Giuseppe da Copertino* (2002), which reproduces much of the poetry and discusses it.

36. I will not discuss here the contemporary world of performance art, which would take us too far afield, but I will say that some of the more well-known modern practitioners in this field (such as Marina Abramovic) are preoccupied with pushing the limits of bodily pain and torture and play off the spectacle of asceticism that Joseph specialized in, but without the attendant religious beliefs.

37. See Butcher, *Poetics*, p. 29.

38. See Batcheldor, pp. 105–122.

39. The reference here is to the fact often noticed of Joseph floating above candle flames that never ignited his robe or burned his feet or legs.

40. For an amusing account of this, see Popolizio, 1955, p. 194.

41. Chiappinelli, 2008, p. 145, and end of chapter 1.

Chapter 8

Speculations on the Physics of Levitation

> Perhaps in the dim future of mankind, if it then exists, we will look back to the queer, contracted three-dimensional universe from which the nobler, wider existence has emerged.
>
> —Alfred North Whitehead, *Modes of Thought*

Joseph's story begins to make sense in light of his ecstatic extremes of love and near death, the psychic tensions induced by fear of the Devil and his Kafkaesque troubles with the Inquisition, and from the suggestiveness of his theatrical baroque culture: all part of the matrix that primed him for the "explosions" of his impossible *voli*.

Still, the problem of physics remains. Something needs to be said about this, however speculative; with luck it may spark conversation among scientists. If Joseph rose in the air when he went into ecstasy, as the evidence repeatedly shows, it is a curious challenge to physics. One conclusion is hard to avoid: levitation implies dramatically extended mental power. Chapters 2 and 3 reported on mind/matter interactions, more or less well observed and well documented, which point to such extended capacities. But what do physicists have to say about the role of mind in nature?

AN UNEXPLAINED FORCE

As noted in chapter 2, William Crookes made claims for an unexplained psychic force, in some obscure way related to the human organism. In 1870, prompted by colleagues, he announced he was going to investigate the phenomena of Spiritualism. The press was jubilant, expecting that the elected fellow of the Royal Society was going to expose the nonsense of Spiritualism. The press and the skeptics were disappointed; the experiments produced positive results.

Crookes, along with his assistants and brother, Sir William Huggins, physicist and astronomer, and Sergeant Cox, a prominent lawyer, launched a series of experiments with Daniel Dunglas Home, the medium slandered by Robert Browning in his poem "Mr. Sludge, the Medium." In his report to the Royal Society on June 15, 1871, Crookes submitted his findings. Because they did not invalidate claims about Home, the report was rejected. Disappointed disbelievers insulted Crookes and called him incompetent, dishonest, a victim of fraud, and so on. Crookes replied:

> The phenomena I am prepared to attest are so extraordinary, and so directly oppose the most firmly rooted articles of scientific belief—amongst others, the ubiquity and invariable action of the force of gravitation—that, even now, on recalling the details of what I witnessed, there is an antagonism between reason, which pronounces it to be scientifically impossible, and the consciousness that my senses, both of touch and sight—and these corroborated as they were, by the senses of all who were present—are not lying witnesses when they testify against my preconceptions.[1]

Crookes never ceased to insist that he had demonstrated the existence of a new and unknown "psychic force." In the report he added: "These experiments *confirm beyond doubt* the conclusions at which I had arrived in my former paper, namely, the existence of a force associated, in some manner not yet explained, with the human organization."[2]

Later he went on to write:

> The Theory of Psychic Force is in itself merely the recognition of the now almost undisputed fact that under certain conditions, as yet but imperfectly ascertained, and within a limited, but as yet undefined, distance from the bodies of certain persons having a special nerve organization, a Force by which, without muscular contact or connection, action at a distance is caused, and visible motions and audible sounds are produced in solid substances.[3]

Clearly, Joseph had "a special nerve organization," a by-product of his intense mental, spiritual, and physiological practices and of his temperament.

Under controlled conditions Home produced effects that Crookes believed proved the reality of the new force: (1) movements of heavy bodies with contact but without mechanical exertion; (2) unexplained percussive sounds; (3) the alteration of the weight of bodies; (4) the levitation of chairs and tables—and pertaining to our story—the levitation of human bodies; (5) the movements of small objects without contact; (6) the appearance of solid luminous hands that melted away upon being touched; (7) direct writing (luminous hands that take up pencils and write messages); (8) the appearance of phantom faces; (9) indications of an external intelligence; (10) and finally, a miscellany of complex occurrences that exhibited various effects of the hypothesized force.[4]

Contrary to the somewhat biased Thurston (1952), Crookes claimed that many witnesses observed Home levitate (about a hundred times, he says) and thought the evidence for his levitations "overwhelming."[5] For example; movements of objects without contact were observed: an accordion held in Crookes's hands that played, a coral necklace that rose up on end, window curtains and Venetian blinds that were raised—all without the action of any known physical force.

A similar list of phenomena has been drawn up by the English researchers of Eusapia Palladino—the most widely investigated physical medium.[6] Three highly skilled researchers isolated the Italian medium in a hotel suite in Naples to study her.[7] One of the most carefully controlled series of experiments with a physical medium on record is described in minute detail. W. W. Baggally and Hereward Carrington were present, both experts in conjuring and seasoned psychical researchers.

In Eusapia's case, the hands that appeared touched the experimenters, sometimes a bit forcefully; one preposterous but often observed phenomenon was the sensation of a cold breeze blowing from a scar on the medium's brow. The three investigators who observed and recorded every movement of Palladino concluded that "the ordinarily recognized laws of dynamics have to be enlarged by the assumption that there does actually exist some hitherto unascertained force liberated in her presence and for the existence of which, both in her and certain other persons, the body of evidence is, we think, not inconsiderable."[8]

As it was with William Crookes, Feilding and company believed the force was animated by intelligence; the intelligence was evident in its observed physical effects and—perhaps more striking—its observed materializations, the hands that emerged and touched the investigators.

As Feilding said, it was easier to yield to the evidence of the former (levitation) but not so easy to accept "that this force should be able to manifest itself as tangible matter and assume an organic form like a hand, capable of grasping."[9] So as far back as the late nineteenth century we have a physicist and several serious investigators affirming the reality of a psychic force, said to show intelligence, cause the levitation of physical objects, and materialize objects such as living hands. Clearly, the Victorian researchers found in Eusapia's mediumship evidence of mind as a force of nature.

NEO-PLATONISM REDUX

There are tendencies today that would reinsert mental agency into the basics of scientific reality. Roger Penrose, for example, argues for a Platonic theory of mathematics. Children, he observes, spontaneously learn to use the concept of natural numbers *before they learn to compute*; numbers are a type of Platonic idea that constitutes an intelligible world. Mathematics is preeminently a mental construct. And we use it to capture equations of the "laws" of physical reality. Penrose writes: "It seems to me that there is a fundamental problem with the idea that mentality arises out of physicality. . . . The things we talk about in physics are matter, physical things, massive objects, particles, space, time, energy and so on. How could our feelings, our perception of redness, or of happiness have anything to do with physics? I regard that as a mystery."[10]

Penrose rejects the idea that awareness could be produced by a computational machine; noncomputability, he asserts, is a fundamental feature of consciousness. Our natural capacity for mathematics refutes computational materialism; Penrose infers this from the innate facility of children to understand numbers. Penrose's ideas here shed no direct light on the Joseph effects under discussion; but his argument does bring mentality back into our basic description of nature, which is where we are going in this chapter.

In order to make intelligible the idea of D. D. Home, Joseph of Copertino, and others in flight, we have to posit *some* kind of force that directly affects gravity. And it must be a *psycho*physical force, generated, as it appears, in the ecstatic phase that leads to manifest levitation. As already noted, levitation does not *violate* the law of gravity; it indicates the presence of an unrecognized force, associated, as Crookes said, with the "human organization." But the question remains: how could an intangible mind (without mass) be involved in doing this?

MIND AND QUANTUM MECHANICS

There is no doubt that hints of large changes in cosmology are on the horizon. Perhaps the most startling claim to come from some quantum physicists is that *consciousness creates reality*. This inverts the metaphysics of classical physics, in which mind is a passive onlooker, as it were hanging on to matter by its shirt-tails; in quantum mechanics, mind makes a comeback onto the stage of reality, this time as a sovereign performer.

Since Galileo, measurement and experiment in physics necessarily eliminate subjectivity. Forced to exclude subjectivity from objective measurement in the kind of mechanistic experimental science he was inventing, Galileo distinguished "primary" and "secondary" qualities—a ranking relevant *only* to his experimental method. He wrote in *The Assayer* of 1623: "These tastes, odors, colors, etc., so far as their objective existence is concerned, are nothing but mere names for something that resides exclusively in our sensitive body, so that if the perceiving creatures were removed, all of these qualities would be annihilated and abolished from existence."[11]

Classical physics became tied to a dualism of measurable matter and unmeasurable mind, setting the stage for a fateful *non sequitur*—the demotion of the mind's reality-status in nature. In fact, there is nothing in Galileo's statement that warrants that demotion. "As far as their objective existence," Galileo *correctly* says, tastes, odors, and colors are "annihilated." All he is saying is that tastes, odors, and colors have *subjective* existence, and are as such irrelevant to measurement in mechanics. Many took an erroneous turn and went from Galileo on to become materialists, reductionists, and invalidators of subjectivity.

The situation has changed with the new physics. As Henry Stapp states, concisely and emphatically: "Classical physics leaves out consciousness; quantum physics requires and is based on consciousness." With quantum mechanics, consciousness becomes crucial to the process of measurement and therefore to the reality of what is measured.

We have made it a point to reject the idea that consciousness is an emergent property of the brain. More recently, the physicist Nick Herbert in his book *Elemental Mind* also explicitly rejects the idea that minds emerge from brains. "Far from being a rare occurrence in complex biological or computational systems, mind is a fundamental process in its own right, as widespread and deeply embedded in nature as light or electricity."[12]

Herbert holds that quantum mechanics provides the basis for a new science of mind and questions the materialist assumption that consciousness must be a rare and quirky phenomenon. About the place of consciousness in nature, he proposes "*quantum animism* in which mind permeates the world at every level." One argument for this panpsychist view is derived from John Bell's theorem and John Clauser's "experimental proof of nature's nonlocality."[13] Elemental mind is nonlocal. For Herbert, "The behavior of matter at the quantum level affords both the opportunity for mind to manifest itself in the material world and the means for us to explore the details of the mind's operations."

In short, the new physics—unlike "classical" Newtonian physics—provides openings through which mind may influence, penetrate, and transform nature. The "mechanism" revolves around the *potential* nature of quantum reality. There is a sense among some physicists that because matter has certain *mindlike* properties, mental agents like ourselves may in principle be able to causally interact with physical nature.

Quantum mechanics paints an unexpected picture of elemental physicality; it turns out to be rather fuzzy, and not just puzzling but mysterious. No wonder most down-to-earth physicists refuse to talk about it! Consciousness is, as physicists Bruce Rosenblum and Fred Kuttner say, the "skeleton in physics' closet." It seems ironic that the most exact of sciences has led to the discovery of quantum nature with *mindlike*, apparently nonlocal properties.

Rosenblum and Kuttner write of the twin enigmas of consciousness and quantum mechanics; to highlight the enigma they contrast classical with quantum ideas of probability, the former subjective, the latter, objective. In the shell game, there is a pea hidden under one of two shells; to the player, the probability of picking the shell with the pea under it is one half. That calculation depends on a real pea being under the shell before the choice is made. Quantum probability is a different matter entirely: the quantum "pea" (say, an electron) in its unobserved state consists of a certain "waviness," described by Schrödinger's equations, which is spread over many possible locations.

The uncertainty is not in the eye of the beholder, as in the shell game; it is in the object itself. In other words, according to Rosenblum and Kuttner,[14] "the object was not there before you found it there. Your happening to find it there *caused* it to be there. This is tricky and the essence of the quantum enigma." It's tricky because it implies that somehow consciousness creates, completes, and ratifies physical reality, and brings it out of the shadows of probability and potentiality into actual existence.

That indeed is a totally unexpected idea coming from the frontiers of physics! Pascual Jordan, one of the founders of quantum mechanics, wrote: "Observations not only *disturb* what is to be measured, they *produce* it." Truly this is—as Niels Bohr famously said—"shocking."

Classical physics and its great success with technology has misleadingly led many to believe that the subjective world is somehow made of second-rate stuff, less truly real, less effective and important than things measurably physical. With quantum physics this misconception is upended. The new unexpected claim is that subjectivity—a state of consciousness—is a necessary condition for something physical to become actual. Without consciousness there is no world; there are only possible worlds. Rosenblum and Kuttner, in their cautiously bold treatment, say:

> Consciousness and the quantum enigma are not just two mysteries: they are *the* two mysteries. The first, the physical demonstration of the quantum enigma presents us with a fundamental mystery of the objective world "out there"; the second, conscious awareness, presents us with the fundamental mystery of the subjective, mental world "in here." Quantum mechanics appears to connect the two.[15]

The authors—in accord with Henry Stapp and Nick Herbert—single out the work of John von Neumann as pinpointing the necessary theoretical step. Von Neumann argued that when a Geiger countermeasures the behavior of a wave function, a conscious observer is still necessary to yield any result of the collapsed quantum state. The Hungarian master mathematician of quantum mechanics and inventor of the digital computer argued that the whole of macro-nature obeys Schrödinger's equations and therefore possesses the uncertainty of the quantum state.

With von Neumann placing consciousness outside physical nature *and* conceptualizing the whole of nature as quantum-like, we see a way in which consciousness determines physical reality. Von Neumann influenced Henry Stapp, who bridles at the idea that classical physics assumes that the "incessantly reconfirmed idea that our conscious efforts can influence our "physical actions" is delusional. Quantum mechanics is the theoretical wedge for making our mental efforts "causally efficacious." Quantum uncertainties affect the dynamics of the brain by enabling influence on ionic behavior in neural tissues that mediate goal-directed behavior. The quantum Zeno effect, according to Stapp, influences a quantum template in the brain that facilitates the action. If this consciously directed effort does occur, and activates a rapid sequence of similar queries, then that template could be held in place for an extended period, which can cause that action to occur.[16]

Stapp follows William James in analyzing "free will" in terms of holding attention on one's aim or task, repeatedly calling it to mind, thus tending to make the action more likely.[17] The phrase "a rapid sequence of similar queries" used by Stapp calls to mind the rapid and incessant fire of Joseph's "queries," his repeated acts of attention on the same cluster of up-oriented, heaven-related ideas and images. Might the efforts of an extremely focused individual like Joseph give rise to a brain dynamic that frees up the "new force," enabling his phenomena to occur more readily? Stapp breaks from von Neumann, who thought that consciousness only collapsed the wave functions of its own brain. But Stapp is prepared, in the face of sufficient empirical evidence, to relax that restriction and allow mind directly to affect not only its own body but also external bodies.

This extension enlarges the scope of the quantum model of psychic influence. In John von Neumann's version of quantum mechanics, mind and consciousness are subtly woven into the fundamental texture of physical nature. This is a game-changer, for it allows us to consider that there is a property of mindlike responsiveness in quantum nature, a *protomental* mode of being that is continuous with, and potentially responsive to, the interior of human mental life.

Stapp appears to be arguing for a kind of minimalism of sympathy latent in the deep structure of the natural world, a *physical* potential inconceivable in classical physics. Combine the hyperintentionality of the quantum Zeno effect with the mindlike responsiveness of nature, and we have a model that helps us imagine how a mystic, a saint, a yogi, or any inspired psychic entity might elicit extraordinary physical responses from nature, providing there is the right confluence of events, the right pattern of coincidences.

In view of Stapp's psychically reanimated nature, Joseph and his phenomena acquire a new quantum of theoretical plausibility. We know from the friar's hampered life how powerful were his spiritual needs and how relentless his conscious efforts to realize them; these efforts, moreover, were informed by a "fire of love" for divine union. The historical record suggests that when fire of love and concentration of will converged, Joseph was lifted into space, into a temporary pocket, as it were, of degravitated existence.

With the uncertainties of quantum reality, nature may be malleable enough to handle the psychophysical contortions of a mystic like Joseph of Copertino. Joseph seems to have possessed an extraordinary ability to exploit the quantum Zeno effect. There is a wide spectrum to consider.

About blisters and stigmata, Stapp writes:

> From this perspective, a natural way to account, for example, for the phenomena of blisters and stigmata would be to assume that the intensely focused mental state of the affected person increases the strength of its inputs into the physical realm to the point of their being able to *directly affect* the pertinent parts of the person's body without involving his or her nervous system.[18]

Bypassing the nervous and muscular system and directly affecting a physical target is what is meant by telekinesis or PK. Stapp is open to the empirical possibilities. Again he states concisely: "The scope of the capacities of thinking entities to probe various physical systems is a matter to be settled empirically." Following von Neumann's orthodox quantum conception of the self as a separate entity, he adds that

> the mind can have *direct* effects, not only upon parts of the body lying outside the nervous system, but also upon parts of the physical universe lying outside the observer's body.... Such macro-PK phenomena do seem to occur in connection with certain abnormal psychic states. The case of Saint Joseph of Copertino is an example, as are recurrent spontaneous physical activities associated with psychologically troubled adolescents.[19]

The quantum dimension of physics brings mentality—soul if we dare use the word—back to a disenchanted cosmos. And it might help make sense of Joseph's levitations. In a related fashion, there are other questions we might ask: Could the quantum undergirding of human intentionality also be amplified to account for distant healing or, say, the odor of sanctity?

In sum, two points seem worth underscoring. The first deals with the range of possible mind-body effects. Von Neumann permits a "thinking entity" to causally impact its brain, and its brain alone. For Stapp this limitation "is simply relaxed, in order to accommodate the anomalies." From a logical point of view, the "thinking entity" is as distant from its own body as it is from external bodies. In the quantum world, then, the range of influence of mind on body is in theory massively enlarged.

The second point involves the quantum Zeno effect, in which an agent by repeated free choices produces a "stable or slowly evolving neural state" that persists and facilitates the designated motor activity. The quantum Zeno effect is a potent ally: it suppresses the no's and amplifies the yes's we receive in response to our "probings" of nature. The way the quantum Zeno effect is supposed to work fits what we know about Joseph's relentlessly focused intentionality.

SCHMIDT MACHINES AND GOAL-ORIENTED PK

Consider now another possible approach. Physicist Helmut Schmidt experimented with PK, using as quantum targets samples of strontium 90, and came to a surprising conclusion. Using machines of various complexity in PK tests had no effect on the subject's scoring ability. To succeed, the agent's sole task was to attend to the target, the goal or end-state, which was to cause one of a panel of small lights to turn on. Dwelling on the how—the intermediate electronic, mechanical, and quantum mechanical connections triggering the target light—was unnecessary and counterproductive. The analytic intelligence does not come into play and must be laid aside. Asking, "How can I do this?" is useless. Schmidt wrote:

> This suggests that PK may not be properly understood in terms of some mechanism by which the mind interferes with the machine in some cleverly calculated way but that it may be more appropriate to see PK as a goal-oriented principle, one that aims successfully at a final event, no matter how intricate the intermediate steps.[20]

In this concept, we apparently take the heretical step of introducing teleological or final causation back into scientific discourse. Goal-oriented thinking fits well with the idea of levitation. Joseph levitates like a subject achieves a hit on a random event generator; without trying to fly like a bird by flapping his arms, all his attention is on the goal of becoming one with God, the Madonna, or Heaven—somewhere on a higher plane.

In one of his strophes, he raps, *Levati anima mia, levati su*, "Raise my soul, raise it high!"[21] Since the end-state is conceived and imagined to reside *somewhere above*, his body is lifted *above*, toward heaven, a surprising and unintended effect we end by labeling levitation.

Goal-oriented thinking pervades magic and religion; spells and petitionary prayer are a kind of goal-directed thinking. One petitions God for a favor; the favor is the goal; the petitioner leaves it to God: to the subliminal mind, to the archetypes, to whatever the notion happens to be named: the goal's the thing—the *telos*, in ancient Greek. Schmidt speaks of one who "aims successfully at a final event." Most of us are clueless as to how this is done, in part because we're addicted to linear habits of thought. Joseph knew how to aim successfully at final events by handing the task over with complete unwavering confidence to the appropriate symbol of transcendence.[22]

Experiments performed by Helmut Schmidt speak to the rehabilitation of mind in nature. The extra chance results at odds of a thousand to a billion to one seem to have demonstrated that human intention—pure thought—can bias events occurring in the quantum world.[23] And this seems compatible with Stapp's emphasis on the quantum Zeno effect. This account of how one scores on a Schmidt machine matches our portrait of Joseph during ecstatic levitation. Joseph found that to achieve his goal he had to withdraw attention from everything but the goal. He used metaphors of aiming right, holding the bow firmly, all goal-oriented in spirit. Joseph had no idea why or how his body rose in the air when he thought of heaven, or the Madonna, just as Schmidt's PK agent has no idea of the machinery involved to affect the light panel he's trying to influence. Everything depends on the ability to hold a picture of the desired state, the final outcome, firmly in mind. Unlike most of us who are poorly developed in this regard, Joseph seems to have had a genius for "goal-oriented" thinking.

SCHRÖDINGER, ONE MIND, TIME ABOLISHED

Now to one of the founders of quantum mechanics for ideas that help us reinstate the concept of mind in nature from yet another angle. Irwin Schrödinger (1969) wrote two books close to our concerns, one on the nature of life, the other on mind and matter. Like the "quantum animists" that Nick Herbert alludes to, Schrödinger asserts that, numerically, there can be only one mind, one consciousness.

Schrödinger believed that the separateness we experience in ordinary life is an illusion. But then we need to ask: How does the one mind, the one consciousness splinter into many individual minds? How did the one get to be a multitude? By what mischievous trick have we been broken up into hordes of selfish, separate, and antagonistic egos?

In *Mind and Matter*, Schrödinger explains: "Consciousness finds itself intimately connected with, and dependent on, the physical state of a limited region of matter, the body." The "connection," through habit, turns into the delusion that we are helplessly mired, fatally entangled, in matter: trapped in one isolated, vulnerable body.

Each of us is conscious through a body in time that colors our unique personal awareness, to which we become accustomed and powerfully attached. The sense of a hidden, subliminal oneness of mind is for all practical purposes nearly meaningless. Countless human ills result from an exaggerated sense of our isolation and separateness; Schrödinger thought we needed a concept of mind that affords a deeper sense of our ultimate self-identity. He was fond of quoting from the Katha Upanishad and thought it possible to attain liberation by meditating on "the Birthless, the light of whose consciousness forever shines . . . the immortal Self."[24]

The physicist asks how billions of neurons can give rise to the experience of one conscious self? How indeed do you get one self-reflective consciousness of will and memory out of billions of tiny bits of electrified matter? Schrödinger thought that as one mind presides over a multitude of neurons, so the multitude and diversity of minds is grounded in and overseen by one great mind.

Schrödinger marvels at the mysterious "place" where the physical stimulus in the cortex is metamorphosed into a mental perception. Beyond the unity of consciousness, he dwells on the sheer fact of being conscious, of being present to awareness but irreducibly other than the cerebral apparatus. One more reflection of Schrödinger is notable: I'm not sure how he gets there, but the idea is daring metaphysics. He says that the fact that humans have constructed quantum mechanics frees us from "the tyranny of old Chronos. What we in our minds construct ourselves cannot, so I feel, have dictatorial power over our mind, neither the power of bringing it to the fore nor the power of annihilating it. . . physical theory in its present stage strongly suggests the indestructibility of Mind by Time."[25]

Our minds are not caught in the net of time and space. A teaching of the Upanishads, this view shades into a belief in immortality. One of the perennial intuitions of the human spirit: it appealed to Schrödinger, a founder of the new physics who refused to acquiesce in the materialist creed.

HIGHER DIMENSIONAL SPACE

In trying to reinvest the universe with a more spacious concept of mind, theories of higher dimensional space are highly suggestive. It should be noted that Joseph in ecstatic levitation found himself in a space with very peculiar properties. Not least of the reported oddities was the abeyance of standard gravitational force, the very thing that so intrigued William Crookes in his dealings with D. D. Home.

In these states the friar had the ability to impart unexplained lightness to other people and to objects like heavy crosses. There were sudden dramatic ascents of meters and prolonged hoverings where his toes dangled inches above the ground. On one occasion in Pietrarubbia, the curious "sacristan had even crouched down to see if his toes were touching the ground . . . in order to be able to understand how it was possible for his slippers to remain attached to his feet."[26]

The detail about the slippers is important; it shows that the counter-gravitational force was not just acting on Joseph's body but on the space around his body. His garments remained stiff, unaffected by his movements through air. He was also observed to hover over candle flames, in which he was not burned nor did any of his garments. Inside this ad hoc levitational space, gravity appears to change along with other properties. It all seems to occur inside a bubble around Joseph, with ordinary observers peering in at what was going on. So what is happening here?

Bernard Carr is a theoretical physicist with the Astronomy Unit of Queen Mary University of London—also one-time president of the British Society for Psychical Research. Carr, interested in a comprehensive theory of consciousness, adverts to the concept of higher dimensional space. I'm intrigued by his view that some "form of communal mental space" is necessary to account for mental life.

Although our bodies enclose us in separate physical shells, is there an extra-bodily way to communicate *through mental space*? A way to participate in the human community more directly than by the usual sensory means? Or are we naturally confined to our personal mental spaces?

Carr lists normal, paranormal, and mystical forms of experience that call for hypothetical mental spaces: for example, ordinary sensory percepts, afterimages, memories, visualizations, hallucinations, ordinary and lucid dreams, nightmares and haggings, telepathic and clairvoyant impressions, apparitions of the dead and the demonic, and of course ecstatic and mystical states. He conceptualizes the functionally different spaces as manifestations of a single uber-space, "a universal structure or information space."

The history of physics, says Carr, has been a series of paradigm shifts in which the dimensionality of the world progressively increases: from the 3-D space of Newton to the 4-D space of Einstein (where time is the fourth dimension) to the 5-D space of Kaluza-Klein theory to the 10-D space of superstring theory to the 11-D space of so-called M-theory. He proposes that these higher dimensions may provide the basis of a unified theory of mind and matter that would accommodate the psychical and mystical outliers.

Speculations on the Physics of Levitation

The Big Bang involved the creation of time and space, according to the new story. At what point mind and its multispaces came into being is unknown. Let's assume with Carr that every novel form of mental evolution creates its own peculiar mental space. Could such mind spaces be clues to understanding how ecstatic levitation is possible?

To repeat: there were dramatic changes in the space around Joseph during his raptures. Suppose these changes occurred, and imagine a local bubble of space in which the ecstatic is enclosed. The properties displayed must somehow be effects of his ecstasy, for they only manifest when he is in ecstasy. Besides the gravitational change, he appears immune to the effects of fire; and he seems immune to pain—observers pinch, poke, or wrench his body, but he's unresponsive. Impervious to mechanical pressure like wind, he moves through space, but his tunic and sash remain "composed," as if he were a floating diorama, or a statue or painted figure. None of what is occurring inside the ecstatic's space bubble are possible in normal 4-D space.

As it appears, Joseph's experience seems like an excursion into dream space. In our *dream spaces*, we may move about free from gravity, are not burned or pained by fire, or mechanically affected by physical objects or forces. We experience our dream bodies as free from the constraints of physics; as with Joseph's levitated body, we inhabit a different space.

Imagine watching Joseph lifted up, displaying all these temporary irregularities. It would be as if we were watching him inside his dream but from the standpoint of our waking space. The strangeness is occurring only inside the bubble, inside Joseph's lucid-dream world. But somehow—and this is the mystery—we are able to observe him there.

Joseph's rapture appears very much *like a dream*: he floats in the air, not a ruffle in his clothing, his feet resting in tapering flames, people jabbing his ribs as a fly crawls on his glazed eye, his arms outstretched in bliss; meanwhile outside the bubble waking people are moving about confusedly, understandably startled by what they see.

It appears that inside this bubble we observe a fusion, a compaction of dream and waking space; a perfect illustration of what Andre Breton meant by surreality.[27] Joseph's surreality—mechanism unknown—consists of a literal coupling of dream and reality. Normally, we dream and wake in cycles, one or the other, always in succession.

What appears to be happening (I am describing, not explaining): in defiance of the normal succession of dream and waking states, Joseph appears to observers as if he were in a waking dream, the two simultaneously conjoined in one space. The phenomenological picture shows a compaction of spaces; the region immediately around Joseph's uplifted body fuses public space and dream space into a surreal amalgam, a space simultaneously subjective *and* objective.

Carr points to a parallel with what happens at the "event horizon" of a black hole. This is the boundary of the region that is accessible to an outside observer, a place where time seems to freeze. At the event horizon, 4-D space is compacted into 2-D space. This compaction of realities raises an interesting question: Is there a "special nerve organization," as Crookes put it, a special psychophysical condition, which can cause dream and waking space to compact into one surreal space where levitation becomes possible?

Certain kinds of experience, Carr suggests, "encourage the view that there is an independent dream space, with its own set of images and memories." So each time we dream we cross over into another spatial world, less continuous with our ordinary world and with a different physics and geometry. The Oxford philosopher H. H. Price (1995) has written about this possibility: "We inhabit two worlds simultaneously, the world of common experience governed by physical law and another space, quite as real, which obeys other laws. . . . *Continuous dream-life goes on throughout our waking hours* [italics added] and occasionally we may catch a glimpse of it."

The idea that we are dreaming all the time is analogous to something else, equally plausible; if there is such a thing as ESP, it is probably occurring all the time, but below the surface awareness of our mental life. On this view, we are in continuous telepathic interaction with a larger mental environment, but conscious or half-conscious of it only intermittently and fleetingly.

C. D. Broad worried about being exposed to alien influences, yet he too suggested that in dreams we merge in a single communal dream space.[28] According to Carr, "The suggestion that dream-space could be *communal* adds a crucial new ingredient to the discussion, tantamount to some form of Universal Mind." Like Price and Broad, Carr speculates that our dreams may be part of a universal mental space that we subliminally inhabit even as we walk about fully alert in our waking world, busily attending to its concerns. Most of the time the two worlds are clearly demarcated. Now and then the poet, mystic, shaman, or madman creates a fissure in the partition, and waking space is infused with dream space.

Is the ecstatic compaction of waking and dream space the way toward Whitehead's "nobler, wider existence" of the future? Was Joseph one of the great explorers of Carr's common mind space? The answers to these questions will have to lie in the future of a new mind-empowered physics.

UNUS MUNDUS AND JOSEPH *IN VOLO*

How a mental state like ecstasy could affect gravity is the enigma. We have the phenomenon, it would seem, but what to make of it? Let's glance at another possible approach based on two major figures in their fields, C. G. Jung and Wolfgang Pauli. Their views provide an intriguing but difficult perspective on what may be going on with the friar's levitations.

Harald Atmanspacher (2012) has written about dual-aspect monism, or the Pauli-Jung conjecture.[29]

According to this conjecture, psyche and matter don't causally interact but are complementary aspects of one underlying reality that Jung named *unus mundus*, the "one world." Jung apparently got this idea of an underlying one world from a life-changing experience he had. Analytical psychologist Erich Neumann remarked: "Strangely unaware of his own nature, Jung forgets that his experience is altogether out of the ordinary, that in scope and content it transcends by far that of his fellow mortals and on that account must be rated "mystical." [30]

Jung's extraordinary experience led him to an extraordinary hypothesis. An ancient hypothesis, it holds that behind the multiplicity of the world's appearances is one transcendent reality. Jung believed that meaningful coincidences or "synchronicities" were a way that the *unus mundus* periodically reveals itself in our experience. According to the Pauli-Jung conjecture, synchronicities are *acausal*.

Consider an example, recounted to me by a scientist who loved opera: on the morning a noted opera singer died, a songbird fell dead from the sky by the door of his house. A striking synchronicity, it was as if the singer's death called forth a gesture, a response from the sky, a beautiful if uncanny way of underscoring the music-maker's passing. But the one event did not *cause* the other; the puzzle is in the timing, the *synchronicity*; but also, and crucially, the two deaths reflect each other and echo each other in a shared meaning—the death of the singer. Synchronicities reveal the power of the *unus mundus* to discover or create deep, soulful connections. He also thought that psychic experiences reveal the presence of the great unifying force, the *unus mundus*. The question here is how this master conjecture might relate to psyche and matter in Joseph's levitations. We could begin by wondering how, and in what sense, is levitation a type of synchronicity?

For Pauli, reality is deeper than what appears to us as mind and matter in our bifurcated world. There is a deeper reality that contains both mind and matter; in some sense (impossible to imagine) that deeper reality is one reality. Mystics (a Jung, a Joseph or an intuitive genius like Pauli) appear to have direct experience of this transcendent *unity*. We might then ask, as far as Joseph's levitations: Is the *unus mundus* of Pauli and Jung also *unifying*? For so it appears: the ecstatic ascent of Joseph's thoughts toward heaven is followed by his body *in unity with his mind*, a mind absorbed in the oneness of divine reality. According to Pauli, the symbolic imagination somehow contains the mental and the physical in a unified reality. Joseph was so attuned to his symbolic imagination that in ecstasy his body rose with his mind in flight toward the divine. Were these the strange fruits of his powerful symbolic imagination?

Von Franz, reviewing forerunners of the idea of synchronicity, quotes Albertus Magnus on Avicenna (980–1037):

> I discovered an instructive account in Avicenna . . . , which says that a certain power to alter things indwells in the human soul and subordinates the other things to her, particularly when she is swept into a great excess of love or hate or the like. When therefore the soul of a man falls into a great excess of a passion, it can be proved by experiment that it binds things and alters them.[31]

This well describes Joseph, falling into great excesses of passion and having the power to "alter" and "bind" things. Joseph in levitation, we may speculate, would signify mind and matter restored to perfect oneness in harmony with the *unus mundus*.

The oneness of being that eludes ordinary perception and ordinary life occasionally breaks through our divided consciousness: perhaps in the form of meaningful coincidences, psychic interactions, moments of love and inspiration, or through the transports of a mystic or a poet. For many of us the sense and glimmer of the *unus mundus* may only suggest itself in certain dreams, or in works of music or art that haunt us for reasons we cannot understand but cannot ignore or forget.

To make sense of Joseph's phenomena, then, we need to upgrade our view of human mental potential. If one thinks of mind as a pale derivative of our brains, talk of it "causing" levitation (or anything interesting) makes no sense. But expand the concept of what mind is and can do, and how it relates to physics, and our idea of what is possible begins to mutate. Signs of such mutation are evident today: in physics, as suggested in this chapter, and in philosophy, anthropology, scholarship in religion, and psychology. Just as the physical universe is more vast, more profound, and more mysterious than we thought, the same can be said for the universe of consciousness. In the next final chapter we touch on some implications of all this for that most seductive of characters to appear on the stage of human evolution—"religion."

NOTES

1. Fodor, 1966, p. 70.
2. Medhurst, 1971.
3. Ibid., p. 29.
4. See Braude's discussion of D. D. Home in Braude, 1991.
5. Ibid., p. 116.
6. Feilding, 1963.
7. Ibid., pp. 15–28.
8. Ibid., p. 54.

9. Ibid., p. 273.
10. Penrose, 1995, p. 94.
11. Danto and Morgenbesser, 1960, p. 28.
12. Herbert, 1993, p. 3.
13. Ibid., p. 5.
14. Rosenblum and Kuttner, 2006, p. 75.
15. Ibid., p. 183.
16. This passage is from a personal communication, but for this and other ideas of Stapp, see his chapter in *Beyond Physicalism*, pp. 157–94.
17. See James, 1971, pp. 74–89.
18. Stapp, "On a Quantum Mechanical Theory of the Mind-Brain Connection and Its Capacity to Accommodate the Targeted Phenomena," p. 28, unpublished manuscript.
19. Ibid., p. 28.
20. Schmidt, 1974, p. 190.
21. Chiappinelli, 2008, p. 177.
22. See the discussion in chapter 9.
23. Schmidt, 1974, p. 185.
24. Prabhavananda and Manchester, 1957, p. 22.
25. Ibid., p. 165.
26. GP3, p. 253.
27. Breton, 1972, p. 14.
28. Broad, 1962, p. 313.
29. Another useful book that discusses this approach is *Psyche and Matter* (1988), by the Jungian analyst Marie-Louise Von Franz.
30. Quoted in Jaffe, 1975, pp. 56–57.
31. See Von Franz, 1988, p. 191.

Part III

CONCLUDING REFLECTIONS

> There are always topics on which otherwise scrupulous minds will cave in to the grossest prejudice with hardly a struggle.
>
> —Terry Eagleton, *Reason, Faith, and Revolution: Reflections on the God Debate*

Parts I and II told the story of Joseph and looked for footholds to understanding the stranger highlights of his achievements. In this concluding chapter, Joseph's story is background for a more general discussion of the parapsychology of religion—an underappreciated approach to the old debate between science and religion. The academic term for what I want to do is *hermeneutics*, from Hermes, the versatile Greek god of thieves and messengers.[1]

Parapsychology, the broad field of consciousness studies, adds new dimensions of meaning to certain religious ideas and experiences. An example would be Frederic Myers finding in telepathy (a word he happened to invent) a way to throw new light on the meaning of love. In the epilogue of his great work, he wrote: "Love is a kind of exalted, but unspecialized telepathy—the simplest and most universal expression of that mutual gravitation, or kinship of spirits which is the foundation of the telepathic law."[2]

For Myers, telepathy is used to create an expanded idea of love. It might mean something entirely different to somebody else; it could be taken to imply that our privacy is threatened, fear that others could snoop on our secret thoughts. Yet a third person might see telepathy as a chance to train for a career in espionage. In the psi zone we can imagine a wider but less tractable universe: a place with novel possibilities but also rife with unknown risks.

Expanding the concept of mind is a way of expanding the concept of life. Acquaintance with new realms of the possible opens for each of us new ways to tell and live our stories. Men and women live by the meanings they create and imagine—or fail to create and imagine. It is a challenge to fashion a story of going beyond that speaks to our humanity. No easy thing, but Jeffrey Kripal beckons the daring inquirer:

> Such a project is based on the wager that new theory lies hidden in the anomalous, that the paranormal appears in order to mock and shock us out of our present normal thinking. Seen in this way, psychical and paranormal phenomena become the still unacknowledged, unassimilated Other of modern thought, the still unrealized future of theory, the fleeting signs of a consciousness not yet become a culture.[3]

NOTES

1. Brown, 1990.
2. Myers, 1903, vol. 2, p. 282.
3. Kripal, 2010, p. 23.

Chapter 9

The Parapsychology of Religion
A New Science of Spirit?

> Science and religion have changed places: today, science provides the security religion once guaranteed. In a curious inversion, religion is one of the possible places from which one can deploy critical doubts about today's society. It has become one of the sites of resistance.
>
> —Slavoj Zizek, *Violence*

> I would not speak about "absolute" truths, even for believers. . . . Truth is a relationship. As such, each one of us receives the truth and expresses it from within, that is to say, according to one's own circumstances, culture, and situation in life.
>
> —Pope Francis, *Evangelii Gaudium,* 2013

The story of Joseph provides a provocative reason to broach the parapsychology of religion. As the venerable science-religion debate evolved, it has for many come to turn mainly on discrepancies between biblical and scientific accounts of creation and cosmology. But is this so important? For a religion like Buddhism, in which enlightenment consists of a special state of mind called nirvana, the question of cosmology is irrelevant. Enlightenment is to achieve a form of consciousness that goes beyond propositional thought (i.e., the earth is of a specific age, life evolved by chance or design, there is one God with the following properties, and so on).

Nirvana or any mystical form of beatitude has nothing to do with the correctness of claims about the constitution of the cosmos. If we think of the essence of religion in terms of special inner states and practices, the specifics of biology, geology, and astronomy are beside the point.

About Samkhya yoga, Christopher Chapple writes: "Cosmological explanations are simply irrelevant to the Samkhyan thrust: questions about the origins of things can only be asked or answered by a limited sense of self."[1] As far as questions about yogic release or enlightenment, it doesn't matter whether we came about by inscrutable fiat, a lucky streak in cosmic roulette, or gradual effortful evolution.

What does matter for the Buddhist, Samkhya yogi, prophet, or mystic of tradition is inner disposition, transcendence, the quality and scope of consciousness. Religion, in its mystical guise, is spiritual mountain climbing and generally concerned with the transformation of consciousness. Astronomy and biology provide the stage for an inner drama to unfold, but no more. There are different kinds of "stages" and cultural settings; still, the main action lies in the struggles and high adventures of subjective existence.

At all times and in all cultures, people have transcendent experiences. The more subjective the experience, the less important the specifics of the prevailing cosmology. Was the Buddha any less enlightened because he knew nothing of the periodic table?

Rosmi quotes Joseph as saying that what counts is "the heaven of the interior life," not "external devotions." The important thing is learning "the spiritual philosophy. Others may study natural philosophy and learn to know the things of nature but do not learn to know themselves."[2]

A NEW SCIENCE OF SPIRIT?

In the mainstream debates about science and spirituality, parapsychology rarely, if ever, comes up. But parapsychology speaks to many points of religious discourse. Under "parapsychology of religion," I include psychical research,[3] the whole range of consciousness studies—meditation, hypnosis, psychedelics, hallucinations, near-death data, placebo studies, and so on. Questions of cosmology and evolution lurk in the background of the science-religion debate, but parapsychology goes to the heart of religious experience in ways that no other science does.

Parapsychologists, an embattled minority, generally do not discuss the implications of their work for religion and spirituality, which, it is feared, might imperil their reputation and livelihood. Nevertheless, such ideas connecting religion and psychical research have been around for a long while.

NOTES ON A HIDDEN HISTORY

The parapsychology of religion lacks a mainstream academic niche, but it has a hidden history.[4] I will glance at some highlights, enough, I hope, to indicate the background of an approach worthy of some interest.

Looking back to ancient times we find the yoga sutras of Patanjali in which siddhis or psychic attainments are discussed in relationship to the role of intense mental concentration (*samyama*).[5] Or we might begin by scanning St. Augustine's *City of God* where he often wrote reflexively about extraordinary phenomena (e.g., his prescient remark that a portent or miracle "does not occur contrary to nature, but contrary to what is known of nature".[6] In his own way respectful of matters of fact, Augustine stressed the value of eyewitness testimony and offered observations on healing phenomena.

Moving quickly ahead, Joseph Glanvill, antischolastic of the English Royal Society, was a seventeenth-century forerunner. Opposed to the facile dismissal of "witchcraft" (*mediumship*, we say) and ghostly apparitions (reported then as now), he invoked the "experimental philosophy" of Bacon as his ally. The question must be settled by appeal to matters of fact, he insisted. The materialists argued that narratives about spirits were creatures of the imagination, but Glanvill countered: "If all these facts were but the result of imagination, it would be very strange that imagination, which is of all things the most changeable, should repeat the same conception hundreds of times in all epochs and all lands."

Another remark of this English contemporary of Joseph of Copertino shows something of his method: "Matters of fact well proved ought not to be denied because we cannot conceive how they can be performed. Nor is it a reasonable method of inference, first to presume the thing impossible, and thence to conclude that the fact cannot be proved."[7]

Even the skeptical Pierre Bayle (1647–1706) was prepared to admit: "The history of all lands register facts so numerous and astonishing that those who deny them all must be suspected either of insincerity, or of a defect in intelligence which prevents them from discerning the sources of proof."[8]

Moving ahead, William James made many rich contributions to the theory of religion. *The Varieties of Religious Experience* is a classic study, but a statement from his last book, *A Pluralistic Universe*, speaks to our aim: "Let empiricism once again become associated with religion . . . and I believe that a new era of religion as well as of philosophy will be ready to begin."[9] The new era will come when we learn to lay aside our hackneyed assumptions of what we think religion is and confront the varieties of psychic and spiritual experience.

Like James, his colleague across the pond, Frederic Myers was one of the founders of psychical research and a visionary of future religion. Being a classical scholar, essayist and poet, the loss of his inherited worldview affected him deeply. In *Fragments of Inner Life*, he describes his gradual disillusionment and despair with a grim clarity worthy of the arch-pessimist, Giacamo Leopardi.

> There is no need to retrace the steps of gradual disillusion. This came to me, as to many others, from increased knowledge of history and of science, from a wider outlook on the world. Sad it was, and slow; a recognition of insufficiency of evidence, fraught with growing pain. Insensibly the celestial vision faded, and left me to pale despair and cold tranquility.[10]

This marked the death of his belief in Christianity, after which he fell into agnostic depression. The triumph of materialism "was a dull pain borne with joyless doggedness, sometimes flashed into a horror of reality that made the world spin before one's eyes—a shock of nightmare-panic amid the glaring dreariness of day. It was the hope of the whole world, which was vanishing, not mine alone."

For Myers the new reign of materialism was depressing and seemed to throw an evil pall over all human relationships. "Nightmare-panic amid the glaring dreariness of day" may be the best line of poetry he ever wrote. "In that foreseen futility of the life of individual and of race," he added, "sympathy itself seemed a childish trifling with the universal despair." The times were undoubtedly changing. It "was the very flood-tide of materialism, agnosticism—the mechanical theory of the Universe, the reduction of all spiritual facts to physiological phenomena."[11] With "triumphant Darwinism," it seemed a black wave of nihilism was rolling over his world, engulfing him with malaise.

During this period of spiritual depression a conversation with the great moral philosopher Henry Sidgwick sparked his vision of a new science of human personality. Perhaps it was possible to winnow from human experience the basis of a new vision of the transcendent. So Myers, with Sidgwick and maverick physicist Sir William Barrett, founded the British Society for Psychical Research in 1882.[12] The aim was to methodically study certain types of phenomena that could not be explained in terms of the prevailing materialist assumptions. The early researchers quickly amassed a large body of experience-centered data, including much that suggested postmortem survival.

In the epilogue of Myers's major work, we find a "Provisional Sketch of a Religious Synthesis,"[13] where he writes of the "religion of the ancient sage," citing Lao-tzu, Buddha, Plato, Christ, and Mohammed as exemplary figures. Central is the belief in a spiritual world that infuses the material world, "a belief driven home to many minds by experiences both more weighty and more concordant than the percipients themselves have always known."

Religion for Myers was a part of our natural evolution as a species, a gradual awakening to a greater consciousness. "Our race from its very infancy has stumbled along a guarded way; and now the first lessons of its early childhood reveal the root in reality of much that it has instinctively believed."[14]

The "root" is the enlarged mental and spiritual faculties Myers and his colleagues were investigating by means of "observation, experiment, inference." The most remarkable features of Joseph Copertino's life were related, as we saw, to his gift for ecstatic experience. Myers singled out ecstasy as perhaps the key to unlocking the greater potentials of human consciousness:

> From a psychological point of view, one main indication of the importance of a subjective phenomenon found in religious experience will be the fact that it is common to all religions. I doubt whether there is any phenomenon, except ecstasy, of which this can be said. From the medicine-man of the lowest savages up to St. John, St. Peter, St. Paul, with Buddha and Mahomet on the way, we find records which, though morally and intellectually much differing, are in psychological essence the same. At all stages alike we find that the spirit is conceived as quitting the body; or, if not quitting it, at least as greatly expanding its range of perception as some state resembling trance.

He cites examples:

> The remembrance of ecstasy has inspired religions, has founded philosophies, has lifted into stainless heroism a simple girl (Joan of Arc). Yet religions and philosophies—as these have hitherto been known—are but balloon-flights which have carried separate groups up to the mountain summit, whither science at last must make her road for all men clear.[15]

The metaphor frames the early religions and philosophies as "balloon-flights" exploring the "mountain summit" of human consciousness; the business of science is to research this realm of phenomena for the benefit of the human race. For Myers, for whom ecstasy was the high point of religion, there was no conflict between science and religion.

He also stated: "We do not find, indeed, that support is given by souls in bliss to any special scheme of terrene theology." Despite being detached from theology, Myers falsely predicted that a hundred years hence all people would embrace as true the resurrection of Christ. But this ought not to surprise us. "Copernicus kept the circle as perfect celestial motion, and Kepler spaced the planets according to the Platonic solids, and Newton pursued alchemy—it's hard to get it all right the first time," observes historian Robert Rosenberg.[16]

Myers was on stronger ground when he claimed that the evidence for a postmortem existence would grow stronger; accounts of reincarnation and the NDE have been added to earlier studies of mediumship and veridical apparitions. In Myers's sketch of a religious synthesis, he wrote in a burst of romantic hope of "an ultimate incandescence where science and religion fuse in one; a cosmic evolution of Energy into Life, and of Life into Love, which is Joy."[17] The basis of this soaring vision was the massive accumulation of observations, experiments and inferences that filled the pages of his great study of human personality (1903). Myers's work has been gaining recognition among scholars.[18]

The French philosopher Henri Bergson was drawn to psychical research. In 1913—a hundred years ago as I write—he gave the presidential address to the British Society for Psychical Research, presenting a model of mind and brain based on the phenomena studied by the Society. Bergson understood creative evolution as the ongoing struggle of consciousness to master the material constraints of nature. He ended his last book contrasting two types of religion with the spectacular claim that sums up his evolutionary vision of divine reality:

> Men do not sufficiently realize that their future is in their own hands. Theirs is the task of determining first of all whether they want to go on living or not. Theirs the responsibility, then, of deciding if they want merely to live, or intend to make just the extra effort required for fulfilling, even on their refractory planet, the essential function of the universe, which is a machine for the making of gods.[19]

Andrew Lang attacked the standard view of anthropologists for its incompleteness: religious belief, this view claimed, is based on illusions, dreams, and hallucinations, which in the minds of early people were said to morph into ghosts, spirits, demons, gods, and goddesses. *The Making of Religion* (1898) argued that this fails to cover all the possibilities. "Primitive concepts of soul may be based, at least in part, on experiences which cannot, at present, be made to fit into any purely materialistic system of the universe." We should, he wrote, postulate the "X region of our nature. Out of that region, out of miracle, prophecy, vision, have certainly come forth the great religions."

Lang's method was comparative. We find in history records of beliefs and practices that, although colored by idiosyncratic culture, reveal similar types of experience and practice; modern evidence sheds retrospective light on stories and beliefs of antiquity. For example, acquaintance with table-tilting experiments might prompt one to suppose that Jesus walked on water after all; of course, the evidence of Joseph's levitations might serve the same purpose, more effectively, to be sure. Almost any modern evidence for PK could provide the necessary hypothetical fulcrum. Newly certified facts can change the way we interpret old narratives, once we bring in the psychical dimension. Lang wrote of his method: "I shall compare the ethnological evidence for savage usages and beliefs analogous to thought-transference, coincidental hallucinations, alternating personality, and so forth, with the best attested modern examples, experimental or spontaneous."[20]

Instead of arguing from *a priori* notions of violated law and the supposed uniformity of nature, as Hume did, Lang brought new empirical materials to the discussion of religious experience.

Closer to our time, Cesar de Vesme (1862–1938) was also a pioneer in the parapsychology of religion. Like Lang, de Vesme compared well-attested phenomena of modern times with accounts from ancient and preliterate cultures. He wrote:

> The origin of religions is . . . specially due to the observation of "supernormal" facts whose true interpretation is still undecided, and of which further study may, therefore, well show that the basis of religion is legitimate; and this, be it clearly understood, without touching on questions of revelation, faith, or dogma, but strictly confined to experimental and scientific grounds.[21]

It is an argument that carries some weight, depending on how we take his term "legitimate." He means, I think, grounded in some measure of empirical fact: "When it is common to a large number of people who have had no intercommunication, we cannot easily admit that the coincidence is due to a simple effect of imagination; there must be at the back of this belief some fact produced everywhere, and better or worse interpreted."[22]

De Vesme, like Lang, focused on religious beliefs and practices, intent on furnishing a global survey. The first volume on the "primitive" has chapters on Africa, Oceania, North and South America, and certain Northern tribes, the Hyperboreans, finding in all these cultures spiritist séances, clairvoyance, divination, methods of becoming sorcerers, use of psychedelics, ordeals, possession, techniques for inducing ecstasy, fetishes, sacred images, talismans, charms, amulets, mana, healing, shape-shifting, and sundry supernormal faculties.

The second volume covers "peoples of antiquity," Chaldeans, Assyrians, Egyptians, Hebrews, Persians, Celts, Germani, Slavs, Aztecs, and of course Greeks and Romans. Oracles, divination, prophecy are ways of negotiating the crises of existence and procedures for invoking sacred powers. De Vesme tried to bring paranormal psychology to bear on a vast miscellany of topics in religious studies, and his books are interesting because of their attention to detail. The same can be said for another learned and slightly more combative forerunner of the parapsychology of religion.

Joseph Ennemoser (1787–1854) was a prominent German physician and professor at the University of Bonn who believed that the phenomena of mesmerism (hypnotism) offered insights into the psychology of religion. His two-volume history of "magic" appeared in 1843. The books view magic and religion through the lens of "magnetism," the new psychology heralded by Anton Mesmer. According to Ennemoser, "magnetism, by its remarkable phenomena, in modern times has led us into a sphere which still, like a closed book, contains secrets of a higher order of things lying beyond the familiar, every-day history of nature."[23]

The main thesis of Ennemoser is: "True magic lies in the most secret, inmost powers of our mind." With this statement he opens a door to exploring magic, miracle, and religion, but strictly in light of specific psychological phenomena: "The intensity and vastness of the human mind are not fathomed by the most faithful observations of physiologists; and these psychological wonders are still frequently enough ascribed to the gods."[24]

Ennemoser's main idea is that one should look to the creative powers of mind for an explanation of the supposed actions of gods. This is similar to the *Tibetan Book of the Dead*[25] where the deities we encounter at the moment of death are said to be projections of our psychic propensities. Ennemoser was not an ungrounded speculator but a subtle, ironical thinker immersed in the kind of empiricism that foreshadows the work of Frederic Myers: both authors who saw in paranormal psychology a bridge to a new kind of dialogue between science and spirituality.

Another forerunner is a major figure in the history of science. Alfred Russell Wallace (1823–1903) shared with Darwin the honor of having conceived the principle of natural selection, one of the cornerstones of the modern theory of evolution.[26] Wallace, curious about the natural world, became interested in the phenomena of mediumship and doubted that natural selection could explain all aspects of evolving life.

Having, as he put it, been "beaten by the facts," he was attracted to Spiritualism, which seemed, from his perspective, like an evidence-based religion. Many disapproved of an eminent man of science like Alfred Russell Wallace embracing psychic phenomena as support for a new religion, a movement that began in the 1840s in upstate New York with the Fox sisters, later embroiled in much controversy. Even so, Wallace remained convinced that his findings justified his belief in a world of spirits.

He was not the only public figure attracted to Spiritualism. Sir Arthur Conan Doyle's commitment is well known, and should be mentioned. Indiana Congressman Robert Dale Owen (1801–1875) introduced the bill that led to creating the Smithsonian Institution. An encounter with D. D. Home while serving as diplomat in Naples prompted him to investigate Spiritualism, which before long convinced him of life after death. Two books, *Footfalls on the Boundary of Another World* (1899) and *The Debatable Land* (1871), are highly readable accounts of his findings. Anne Braude (1989) studied the progressive ideals of the Spiritualist movement that favored the abolition of slavery, woman's suffrage, animal rights, vegetarianism, "free" love (*not* promiscuity), and other ideals. American Spiritualists, according to Braude, used trance speaking to express demands for women's rights and other socially progressive causes.[27]

In the last century, the American Joseph Banks Rhine and his wife, Louisa Rhine, launched modern experimental research in parapsychology. Rhine was interested in the implications of parapsychology for religious studies, and was perhaps the first to speak of the "parapsychology of religion." He began by studying mediumship, but with William McDougall's support at Duke University, chose to pursue experimental parapsychology. Publicly, Rhine laid aside his interest in the evidence for life after death and for the phenomena people call miracles. Seymour Mauskopf and Michael McVaugh discuss the religious interests behind Rhine's attraction to parapsychology. The following from Rhine could be the epigraph of this chapter: "Religious communication is basically psi communication, pure and simple: it is neither sensory nor motor; it is unequivocally extrasensory. . . . All the physical miracles, whether in the healing of disease, the miraculous movements of objects, or the control of the elements, had to be manifestations of PK."[28]

This remark underscores the importance of parapsychology for the interpretation of so-called religious claims and texts. We have, in effect, the psi-mediated "mechanics" of religion laid bare; clearly, we have new ways of thinking about sacred writings, art objects, symbols, methods of divination, and the like. Scholars adopt what are *hermeneutical* stances: for example, the Deistic (Jefferson just redacted anything that looked like a miracle), the Fundamentalist and literalist, the Psychoanalytic, the Jungian, the Marxist, the Feminist, the Atheist, and so on. Why not then a full-blown *parapsychological* hermeneutics of religious experience?

To start us off, I will write of five core religious beliefs found the world over, and argue that for each belief, parapsychology has matters of vital importance to contribute—not pat solutions but pointers toward deeper understanding. The number five is not definitive; there are different ways of parsing themes and points of entry. This list covers basic beliefs found in most types of religious experience and worldview. The treatment will be selective, not exhaustive.

BELIEF IN A SPIRITUAL WORLD

This of course is a core and very broad belief. In all religions we find a belief in types of divine being or transcendent reality; they go under various names, ranging from the Hindu Atman and Brahman, the Great Spirit of Native American traditions, the God of the Abrahamic traditions, the transcendent state of nirvana, and so on. For traditional believers like Joseph, there was the

Church as the "mystical body" of Christ; among the Iroquois Indians we find belief in the "long body," not unlike the Christian "mystical body."

There is no end of variety on the theme of spiritual beings and spiritual dimensions of reality. The whole thing is apt to seem alien and incredible to the modern educated temperament. Clearly, much—though not all[29]—of the world-dominant scientific culture is out of touch with this enormously varied aspect of human experience, which has become disposable. My point here is modest: various forms of experience can help us imagine the possibility of higher beings and spiritual worlds. For example, William Braud and Marilyn Schlitz did experimental work on distant intentionality in 1997.

Distant intentionality is an idea of importance to our question, implying that our thoughts, feelings, and desires can affect each other at a distance, apart from the limits of time and space. Research of this type, and all the empirical evidence for PK and ESP, offers a factual basis for inferring that our individual minds extend into a wider mental environment, and are therefore in touch with much more mental reality than our everyday awareness would suggest.

Modern terms exist for this (I hold) highly grounded notion of extended or big mind. Aldous Huxley spoke of "mind at large"; Myers, of the "world-soul"; Emerson, of the "over-soul"; Richard Bucke, of "cosmic consciousness; all religious and mythic systems evolve their own terminologies, growing out of their unique histories, experiences, and cultural settings. Are they just vague terms or are they based on something real and powerful, and (wild surmise) perhaps even good, and even (dream on) beautiful?

I believe that terms signifying transpersonality, the notion of a big, great, or extended mind, make perfectly good sense in light of the many kinds of phenomena canvassed here in this book and elsewhere. Introduce telepathic and clairvoyant capacity, and a significantly greater mind seems still easier to imagine. And now add another crucial piece of data. Based on the phenomena of PK, some of which we have surveyed and assessed in this book, we may now enrich our hypothesis with an extended capacity for action, an ability to perform deeds on the world stage. Aldous Huxley wrote in the *Perennial Philosophy*: "If a human mind can directly influence matter not merely within, but even outside its body, then a divine mind, immanent in the universe or transcendent to it, may be presumed to be capable of imposing forms upon a pre-existing chaos of formless matter, or even, perhaps, of thinking substance as well as forms into existence."[30]

This is a bold stroke and widens the scope of the parapsychology of religion. If there is evidence for human-scale PK, a greater mind at large might well have correspondingly greater physical powers. In light of this feature of the greater mental entity, we may now entertain the possibility of dramatic healings, levitations, unexplained fragrances, and the like; once, that is, we coalesce the extended aspects of human mental life into one hypothetical uber-entity.

In history, the *greater mind*, whose reality we are constructing hypothetically from empirical data and trying to imagine, would assume different identities, reveal and be invested with different properties, and become the center of its own cult and mythologies, all things (as usual) depending on time and place, culture and context. And so, the idea we may entertain: relying on many findings typically ignored by mainstream academics, we may form a notion of a super-personal mental entity with extraordinary powers that throughout history appears to have interacted in unpredictable ways with human beings.

This entity, of course, is not the perfect deity of any known religion or school of theology. The parapsychological "God" we can plausibly construct out of the raw materials of psychic experience is imperfect, struggling, flawed, full of blind spots, malicious, sometimes stupid; its multiple identities and gross limitations reflect the waffling human instrument through which its evolution has unfolded on earth. Nothing could be more modest, our patching together this minimalist deity. Minimalism in theology is no doubt a novelty; most of us like our gods almighty and all right and all knowing. So the present nascent god should be treated with patience and forbearance. And nothing will be understood unless it is clear that the deity we have formed needs us as much as we need it, since it is nothing if not the collective expression of our evolving mental history.

BELIEF IN THE POWER OF BELIEF

Broadly conceived, what's called *religion* cherishes faith over reason. In all but few forms of religion, conceptual thinking is ultimately put in a backseat. The driving force is faith; but faith is more than doctrinal compliance without rational support; it has a volitional side, in Greek, *pistis,* which means "trust," "confidence."[31]

Everywhere in religious experience faith occupies a key role. In the healing stories of the New Testament, Jesus says, "Your faith (*pistis*, trust) has made you whole." *Pistis* can move mountains, according to Jesus, who had a weakness for hyperbole. Joseph's advice to all was "stay happy" and *trust* in the Madonna. Faith trumps reason. "If the Sun & Moon should doubt," said William Blake, also fond of hyperbole, "They'd immediately Go out."[32] With Blake, faith is really a form of imagination. "I believe" must also mean "I imagine." Reducing faith to passive doctrinal compliance is simplistic; the Greek *pistis* suggests an active force, the opposite of mincing self-doubt.[33]

With belief and faith we have a point of contact with parapsychology. The American parapsychologist Gertrude Schmeidler coined the expression "sheep-goat effect."[34] In psychic experiments, subjects (the "sheep") are reported to perform above chance when they *believe* that they will. For belief to be effective it must apply to the task at hand. It's not a matter of general belief but how you feel at the moment. Studies find a connection between ad hoc confidence and paranormal success.

Trust and confidence are related to another psychically enhancing variable, the group mind. There are things individuals do best in a special group setting. Psychologist Kenneth Batcheldor modeled table-tilting experiments he conducted on the Victorian séance. He learned that doubt, hesitation, and uncertainty were fatal to obtaining the desired effects. To succeed, the table tilters had to relax, get into a playful mood, and above all, maintain "unwavering conviction" of success. The reports show they achieved levitation of tables "without contact"—without their hands on the tables.

They learned how to do this thing by practicing a special group skill, harmonious, effortless intentionality, and did so in a psychologically responsive atmosphere.[35] Firm belief and conviction were fundamental. This is crucial. A special group dynamic, based on firm belief and conviction, can amplify latent paranormal powers. Similarly, Joseph's extraordinary performances grew in the special group dynamic of the Baroque Reformation.

John Palmer found that spontaneity is the best predictor of psychic capacity. Rigid, regimented attitudes and lifestyles work against letting psi manifest. Another predictor of psi is the "presence of a hypnogogiclike state of consciousness," which tends "to encourage spontaneity insofar as they (responses) are associated with a breakdown of rationalistic or linear . . . patterns of mentation."[36] Freedom from rationalistic inhibitions, unqualified trust and confidence, increases the probability of a psi event.

If spontaneity favors the occurrence of psi, it seems clear why it can't be produced on demand. For the same reason—the need for incubation—creative works cannot be produced on demand. In John 3:8, Jesus explains to Nicodemus what happens when a person is born "in the spirit": "The wind blows where it wishes and you hear the sound of it, but do not know where it comes from and where it is going: so is everyone who is born of the spirit." The unpredictable nature of the spirit resembles the psi-conducive states of spontaneity and hypnagogia,[37] described in hundreds of modern experimental studies. Modern research supports ancient intuition.

Modern PK research confirms the traditional belief in the power of faith. Recall Jesus bidding Peter to walk with him on water; Peter does so but loses his *pistis* (his confident expectation of success) and starts to sink. "But seeing the wind he became afraid, and beginning to sink he cried out." After saving him, Jesus says to Peter, "O you of little faith, why did you doubt?" (Mat. 14:30–31) The image is iconic of "the power of faith." Could a change of mental state alter our relationship to gravity? Peter walks on water, is frightened out of his *pistis*, and starts to sink.

People who believe in their psychic abilities are more likely to produce effects; people who doubt tend to miss the target, sometimes to a degree exceeding chance. They prove psi in spite of themselves, but in a negative way called "psi-missing." Our intangible beliefs, positive or negative, can directly shape the course of events; belief is a creative force. Assumptions about what is possible make a difference to how we experience the world. This now shades into another typical religious belief.

BELIEF IN THE POWER OF PRAYER

Religious systems affirm belief in higher beings—in gods, goddesses, angels, patron saints, and the like. All manner of spiritual agencies are believed to exist. One might then ask: Can we interact and communicate with these agencies? Ingratiate ourselves with them? Until modern times, people generally believed in the power of prayer and assumed they could indeed interact in meaningful ways with the unseen powers. In religious America, 2013, however, a poll from the Pew Research Center found that 55 percent of the population prayed at least once a day. Our discussion here is for those who find the idea of prayer difficult to entertain.

The physician Larry Dossey has described many historical and experimental studies that show the healing and even the more rare harmful aspects of prayer. Dossey's views on prayer and the parapsychology of spiritual wellness are synthesized in his concretely visionary *One Mind* (2013). This big idea was already present in his earlier, best-selling study, *Healing Words*: "Prayer says something incalculably important about who we are and what our destiny may be. . . . Prayer reaches outside the here-and-now; it operates at a distance and outside the present moment. Since prayer is initiated by a mental action, this implies that there is some aspect of our psyche that is also genuinely nonlocal. If so, then something of ourselves is infinite in space and time—thus omnipresent, eternal and immortal."[38]

From a parapsychological perspective, it is possible to think of prayer as any attempt to interact with the extended mind that Dossey calls "nonlocal." The forms of such interaction are infinite. A Zen meditation is a kind of prayer and so is the sand painting of a Native American. Blake said that art was his prayer and the music of Palestrina and Hildegard of Bingen were prayers as are the dances of the Sufis. Prayer, we could say, is the language of response to belief in the transcendent. Forms of prayer vary from grossly petitionary to cosmically mystical. Some petition for help with everyday troubles; others pray to transcend themselves in contemplation. There are prayers of thanksgiving, prayers for the dead, prayers of adoration, and there are unitive forms of prayer in the contemplative manner of the mystics.

L. R. Farnell[39] studied the "evolution of prayer," and found it began with runes and spells and the assumption that words possessed magical power. These were the rudiments of prayer. The difference between magic and religion is a difference of grammar. Magic is performed in the imperative mood; it tries to coerce the god, force obedience by command or suggestion. Religion politely asks for help and speaks in the optative and potential mood. "Lord, grant me the wisdom to cope with this impossible situation!" The heroes in the Homeric epics call on the gods for strength in the optative mood. Like the subjunctive mood, the optative invokes the potential; the key word is *may* not *must*. Prayer moves on a spectrum from incantatory coercion to optative mysticism. In the higher forms of prayer, the mood shifts toward self-effacement, one strives to merge in love with the supreme One—St. Teresa's prayer of quiet or the prayer of adoration that Joseph practiced.

Is prayer just a symptom of the existentially maladapted? Prayer has been around for a long time and must have served a purpose beyond repeated self-deception. For some religious skeptics, it might be possible to talk about prayer in light of the well-known medical effectiveness of the placebo.[40] Belief that an injection of water received from your doctor is an effective drug, and your medical problem may clear up. We saw how that worked with "Mr. Wright," the cancer patient, and his belief in Krebiozen; belief freed him completely from cancer and kept death at bay until he lost his "belief."

There must be something to believe in and you must sincerely believe in it for the "placebo" to be effective. From one perspective, belief in God is the ultimate placebo; we have something powerful and worthy to believe in and something that many feel motivated to trust and expect results from. There is also the factor of group support, and we know how helpful that can be from parapsychological studies, especially the experiments of Kenneth Batcheldor.[41] In a previous chapter, I tried to show that Catholic Reformation culture was the ideal belief-setting to elicit Joseph's peculiar mystical talents, including the levitations.

A great deal of evidence proves the power of placebo, which takes advantage of the "belief" variable; on the evidence we already have, prayer addressed to a higher spiritual entity should produce extra chance rates of effective results, *at least as much as the average placebo*.

Placebos are barely less effective than antidepressant drugs. Whenever some new drug or procedure is put on the market and tested, the placebo works almost as well as the real drug. The persistent percentage of responsiveness to the sheer power of belief, evident from so many varied systematic studies, explains the perennial appeal of prayer. The general experience of humankind seems to be that prayer works: not reliably, or fairly, but in odd, unpredictable ways for a certain percentage of people.

There is another possible connection between prayer and parapsychology. Recall the discussion of Helmut Schmidt's micro-PK experiments and the role of goal-oriented thinking in achieving results. The subject concentrates on the goal, but doesn't worry about how to realize the goal. When a person is praying, she thinks about the desired goal and leaves it to the higher power to do the job. Some people might be better at doing this than others; better at imagining the end-state, better at not pushing too hard, better at letting go and leaving things to the other.

The placebo must work because of how the believer imagines the end-state; the more steadfast the image of the outcome, the more likely results will follow. Of course, as John Palmer concluded in his classic 1978 review, parapsychology is a probabilistic science. So is prayer a probabilistic art. Joseph would agree. He made the proposals, he said, the rest was up to God. Joseph's intercessions, as recounted by his chroniclers, were sought after by everyone; the intense belief in him as intercessor might well have produced an *extra potent* placebo effect.

In the nineteenth century, Francis Galton put prayer to the test but without conclusive results. An often-quoted study by cardiologist Randolph Byrd of the San Francisco General Medical Center describes the therapeutic effects of intercessory prayer on 192 patients measured against a control group of 201 patients who were not prayed for. The experiment went on for ten months in a coronary care unit.[42] The results showed that the prayed-for group significantly required fewer antibiotics, less ventilator assistance, and fewer diuretics than the control group. Nothing miraculous, but statistically significant improvements.

H. H. Price, the Oxford philosopher, had a theory of petitionary prayer based on two concepts: telepathy and the common unconscious. When I pray for something I need or desire, he said, I am in effect "broadcasting" my request by telepathy to the common unconscious. Sometimes my call may elicit a response, perhaps in the form of a favorable coincidence, a rush of confidence to do such and such, leading in some unforeseen way to the prayer being answered.

In my opinion, the possibility of effective prayer follows from some basic mental facts often not properly appreciated. But grant the existence of psi—ESP *and* PK—and it is not hard to imagine how petitionary prayer might occasionally produce tangible results. Nobody knows how wishes, needs, and goals can mobilize latent extrasensory and psychokinetic capacities. But we know that they sometimes do. That simple fact should change our picture of the world. On the other hand, one should be aware of the whimsical nature of this intelligent force, described by some researchers as systematically elusive and evasive.[43] Still, the bald fact of *psycho*kinesis allows us to imagine how our aims, our hopes, and our goals—in short, our prayers—may be realized by virtue of exercising something we all possess, the capacity for *intentional* acts of consciousness.

Consciousness studies ratify the belief in the power of prayer or what's called distant intentionality. Prayer in this sense might be of interest to nontheists or agnostics, for it involves no necessary assumptions about deity; one's prayers may be answered but how or what answers remains a mystery. As you can believe in life after death and not be tied to any religious doctrine, you can also believe in the power of prayer while laying aside all traditional conceptions of piety and divinity.

Let me end this section with a reference to a survey conducted in 1997 and published in the prestigious *Nature*, which found that 39 percent of mathematicians and scientists entertain the belief in some kind of supreme being with which it is possible to engage in prayer.[44] The parapsychology of religion should speak to this part of the scientific community, or to anybody curious about the links between science and spirituality.

BELIEF IN A LIFE AFTER DEATH

Most religious systems have a story about what comes after life, although it varies from culture to culture. The question in our sophisticated age is whether the belief in a hereafter has any factual support at all. The reply is that psychical research has interesting and thought-provoking things to say about the question. And in the minds of objective reviewers of this research, there exist matters of fact that are best explained by assuming some form of survival. Whether the evidence for life after death is conclusive is another question.

A critical review of the evidence would require lengthy treatment; fortunately, there are some good books on the subject to which we can refer.[45] All that is needed for the purpose of this chapter is to describe the types of afterlife data available for study and to make a few remarks of a general nature.

Belief in a life after death is logically independent of any religious belief; the survival of human personality might just be a natural fact, if it is a fact. In itself, it may have nothing to do with religion. Survival does not automatically imply anything religious. Nevertheless, the different religious belief-systems have taken over the way people imagine what the afterlife will be. So it seems likely that if there is an afterlife the form it takes will be shaped by our cultural expectations. Believers in reincarnation might enter interim states that prepare them for another round of existence, American Indians will go to their Happy Hunting Grounds, and Christians will find themselves in places resembling heaven or hell or, if they are Catholic, purgatory. It is also possible that people convinced there is no afterlife will experience nothing at all when they die; they might just sleep through their afterlife.

Another general point worth making: if materialism is true, survival is almost certainly impossible. If my I-world really resides in my brain, the end of my brain is the end of me, and that's that. Needless to say, the drift of ideas in this book does not support that premise. Survival, I am convinced, must at least be possible. As noted earlier: if consciousness preexists the brain, brain death does not entail consciousness death.

But the big question we need to ask is: Are there any factual reasons to believe that—logic permitting—we *really do* survive? Is survival of death—persisting personal consciousness—really the best explanation of certain facts, observations, or reported narratives? In some cases the answer seems yes, but that is a matter for the reader to decide, and it's not our primary concern here. The present thesis is that psychical research represents a way to more or less confirm or disconfirm the belief in a life after death, and hence speaks to the old quarrel between science and religion. As usual, the devil is in the details; so we need to look at particular case histories, and there are several types.

The Out-of-Body Experience (OBE)

The first I'll mention is interesting mainly because of its subjective impact on the experiencer, often resulting in lifestyle changes and a transformed worldview. People who have this experience are often left with a powerful impression that the afterlife—*their* afterlife—is a real thing. They experience themselves moving about in space, separate from their bodies, a clear center of awareness, memory intact, a sense of freedom and exhilaration. Depending on the clarity and intensity of the experience, it apparently seems like a vivid preview of the next world, of a new dimension of reality. Any number of situations might trigger these out-of-body excursions: extreme fatigue, fasting, fascination, fever, drugs, meditation, trauma, or near death, to mention a few.

An OBE is said to be *veridical* if it involves observing something in the environment made *at a distance* from one's body—later determined to have in fact *been there*. That sort of thing is not supposed to happen, according to mainstream views of perception, but there are plenty of well-documented examples proving the reality of the "outness" of the experience.[46]

But an OBE, even a veridical one, is not proof of life after death. After all, your body is still alive, even if you *feel as if* you have left it behind. But still the experience can alter one's perception of life and death, alter one's sense of identity, of reality, as in the case of St. Paul's famous conversion on the road to Damascus. St. Paul's experience may be described as world-historical, for it led to bringing the Christian "good news" onto the world stage of history: "I know a man in Christ, who, fourteen years ago, was caught up—whether still in the body or out of the body, I do not know, God knows—right into the third heaven . . . into paradise and (who) heard things which must not and cannot be put into human language."[47]

For Joseph, who spent so much time camping out in the next world, "survival" would have seemed a dull way of referring to ecstasy. Increasingly, the idea of another world seems abstract and remote to most educated people today, but for someone like Joseph such experiences were not rare; as a result, from Joseph's perspective, everyday life in a gravity-bound body was what seemed abstract and remote.

Mediumship

William James discovered the gifted mental medium Leonora Piper (1857–1950). The initially skeptical Richard Hodgson, trained in law and philosophy, worked very closely with Piper and was eventually convinced of the reality of postmortem existence by the so-called "G. P." case, on which he laboriously worked.[48] "G. P." were the initials of George Pellew, a young friend of Hodgson who died accidentally in New York City and whose persona was said to turn up shortly after his death at the Leonora Piper's séances. There he reportedly took control of Mrs. Piper's bodily organism and used it as an instrument to articulate his thoughts.

The G. P. case was extraordinary. Once the self-declared presence of Pellew appeared established, Hodgson brought 130 sitters to interact with the entranced Piper and the G. P. persona that seemed to be speaking through her. Among the 130 visitors who were kept blind as to the presumptive presence of Pellew, thirty knew the young man in life.

Hodgson recorded the sittings in painstaking detail (the report is hundreds of pages long). Among the thirty who knew Pellew in life, "Pellew," using the vocal chords of Leonora Piper, spoke, recognized and interacted with all thirty who knew "him" in life, *but with none of the others*. And he did so with the appropriate speech and mannerisms, convincing the most skeptical that they were really interacting with the deceased George Pellew himself.

This was a spectacular exhibition of paranormal deception on the part of Piper's subliminal self *or* one of the most detailed, prolonged interviews with a dead soul. On either interpretation, the resolute materialist is challenged to give a plausible explanation.[49]

After Sidgwick, Myers, Gurney, and the other founders of psychical research died, a new type of evidence appeared, designed, it was concluded, to avoid the criticisms of mediumship that troubled the founders: a series of cases of so-called "cross correspondences" are probably the least known and possibly the most erudite mass of evidence for life after death. The early researchers knew that as long as written or living sources of information could unconsciously be scanned by a living medium's use of her psi powers, proof of the afterlife would fall short.

As the story is told, Myers and his codeceased colleagues devised a new experiment to prove their identity from their postmortem redoubt. The skeleton of the plan was this. The excarnate researchers took control of several mediums who were not in touch with each other and were physically separated, sometimes by continents. Each medium was given obscure references to classical literature, often in Greek and Latin, bits and pieces, which by themselves failed to communicate any meaning.

In effect, they were given isolated clues to a puzzle. As the experiment progressed, it became apparent that a single external intelligence was using the different mediums—who turned out to be the deceased Frederic Myers who had the classical knowledge to perform such an experiment. Everything seemed designed to prove an external, *ex*carnate intelligence, giving the different mediums parts of the puzzle that was slowly solved through the promptings of the communicators. These recondite cross-correspondence experiments went on for thirty years.[50]

From the accrued evidence one might be tempted to conclude that Myers and his colleagues survived death. Call it a postmortem group experiment, performed by the learned founders of psychical research, who sought to prove once and for all that death is just a change of scene in the long play of life. Still, the cross-correspondence evidence may have been a brilliant performance orchestrated subliminally by some very talented but living mediums. If *that* were true, it would still be a momentous achievement and worthy of thought and reflection.

Reincarnation

Ian Stevenson, a psychiatrist from the University of Virginia, investigated reports of children with memories, behaviors, and bodily marks said to stem from previous lives—what he called cases of the reincarnation type (CORT). Stevenson traveled around the world, interviewing his subjects, testing and confirming statements from his various sources. Reincarnation memories rarely persist beyond the age of eight, he found, and then sink below the margins of awareness.

Besides specific cognitive memories—in one case, a boy tracked down the woman he was married to when he died and showed he knew intimate facts of their previous life together—Stevenson found peculiar behaviors, aversions and attractions, skills and mannerisms, carried over from life to life. Also, using medical records, he found that specific bodily marks, linked with a traumatic death, were sometimes physically reproduced in the body of the apparently reincarnated subject.[51]

The research produced a body of accounts that looks like evidence for reincarnation. Without attempting to assess the value of this rich and carefully garnered material, which is certainly "suggestive," we can say that parapsychology *contributes toward* ratifying the widely held religious belief in reincarnation. This in turn enriches the science-religion debate, but it also underscores the limitations of parapsychology. Nothing I'm aware of supports any of the large claims about the moral ideas of karma and reincarnation, used for millennia as the basis of an oppressive caste system.

But the research does lend support to the perennial religious belief that the human personality is not extinguished at death. All this seems like a positive contribution to an important problem in the study of religion, which is the existence, as well as the fate, of the "soul." The soul is a word that has come to sound strange, and yet all it really refers to is our interior, our mental life, the most intimate of things, oneself.

Ghosts and Apparitions

Another type of so-called survival evidence comes in the shape of ghosts, wraiths, specters, dreams, visions—*apparitions* of one sort or another, and staple of the storytelling imagination.

People sometimes ask, "Do you believe in ghosts?" Wrong question. The evidence is overwhelming that people from all walks of life and culture report experiencing things they call ghosts, spirits, or apparitions. The important question is, "What are they?" Beguiling phantoms of deluded brains or revenants of the once living? It turns out that among the family of experiences that come under this heading, a number imply important things about the possibility of conscious survival.[52]

We find, for example, so-called crisis apparitions: at the moment of death, a person appears to another at a distance, a friend or a loved one. Later, it is confirmed that exactly when the apparition occurred, the friend or loved one had died. What to make of this? Meaningless coincidence? How could a soulless biological mechanism produce such a well-timed apparition? As it turns out, around the hour of death curious things do seem to happen.

For example, another expression of departure from this world produces a physical signal, like a clock stopping at the moment of death or a picture of the deceased spontaneously breaking or falling from its hook on the wall. They announce the moment of death, the last stop on their earthly time ride. Ernesto Bozzano[53] published a collection of these "telekinetic events (occurring) at the moment of death." It looks as if spirits parting from this world like to let us know they're leaving. These last farewells may not carry much weight as proof of survival, but they are attention-getters that prompt our curiosity to search for more telling clues.

There is an entertaining class of events that bear on the afterlife belief: stories of haunted houses. The story repeats itself with regularity. An invisible intruder sneaks around a house and causes accidents, destroys or moves objects, gives off stenches, makes noises, affects room temperature, is heard groaning and moaning, causes household pets to flee in terror, seems implicated in unexplained illness or even death, and generally tries to drive the victims out of their infested house or, if need be, their minds. The history of the house is dug up and foul deeds that transpired there are exposed.[54] These infestations do take place, as do the mysterious (and often quite frightening) haggings that David Hufford has described in his classic study, *The Terror That Comes in the Night* (1982).

Among the different kinds of theoretically interesting spooks, there is one I rank as a favorite. There are cases where it appears as if information is revealed that only the deceased person could have known. James Chaffin died in 1921; in his last-known will of 1905, he left his whole estate to his third son, Marshall. In fact, in 1919, Mr. Chaffin wrote but for some reason hid a second will. No living person knew this document existed. Four years after, James Chaffin Jr. began to dream of his dead father, who directed him to the location of the last will, which in the company of witnesses he found hidden in an old Bible. The latest will distributed the estate evenly among all of Chaffin's sons and was probated in the courts of North Carolina.[55] Interesting story, don't you think?

The point to underscore: Psychical researchers—quite apart from faith, scripture, or ideology—have carefully collected, studied, and assessed various kinds of evidence that suggest the real possibility of postmortem survival. Despite the near monumental indifference toward this body of information on the part of most people, the types of evidence are increasing. Prior to 1975, NDE was virtually unknown; that changed after the publication of Raymond Moody's *Life after Life*. There was very little organized study of reincarnation phenomena until Ian Stevenson began his research in the 1960s. Cases of *terminal lucidity* have recently appeared in the literature; people who have lost their mental faculties from brain lesions, from Alzheimer's, schizophrenia, or whatever, regain them just before dying.[56]

This must be puzzling to materialists. Why should a wrecked brain suddenly become functional just before death? Terminal lucidity could be viewed as a consequence of consciousness disengaging from damaged brains at the approach of death. If postmortem survival is real there must be a stage, or process, of the surviving consciousness separating from the dying brain. During that transition, one would repossess his mental faculties and use his body to speak to others, which might explain terminal lucidity. Of course, more work on the puzzle of terminal lucidity needs to be done.

Let me mention one more type of experience that points to the survival of personal consciousness. Cited in the introduction as a "consciousness activist," Mai Lan Gustafsson, the anthropologist, examines a type of case history resulting from modern military technologies that specialize in annihilation.[57] Gustafsson collected 190 case histories mainly from Hanoi about individuals said to be possessed, assaulted, haunted by "angry ghosts" (*con ma*). These were victims living in the psychic wake of a war that officially ended in 1975 and began with the French colonialists returning to Saigon in 1946 after the Second World War.

Accounts of angry ghosts and their victims were epidemic. It was so bad that the Communist government, officially disbelieving in spirits, acknowledged the economic impact of the problem, affirming that angry ghosts were indeed a "public health menace."

According to the Confucian *li* (rites), proper burial is essential to the well-being of the deceased. When the *li* are done properly, the departed become guardian spirits (*lo tien*); they become a source of guidance and good fortune for the family. Done improperly—or not at all—they may become angry ghosts. The *li* cannot be performed without an intact body—a head or a limb won't do.

In the war, Americans killed five million Vietnamese and 300,000 bodies were never found, thus preventing the *li* from occurring in 300,000 Vietnamese families. There were about 300,000 orphans, also a telling statistic. The important number is the 300,000 missing dead bodies—annihilated by the magnificent American war machine.

In Vietnam that meant 300,000 angry ghosts wandering about looking for ways to vent their fury and frustration. Suppose the invisible afterworld corridors do indeed swarm with such agents of ill will, conscious entities without prospect of escape from their psychic inferno? Reading the horror stories recorded by Gustafsson, it's hard to dismiss them as imaginary or self-inflicted.

Regarding the main point of this chapter, psychical research is the only discipline with much to say of intellectual value about what may come after death, if anything. What the facts show from various sources—mediumship; apparitions; reincarnation memories, behaviors, and bodily marks; out-of-body and NDEs; reports of angry ghosts, and so on—is a case for survival *at least* suggestive, and *sometimes* compelling, for me, as the "G. P." case. The religious imagination soars beyond the humble limits of the evidence; the scientific imagination in the main ignores the evidence. The parapsychology of religion explores the rich ground between these worthless extremes.

THE BELIEF IN MIRACLES

There is one more common religious belief deeply at odds with the modern mindset—the belief in miracles. A big part of the problem is the way the word is defined. People talk sensibly about the "miracles" of modern science, and the term is at home in poetry and the arts.

Trouble begins with the theological sense of *miracle*, the sense in which God is assumed to "violate" some law of nature. For instance, some would be troubled by the idea that God violated the law of gravity so Joseph could levitate. But this legalistic conception of miracle misses the primitive sense of the word, which, rooted in the Sanskrit *smi*, makes the word *smile*.[58] Etymologically, a miracle is something that makes us smile with wonder. Fixated on the humorless conception of miracle, David Hume wrote an essay designed to prove nothing miraculous could ever conceivably occur.[59]

What would Hume have said if he witnessed Joseph levitate? How did he in fact respond to the events said to occur at the gravesite of the Abbè de Paris? That riot of psychophysical surreality is known to history as the "convulsionaries of St. Medard."[60] Clearly, things sometimes go perversely against uniformity of experience, as did the strange and frequently grotesque events at St. Medard's cemetery. I'm afraid Joseph would have no less flummoxed Hume.

And yet, according to the philosopher, experience is the basis of our knowledge of matters of fact, proposing "that causes and effects are discoverable, not by reason, but by experience."[61] In that case we cannot say levitation is *impossible*; experience is the sole arbiter in judging matters of fact. Follow Hume and reject every departure from "uniform" or "customary" experience and progress in art, science, and life would be impossible. The first person to start a fire by rubbing twigs together would be routed by the mass of non–fire-starters, if they were Humeans.

We should look more closely at the essay. To his credit, Hume places before us just the evidence we need to question his main claim:

> There surely never was a greater number of miracles ascribed to one person, than those, which were lately said to have been wrought in France upon the tomb of Abbe Paris, the famous Jansenist, with whose sanctity the people were so deluded. The curing of the sick, giving hearing to the deaf, and sight to the blind, were everywhere talked of as the usual effects of the holy sepulcher. But what is more extraordinary; many of the miracles were immediately proved upon the spot, before judges of unquestioned integrity, attested by witnesses of credit and distinction, in a learned age, and on the most eminent theatre that is now in the world. Nor is this all: A relation of them was published and dispersed everywhere; nor were the Jesuits, a learned body, supported by the civil magistrate, and determined enemies to those opinions, in whose favour the miracles were said to have been wrought, ever able distinctly to refute or detect them.

He adds a lengthy footnote providing further details in support of the extraordinary claims, along with useful bibliographical references: "Many of the miracles of Abbe Paris were proved immediately by witnesses of the officialty or bishop's court at Paris, under the eye of cardinal Noailles, whose character for integrity and capacity was never contested even by his enemies."

The new archbishop did not favor the Jansenists, but Hume reports that "22 rectors or curés of Paris, with infinite earnestness, press him to examine those miracles, which they assert to be known to the whole world, and indisputably certain."

He then criticizes (we are still in his footnote) the Molinist (Jesuit) party for unfairly repudiating the case of Mademoiselle le Franc, but who "soon found themselves overwhelmed by a cloud of new witnesses, one hundred and twenty in number, most of them persons of credit and substance in Paris, who gave oath for the miracle."

All these creditable persons testified under oath that something unexplained had occurred.

> Mons. Heraut, the Lieutenant de Police, whose vigilance, penetration, activity, and extensive intelligence have been much talked of. This magistrate, who by the nature of his office is almost absolute, was invested with full powers, on purpose to suppress or discredit these miracles; and he frequently seized immediately, and examined the witnesses and subjects of them: But never could reach anything satisfactory against them.

And neither does David Hume reach anything satisfactory against the reports about St. Medard. What then does he conclude from all this? Returning to the main body of his text we read: "And what have we to oppose to such a cloud of witnesses, but the absolute impossibility or miraculous nature of the events, which they relate? And this surely, in the eyes of all reasonable people, will alone be regarded as a sufficient refutation."

And so, all the eyewitness observations and judgments of numerous, highly credible witnesses—placed in the balance against David Hume's belief in what is possible—are reduced to nothing!

The philosopher could have avoided this embarrassing display of incoherence by using the word *miracle* to refer to any apparently unexplained event in the context of religious experience. Hume's resistance to miracles was political, an indirect way to undermine the authority of the Church. The Church sometimes used miracle claims to bolster its authority, but rather than deny facts as a way to combat the Church, Hume could have saved the phenomena by redefining them as natural but unexplained. Challenge the privileged claims of the Church, by all means, but not at the cost of repressing masses of interesting human experiences.

Records from Catholic hagiography contain testimony that supports our relatively modest but still important sense of the word "miracle."[62] Thanks to a legalistic Catholic Church, eyewitness testimony is required during trials of beatification and canonization. In chapters 2 and 3 we found reports of "miracles" in the sense of the word that suggests realities that cannot be understood by present physical science. In that sense, we are surrounded by the miracles of life and by the most radical miracle, consciousness, without which the entire universe collapses into nonentity.

Stripped of supernaturalistic labels, "miracles" may be thought of as manifestations of latent human capacities, mostly *very* slightly manifest, as Dean Radin's surveys (1997) have shown, but occasionally, in special circumstances, so startling it might evoke a smile of wonder and prompt one to say, "It's a *miracle!*" We have reflected upon examples of this type that center around the story of Joseph of Copertino. And as we saw in making comparisons with other cultures, examples exist in abundance.

Not to be daunted as Hume was, to believe in miracles would signify no more than to believe there are certain facts of experience that transcend the horizons of reductive materialism. We should welcome the extraordinary as provocations to think and to smile and wonder. How to interpret and explore the X dimension of reality we have been dwelling on should be a free, open-ended venture. My conclusion is that parapsychology provides the missing ingredient in Rorty's and Vattimo's vision of the future of religion—the transcendent. The Latin root of this word means "climbing over." We are always trying to "climb over" our limits, always on the move toward the great more, the great next. Transcendent? A sense of the infinite possibilities of life.

NOTES

1. Chapple, 1990, p. 61.
2. GP, p. 375.
3. The expression *psychical research* was used by the English founders and focused on evidence for life after death; *parapsychology* is the more recent term associated with twentieth-century experimental *psi* studies. The Greek letter *psi* refers to the first letter of the word *psyche,* referring to the whole range of paranormal effects, psychokinesis, and extrasensory perception.
4. For a recent example, see the anthology by Charles Tart (1997).
5. See Taimni (1961, passim).
6. Augustine, 1980, p. 980.
7. Redgrove, 1921, p. 68.
8. Quoted in de Vesme, vol. 1, p. xlvii.
9. James, 1971a, p. 133.
10. Myers, 1905, p. 29.
11. Ibid., p. 33.
12. See Gauld, 1968.

13. Myers, 1903, vol. 2, pp. 284–92.
14. Ibid., pp. 286–87.
15. HP, vol. 2. pp. 260–61.
16. Personal communication.
17. Ibid., p. 290.
18. See, for example, Trevor Hamilton, *Immortal Longings* (2009); Kelly and Kelly, *Irreducible Mind* (2007), a massive study inspired by Myers; and a chapter in Jeffrey Kripal's *Authors of the Impossible* (2010). See also Andre Breton, *The Automatic Message* (1933/1997); Breton wrote of Myers's "gothic psychiatry" and claimed him a forerunner of surrealism.
19. Bergson, 1935, p. 317.
20. Ibid., p. 7.
21. De Vesme, 1931, p. xvii.
22. Ibid., p. 127.
23. Ennemoser, 1970, pp. i–ii.
24. Ennemoser, 1970, vol. 1, p. vi.
25. Evans-Wentz, 1960.
26. For a critique of the principle of natural selection, see Fodor and Piatelli, 2013.
27. For a comprehensive historical study of the American metaphysical religions of this period, see Catherine Albanese's *A Republic of Mind and Spirit* (2007).
28. See Mauskopf and McVaugh, 1980, pp. 72–73, 86–87.
29. There are all kinds of exceptions to this, for example, Francis Collins, a Christian who led the effort to crack the code of the human genome. See his *Language of God: A Scientist Presents Evidence for Belief* (2006).
30. Huxley, 1945, p. 28.
31. See Abbott-Smith, 1986, p. 362. The word stresses the sense of trustworthiness and reliability.
32. Keynes, 1972, p. 433.
33. It can also merge with overweening fanaticism.
34. Wolman, 1977, p. 144.
35. Batcheldor, 1984.
36. Palmer, 1978.
37. See the extremely interesting book *Hypnagogia*, by Andreas Mavromatis, 1987.
38. Dossey, 1993, *Healing Words*, p. 6. See also Dossey's *Be Careful What You Pray For* (1997) and the comprehensive *One Mind* (2013).
39. See Farnell, 1905.
40. The article on "placebo effect" in Wikipedia provides access to a huge collection of scientific papers on every aspect of this widely studied phenomenon; the range of the effect is very extensive.
41. See Batcheldor.
42. Hodgson, 1898, pp. 284–582.
43. Kennedy, 2003.
44. Larson and Witham, 1997, pp. 435–36.

45. See Ducasse, 1961; Broad, 1962; Gauld, 1982; Almeder, 1992; Griffin, 1997; Braude, 2003; Grosso, 2004; Kelly and Kelly, 2007.

46. Alvarado, 2000; Tart, 2009, pp. 199–220.

47. 2 Cor. 12:2–4.

48. Hodgson, 1898, pp. 284–582.

49. Hodgson, 1898.

50. Saltmarsh, 1938.

51. For an introduction to Stevenson's extensive research, see Stevenson, 1974, 1987, 1997a, and 1997b.

52. Maxwell-Stuart, 2006.

53. Bozzano, 1948.

54. Flammarion, 1924, passim.

55. Richmond, 1983, p. 43.

56. Greyson and Nahm, 2009, pp. 942–44.

57. Gustafsson, *War and Shadows: the Haunting of Vietnam* (2009).

58. Skeat, 1963, p. 329.

59. Hume, 1748/1955, see sec. 10.

60. Mathieu, 2006.

61. Italics Hume's, 1748/1955, p. 42. All the quotes from Hume are from his discussion of miracles. See Hume 1748/1955.

62. For example, Thurston, 1952.

Appendix

In this book, which raises questions about the mainstream view of mind, I focus on one extraordinary case history as my point of departure. St. Joseph of Copertino, who, although not a popular or famous saint of the stature of St. Paul, St. Francis, or St. Teresa, enjoys a more narrowly focused fame as wonder-worker *par excellence*.

The critical reader will surely want to know the documentary sources of the narrative. I first encountered the story of Joseph in the writings of the Jesuit scholar Herbert Thurston and in an essay by the skeptical writer Eric Dingwall in *Human Oddities*.[1] Dingwall's essay contains an invaluable discussion of sources,[2] in which he asks why in modern times there are fewer and fewer reports of levitation: "Is it because the progress of science renders the exposure of such claims easier to carry out and so makes belief in them more difficult, or is it because this very progress has so transformed our ways of life and thought that, in some subtle manner, the production of such phenomenona is thereby inhibited?"[3] These and other books are cited in the references.

Here I want to call attention to the sources that form the basis of the narrative of Joseph's life and, in particular, the eyewitness testimony to the claims about controversial phenomena such as levitation. I would have had no interest whatsoever in writing this book unless I was convinced there was more than sufficient testimony to justify the efforts required for the project.

Domenico Bernini's *Vita di Ven Giuseppe da Copertino* is singled out for its abundant quotations of eyewitness testimony to Joseph's reported phenomena. It has been reprinted, translated, and abridged several times in several languages. For the present study, Cynthia Clough made the first English translation in a version I edited and abridged. The reader will find many references to Bernini's reproduced sworn eyewitness testimonies in this *Vita*. Bernini was aware of the inherently incredible nature of some of

Joseph's public behaviors and keeps reminding readers that the reports are based on credible eyewitness testimony. Bernini states that his *Vita* of Joseph was nothing but a "transcription" of public records; no doubt an exaggeration, but the intent is clear enough. He was commissioned by Pope Innocent XIII to write the *Vita*, which he dedicated to the pope. It is a work of hagiography, geared to exhibit Joseph as a great servant of God. It doesn't follow that he made things up, though sometimes he repeats stories as if they might be true but offers no satisfactory testimony for them. The abbreviation for the text is DB, and the page numbers refer to our unpublished manuscript.

There are important, earlier documents written by living witnesses—for example, the earliest biography by Roberto Nuti (published in 1678). Books on Joseph, and events celebrating his cult, continued to appear through the eighteenth and nineteenth centuries. In the twentieth century, however, a preeminent scholar studied the friar's case, assembled the pertinent documents, and provides the most complete picture of his life; the books of Gustavo Parisciani have been invaluable for primary materials. Parisciani's 1,083-page *magnum opus* is called *San Giuseppe Da Copertino: Alla Luce dei Nuovi Documenti* (*In Light of New Documents*). Dingwall, in his scholarly account of Joseph, noted how hard it was to locate copies of the various *processi* ("trials"). Part of the problem was that Joseph was moved around so many times by the Church that records and sworn depositions lay in obscure convents scattered around Italy. In fact, a large quantity of eyewitness testimony was formally deposed within two years of Joseph's death, and at different places such as Grotella, Nardo, Assisi, Rome, Naples, Pietra Rubbia, Fossombrone, and Osimo. Parisciani collected as much of these missing documents as he could. Hence the subtitle of his book—"in light of new documents." In the introduction, Parisciani emphasizes his aim to describe the facts and present the real events of the saint's life accurately and chronologically. Accurate history, he says, leaves us with a "living" saint, "above all human" (*sopratutto umano*).

With Bernini, Parisciani provides the main source (five books) apt to contain original testimony for the reports about Joseph's life and phenomena. The 1963 *magnum opus* has appendices listing in detail archives, compendia, summaries, vitas, perorations, panegyrics, even literary dramas (e.g., Theodori Filippo's *Il Volatore Mistico* [1963]), and an opera by Pietro Metastasio. There is an extensive bibliography, including an article from a popular magazine about an American actress, Elizabeth Cobb, from the fifties, describing how she was converted by Joseph to the Catholic faith. This key source contains letters, Joseph's poetry (pp.1016–29), and copies of other major documents such as Prosper Lambertini's statement on his beatification.

The sources for sworn eyewitness testimony are found in the various trials (*processi*), which are listed, described, and quoted at length in the books of

Bernini, Nuti, Rosmi, Parisciani, and others. Don Arcangelo Rosmi, diarist and intimate friend of Joseph, stated that he stopped after recording seventy instances of Joseph's anomalous ascents; many more testimonies would eventually be deposed. Again we have Gustavo Parisciani, *I Tre Diari dell'Abate Arcangelo Rosmi di San Giuseppe da Copertino*. Also, see Archivo Segreto Vaticano, Fondo Riti 2039 (no date given here but Rosmi's diaries were eyewitness documents).

NOTES

1. Dingwall, 1962, pp. 9–37.
2. Ibid., pp. 162–71.
3. Ibid., p. 162.

REFERENCES

Processus Auctoritate Ordinaria in Civitate Assisiensi, Fabricato ab Anno 1666 ad Anno 1669. Archivio Segreto Vaticano, Fondo Riti 2039.

Acta Sanctorum, Sep. vol. 5.

Roberto Nuti. (1678). *Vita del Servo di Dio Fra Giuseppe di Copertino.* Palermo, Italy: Ordine de'Minori Conventuali.

DB: Domenico Bernini. (1722). *Vita Fr. Giuseppe da Copertino.* Roma.

DB: Abridged translation of same into English, used throughout.

Acta Canonizationis Sanctorum—Josephi a Cupertino (p. 35 segg.), Biblioteca Angelica, H. 1928, Roma, 1769.

GP: Gustavo Parisciani. (1963). *San Giuseppe da Copertino: Alla Luce Dei Nuovi Documenti.* Osimo, Ancona: Pax et Bonum.

GP2: Gustavo Parisciani (1967/2003). *San Giuseppe da Copertino.* Padova: Messaggero di Sant'Antonio.

GP3: Gustavo Parisciani (1968). *The Flying Saint.* (Trans. Nevin Hammon) Osimo, Ancona: Pax et Bonum.

Gustavo Parisciani (1988). *San Giuseppe da Copertino e la Polonia.* Padova: Edizioni Messaggero.

Gustavo Parisciani. (1996). *L'Inquisizione e Il Caso S. Giuseppe da Copertino.* Padova: Messaggero di S. Antonio.

Constantinus Suyskenus, *Acta Sanctorum*, Bollandists, September, vol. 5, cc. 992–1060.

Angelo Pastrovicchi. (1753). *St. Joseph of Copertino.* Rome. (English translation and abridgement by Francis Laing).

G. I. Montanari. (1851). *Vita e Miracoli di San Giuseppe da Copertino.* Fermo.

F. Gattari. (1898). *Vita di S. Giuseppe da Copertino.* Osimo.

References

ABBREVIATIONS FOR FREQUENTLY QUOTED TEXTS

DB: Abridged translation into English, used throughout, of Domenico Bernini (1722). *Vita Fr. Giuseppe da Copertino. Roma.*

GP: Gustavo Parisciani (1963). *San Giuseppe da Copertino: Alla Luce Dei Nuovi Documenti.* Osimo, Ancona: Pax et Bonum.

GP2: Gustavo Parisciani (1967/2003). *San Giuseppe da Copertino.* Padova: Messaggero di Sant'Antonio.

GP3: Gustavo Parisciani (1968). *The Flying Saint.* Translated by Nevin Hammon. Osimo, Ancona: Pax et Bonum.

Abbott-Smith, G. (1986). *A Manual Greek Lexicon of the New Testament.* Edinburgh: T & T Clark Ltd.

Adams, H. (1905/1957). *Mont-Saint-Michel and Chartes.* New York: The Heritage Press.

AE (G. W. Russell). (1955). *The Candle of Vision.* Wheaton, IL: Quest Books.

Albanese, C. L. (2007). *A Republic of Mind and Spirit.* New Haven: Yale University Press.

Alberti, L. B. (2011). *On Painting: A New Translation and Critical Edition.* Edited and translated by Rocco Sinisgalli. New York: Cambridge University Press.

Alexander, E. (2013). *Proof of Heaven: A Neurosurgeon's Journey to Heaven.* New York: Simon & Schuster.

Almeder, R. (1992). *Death and Personal Survival: The Evidence for Life after Death.* Lanham, MD: Littlefield Adams.

Alvarado, C. S. (2000). Out-of-body experiences. In E. Cardeña, S. J. Lynn, and S. Krippner, eds., *Varieties of Anomalous Experiences.* Washington, DC: American Psychological Association.

———. (2007). Remarks on Ernesto Bozzano's *La Psichi Domina la Materia*. *Journal of Near-Death Studies* (25.3).
Angus, S. (1925–1975). *The Mystery Religions*. New York: Dover Publications.
Arbman, E. (1968). *Ecstasy or Religious Trance*. Vol. 2. Scandinavian University Books.
Assagioli, R. (1971). *Psychosynthesis: A Manual of Principles and Techniques*. New York: Viking Press.
Atmanspacher, H. (2012). Dual-aspect monism à la Pauli and Jung. *Journal of Consciousness Studies* 19(9/10): 96–120.
Atmanspacher, H., and H. Primas. (2006). Pauli's ideas on mind and matter in the context of contemporary science. *Journal of Consciousness Studies* 13(3): 5–50.
Auden, W. H. (1946). *The Collected Poetry*. New York: Random House.
Augustine. (1980). *City of God*. New York: Pelican Classics.
Avalon, A. (1964). *The Serpent Power*. Madras: Ganesh & Co.
Backman, L. E. (1952). *Religious Dances in the Christian Church and Popular Medicine*. London: George Allen & Unwin Ltd.
Baker, M. C., and S. Goetz. (2011). *The Soul Hypothesis*. New York: Continuum.
Baring-Gould, S. (1914). *The Lives of the Saints*. Vol 10. Edinburgh: John Grant.
Barker, D. (1979). Psi phenomena in Tibetan culture. *Research in Parapsychology*. Metuchen, NJ: Scarecrow.
Barker, J. C. (1968). *Scared to Death: An Examination of Fear, Its Cause and Effects*. London: Frederick Muller Limited.
Barrett, W. (1912). *Proceedings of the Society for Psychical Research*. Vol. XXV.
Batcheldor, K. J. (1964, unpublished). *Psychokinesis, Resistance, and Conditioning*.
———. (1980). Report on a case of table levitation and associated phenomena. *Journal of Social and Personal Relationships* 43(729), 339–56.
———. (1984). Contributions to the theory of PK induction from sitter-groupwork. *Journal for the American Society of Psychical Research* 78.
Bauer, H., and A. Prater. (2001). *Baroque*. London: Taschen.
Bayle, P. (2000). *Various Thoughts on the Occasion of a Comet*. Albany: State University of New York Press.
Beauregard, M. (2012). *Brain Wars: The Scientific Battle Over the Existence of Mind*. New York: HarperOne.
Becker, E. (1973). *The Denial of Death*. New York: The Free Press.
Beichler, J. (2001). To be or not to be!: A "paraphysics" for the new millennium. *Journal of Scientific Explanation* 15(1): 33–56.
Beitman, B. (Forthcoming). *Connecting With Coincidence*. Deerfield Beach, FL: Health Communications Inc.
Bender, H. (1974). Modern poltergeist research. In J. Beloff, ed., *New Directions in Parapsychology*. Metuchen, NJ: Scarecrow Press.
Benedict XIV. (1850). *Heroic Virtue* (3 vols.) London: Thomas Richardson.
Bergin, T. G., and M. H. Fisch. (1984). *The New Science of Giambattista Vico*. Ithaca and London: Cornell University Press.
Bergson, H. (1913). Presidential Address. *Proceedings of the Society for Psychical Research* XXVII: 157–75.

———. (1935). *The Two Sources of Morality and Religion*. Garden City, NY: Doubleday.
Bharati, A. (1970). *The Tantric Tradition*. New York: Anchor Books.
Bloch, E. (1971). *Man on His Own*. New York: Herder and Herder.
Blofeld, J. (1958). *The Zen Teaching of Huang Po: On the Transmission of Mind*. New York: Grove Press.
———. (1970). *The Tantric Mysticism of Tibet*. New York: E. P. Dutton.
Boethius, A. M. (1962). *The Consolation of Philosophy*. New York: Bobbs-Merrill.
Boff, L. (1984). *Saint Francis: A Model for Human Liberation*. New York: Crossroad.
Boniface, E. (1971). *Padre Pio le Crucifié*. Paris: Nouvelles Editions Latines.
Bourguignon, E., and R. Prince, eds. (1968). World distribution and patterns of possession states. In *Trance and Possession States*. Proceedings. R. M. Bucke Memorial Society.
Bozzano, E. (1948). *Psychic Domination of Matter: On Phenomena of Telekinesis Corresponding to Death Events*. Verona: Casa Editrice Europa.
Braude, A. (1989). *Radical Spirits: Spiritualism and Women's Rights in Nineteenth-Century America*. Boston: Beacon Press.
Braude, S. (1991). *The Limits of Influence*. London: Routledge & Kegan Paul.
———. (2003). *Immortal Remains: The Evidence for Life after Death*. Lanham, MD: Rowman & Littlefield.
Breton, A. (1933/1997). *The Automatic Message*. London: Atlas Press.
———. (1972). *Manifestoes of Surrealism*. Ann Arbor: University of Michigan Press.
Breunig, L. C. (1995). *The Cubist Poets in Paris*. Lincoln: University of Nebraska Press.
Broad, C. D. (1962). *Lectures on Psychical Research*. London: Routledge & Kegan Paul.
Brown, N. O. (1990). *Hermes the Thief: The Evolution of a Myth*. Aurora, CO: Lindisfarne Press.
Brown, P. (1981). *The Cult of the Saints: Its Rise and Function in Latin Christianity*. Chicago: University of Chicago Press.
Brown, S. (1970). *The Heyday of Spiritualism*. New York: Hawthorn Books.
Bucke, R. M. (1969). *Cosmic Consciousness*. New York: Dutton.
Bulkeley, K. (2011). Big dreams: the science of highly memorable dreaming. In Sudhir Kakar, ed., *On Dreams and Dreaming*. New York: Penguin/Viking.
Burton, J. (1948). *Heyday of a Wizard*. London: Harrap & Co.
Butcher, S. H. (1951). *Aristotle's Theory of Poetry and Fine Art*. New York: Dover Publications.
Byrd, R. C. (1997). Positive therapeutic effects of intercessory prayer in a coronary care unit population. *Alternate Therapies* 3(6): 87–96.
Cannon, W. (1942). "Voodoo" death. *American Anthropologist* 44: 169–81.
Capek, M. (1961). *The Philosophical Impact of Contemporary Physics*. New York: Van Nostrand.
Carrel, A. (1950). *The Voyage to Lourdes*. New York: Harper & Brothers.
Celano, T. (1963). *St. Francis of Assisi*. Chicago: Franciscan Herald Press.

Cendrars, B. (1949/1996). *Sky Memoirs*. New York: Marlowe & Company.
Chabris, C., and D. Simons. (2010). *The Invisible Gorilla: And Other Ways Our Intuitions Deceive Us*. Crown: New York.
Chapple, C. (1990). The unseen seer and the field: Consciousness in samkhya and yoga. In R. K. Forman, *The Problem of Pure Consciousness: Mysticism and Philosophy*. Oxford & New York: Oxford University Press.
Chiappinelli, W. (2008). *San Giuseppe da Copertino: Il Santo della Meraviglie*. Ancona, Italy: Shalom.
Choong, M. (1999). *The Notion of Emptiness in Early Buddhism*. Delhi: Motilal Banarsidass Publishers.
Coates, J. (1911/1973). *Photographing the Invisible*. New York: Arno Press.
Corbin, H. (1972). *Mundus imaginalis* or the imaginary and the imaginal. Spring Colloquium on Symbolism in Paris, June 1964.
Cory, M. A. (1993). *God and the New Cosmology: The Anthropic Design Argument*. Lanham, MD: Rowman & Littlefield.
Coulton, G. G. (1906). *From St. Francis to Dante*. London: David Nutt.
Crabtree, A. (1993). *From Mesmer to Freud: Magnetic Sleep and the Roots of Psychological Healing*. New Haven and London: Yale University Press.
———. (1997). *Multiple Man: Explorations in Possession and Multiple Personality*. Toronto: Somerville House Books.
Cytowic, R. E. (1998). *The Man Who Tasted Shapes*. Cambridge, MA: MIT Press.
Danielou, A. (1982). *Gods of Love and Ecstasy: The Traditions of Shiva and Dionysus*. Rochester, VT: Inner Traditions.
Danto, A., and S. Morgenbesser. (1960). *Philosophy of Science*. New York: Meridian.
David-Neel, A. (1971). *Magic and Mystery in Tibet*. Baltimore: Penguin Books.
Delehaye, P. H. (1961). *The Legends of the Saints: An Introduction to Hagiography*. Notre Dame, IN: University of Notre Dame Press.
Delumeau, J. (1990). *Sin and Fear: The Emergence of a Western Guilt Culture 13th–18th Centuries*. New York: Saint Martin's Press.
De Vesme, C. (1931). *A History of Experimental Spiritualism, vol. 1, Primitive Man*. London: Rider & Co.
Dingwall, E. (1962). *Some Human Oddities: Studies in the Queer, the Uncanny, and the Fanatical*. New Hyde Park, NY: University Books.
Dioszegi, V., and M. Hoppal. (1996). How Sereptie Djaruskin of the Nganasans Became a Shaman, in *Folk Beliefs and Shamanistic Traditions in Siberia*. Budapest: Akademiai Kiado.
Dodds, E. R. (1968). *The Greeks and the Irrational*. Berkeley: University of California Press.
Donne, J. (1946). *The Complete Poetry and Selected Prose*. New York: Modern Library.
Dossey, L. (1993). *Healing Words: The Power of Prayer and the Practice of Medicine*. San Francisco: HarperSanFrancisco.
———. (1997). *Be Careful What You Pray For: You Might Just Get It*. San Francisco: HarperSanFrancisco.
———. (2013). *One Mind: How Our Individual Mind is Part of a Greater Consciousness and Why It Matters*. Carlsbad, CA: Hay House.

Douglas, J. D. (1982). *New Bible Dictionary*. Wheaton, IL: Tyndale House Publishers.
Douglas, N. (1915/2001). *Old Calabria*. London: Phoenix Press.
Dowling, J. (August 1984). Lourdes cures and their medical assessment. *Journal of the Royal Society of Medicine* 77: 634–638.
Doyle, C. (1918). *The New Revelation*. New York: George Doran Company.
Ducasse, C. L. (1961). *The Belief in a Life after Death*. Springfield, IL: Charles C. Thomas.
Duffin, J. (2009). *Medical Miracles: Doctors, Saints, and Healing in the Modern World*. New York: Oxford University Press.
Eagleton, T. (2009). *Reason, Faith, and Revolution: Reflections on the God Debate*. New Haven & London: Yale University Press.
Eisenbud, J. (1967). *The World of Ted Serios*. New York: Pocket Books.
———. (1977). Paranormal photography. In B.Wolman, ed., *Handbook of Parapsychology*. New York: Van Nostrand Reinhold.
Eliade, M. (1964). *Shamanism: Archaic Techniques of Ecstasy*, Bollingen Series LXXVI. New York: Random House.
———. (1970). *Shamanism: Archaic Techniques of Ecstasy*. Princeton, NJ: Princeton University Press.
Elkin, A. P. (1977). *Aboriginal Men of High Degree*. New York: St. Martin's Press.
Ellenberger, H. F. (1970). *The Discovery of the Unconscious: The History and Evolution of Dynamic Psychiatry*. New York: Basic Books.
Ellis, D. J. (1978). *The Mediumship of the Tape Recorder*. Harlow Essex: Dorset Press.
Ennemoser, J. (1970). *The History of Magic* (2 vols.). New Hyde Park, NY: University Books.
Evans-Wentz, W. Y. (1928). *Tibet's Great Yogi Milarepa*. London: Oxford University Press.
———. (1960). *The Tibetan Book of the Dead*. New York: Oxford University Press.
Farnell, L. R. (1905). *The Evolution of Religion: An Anthropological Study*. New York: Williams & Norgate.
Feilding, E. (1963). *Sittings with Eusapia Palladino and Other Studies*. New York: University Books.
Fergusson, E. (1931). *Dancing Gods: Indian Ceremonials of New Mexico and Arizona*. Albuquerque: University of New Mexico Press.
Feyerabend, P. (1987). *Farewell to Reason*. New York: Verso.
———. (2011). *The Tyranny of Science*. Cambridge, UK: Polity Press.
Flammarion, C. (1924). *Haunted Houses*. London: Fisher Unwin.
Flower, M. A. (2008). *The Seer in Ancient Greece*. Berkeley: University of California Press.
Fodor, J. (July 3, 1992). The big idea: Can there be a science of mind? *Times Literary Supplement*.
Fodor, J., and M. Piattelli-Palmarini. (2010). *What Darwin Got Wrong*. New York: Farrar, Strauss and Giroux.
Fodor, N. (1964). *Between Two Worlds*. West Nyack, NY: Parker Publishing.
———. (1966). *Encyclopedia of Psychic Science*. New York: University Books.

Forman, R. (1990). *The Problem of Pure Consciousness: Mysticism and Philosophy.* New York: Oxford University Press.

Foster, G., and D. Hufford. (1985). *The World Was Flooded with Light: A Mystical Experience Remembered.* Pittsburgh: University of Pittsburgh Press.

Frank, J. (1974). *Persuasion and Healing.* Baltimore and London: Johns Hopkins University Press.

Frankl, V. E. (1963). *Man's Search for Meaning: An Introduction to Logotherapy.* New York: Washington Square Press.

Freud, S. (1966). *Studies in Parapsychology.* New York: Collier Books.

Gardner, E. G. (2009). *The Road to Siena: The Essential Biography of St. Catherine.* Brewster, MA: Paraclete Press.

Gardner, R. (1983). Miracles of healing in Anglo-Celtic Northumbria as recorded by the Venerable Bede and his contemporaries: A reappraisal in the light of twentieth-century experience. *British Medical Journal* 287: 1927–1933.

Gauld, A. (1968). *The Founders of Psychical Research.* London: Routledge & Kegan Paul.

———. (1982). *Mediumship and Survival.* London: Heinemann.

Geiger, J. (2009). *The Third Man Factor: Surviving the Impossible.* New York: Weinstein Books.

Germanus, F. (1933). *Blessed Gemma Galgani: The Holy Maid of Lucca.* London: Sands.

Geuss, R. (1981). *The Idea of a Critical Theory: Habermas & the Frankfurt School.* Cambridge: Cambridge University Press.

Gissurarson, L. R., and E. Haraldsson. (1995). In A. Imich, ed., *Incredible Tales of the Paranormal.* New York: Bramble Books.

Grad, B. (1965). Some biological effects of the "laying on of hands": A review of experiments with animals and plants. *Journal of the American Society for Psychical Research* 59: 95–127.

Greyson, B., and M. Nahm. (2009). Terminal lucidity in patients with chronic schizophrenia and dementia. *The Journal of Nervous and Mental Disease* 197(12): 942–44.

Griffin, D. R. (1997). *Parapsychology, Philosophy, and Spirituality: A Postmodern Examination.* Albany: State University of New York Press.

Grosso, M. (1995). *The Millennium Myth.* Wheaton, IL: Quest Books.

———. (1997). Inspiration, mediumship, surrealism: The concept of creative dissociation. In S. Krippner and S. M. Powers, eds., *Broken Images, Broken Selves.* Washington, DC: Brunner Mazel.

———. (2004). *Experiencing the Next World Now.* New York: Simon & Schuster.

———. (2015). The "transmission" theory of mind and brain: A brief history. In E. Kelly, A. Crabtree, and P. Marshall, *Beyond Physicalism: The Reconciliation of Science and Spirituality.* Lanham, MD: Rowman & Littlefield.

Guillaume, A. (1938). *Prophecy and Divination among the Hebrews and Other Semites.* New York: Harper and Brothers.

Gustafsson, M. L. (2009). *War and Shadows: The Haunting of Vietnam.* Ithaca and London: Cornell University Press.

Hamilton, T. (2009). *Immortal Longings: FWH Myers and the Victorian Search for Life after Death.* Charlottesville, VA: Imprint Academic.

Hannah, B. (1981). *Encounters with the Soul: Active Imagination as Developed by C. G. Jung.* Salem, MA: Sigo Press.

Hanson, G. (2001). *The Trickster and the Paranormal.* Bloomington, IN: Xlibris Corporation.

Harding, E. (1869). *Modern American Spiritualism.* New Hyde Park, NY: University Books.

Hardy, A. (1966). *The Divine Flame: An Essay towards a Natural History of Religion.* London: Collins.

Haynes, R. (1970). *Philosopher King: The Humanist Pope Benedict XIV.* London: Weidenfeld & Nicholson.

Heisenberg, W. (1958). *Physics and Philosophy: The Revolution in Modern Science.* New York: Harper & Row.

Herbert, N. (1993). *Elemental Mind.* New York: Dutton.

Hillman, J. (1975). *Re-Visioning Psychology.* New York: Harper & Row.

Hind, A. M. (1912). *Rembrandt's Etchings: An Essay and a Catalogue.* Vol. 2. New York: Charles Scribner's Sons.

Hodgson, R. (1898). A further record of observations of certain phenomena of trance. *Proceedings of the Society for Psychical Research* 13: 284–582.

Hufford, D. (1982). *The Terror that Comes in the Night: An Experience-Centered Study of Supernatural Assault Traditions.* Philadelphia: University of Pennsylvania Press.

Hughes, R. (1968). *Heaven and Hell in Western Art.* New York: Stein & Day.

———. (2011). *Rome: A Cultural, Visual, and Personal History.* New York: Alfred J. Knopf.

Hume, D. (1748/1955). Of miracles. Sec. 10, *An Inquiry Concerning Human Understanding.* New York: Library of Liberal Arts.

Hunter, J. (March 2012). Anthropology and the supernatural. *EdgeScience.*

Huxley, A. (1945). *The Perennial Philosophy.* New York: Harper Colophon Books.

Imich, A. (1995). *Incredible Tales of the Paranormal.* New York: Bramble Books.

Jaffe, A. (1975). *The Myth of Meaning.* New York: Penguin Books.

James, W. (1958). *The Varieties of Religious Experience.* New York: Mentor.

———. (1971a). A pluralistic universe. In *Essays in Radical Empiricism and a Pluralistic Universe*, pp. 121–84. New York: E. P. Dutton.

———. (1971b). *A William James Reader.* Edited by Gay Wilson Allen. New York: Houghton Mifflin Company.

Jenkins, P. (2007). *The Next Christendom.* New York: Oxford University Press.

Jung, C. G. (1958). Transformation symbolism in the Mass. In *Psychology and Religion.* London: Routledge & Kegan Paul.

Jung, C. G., and W. Pauli. (1955). *The Interpretation of Nature and Psyche.* London: Routledge & Kegan Paul.

Kandinsky, W. (1912/1966). *Concerning the Spiritual in Art.* New York: Wittenborn.

Kant, I. (1951). *Critique of Judgment.* New York: Hafner Publishing.

Katz, S. T. (1978). *Mysticism and Philosophical Analysis.* Oxford: Oxford University Press.

Kaufmann, W. (1968). *Nietzsche: Philosopher, Psychologist, Antichrist.* New York: Vintage Books.

Keener, C. (2011). *Miracles: The Credibility of the New Testament Accounts*. Grand Rapids, Michigan: Baker Academic.

Kelly, E. F. (2003). Book review: *The Illusion of Conscious Will* by Daniel M. Wegner. *Journal of Scientific Exploration* 17: 166–71.

Kelly, E., A. Crabtree, and P. Marshall, eds. (2014). *Beyond Physicalism: Toward the Reconciliation of Science and Spirituality*. Lanham, MD: Rowman & Littlefield.

Kelly, E. F., and E. W. Kelly, eds. (2007). *Irreducible Mind: Toward a Psychology for The 21st Century*. Lanham, MD: Rowman & Littlefield.

Kelly, E. F., and R. Locke. (2009). *Altered States of Consciousness and Psi: An Historical Survey and Research Prospectus*. New York: Parapsychology Foundation.

Kelsey, M. T. (1973). *Healing and Christianity: In Ancient Thought and Modern Times*. New York: Harper & Row.

Kennedy, J. E. (Spring 2003). The capricious, actively evasive, unsustainable nature of psi: A summary and hypothesis. *The Journal of Parapsychology* 67: 53–74.

Kerenyi, C. (1976). *Dionysos: Archetypal Image of Indestructible Life*. Princeton, NJ: Bollingen Series.

Keynes, G. (1972). *Blake: Complete Writings*. London: Oxford University Press.

Kirk, G. S., and J. E. Raven. (1957). *The Presocratic Philosophers: A Critical History With a Selection of Texts*. New York: Cambridge University Press.

Kirsch, I. (2011). *The Emperor's New Drug: Exploding the Antidepressant Myth*. New York: Basic Books.

Knox, R. (1950). *Enthusiasm: A Chapter in the History of Religion*. New York: Oxford University Press.

Koons, R. C., and G. Bealer. (2010). *The Waning of Materialism*. Oxford: Oxford University Press.

Kothari, L. K., A. Bordia, and O. P. Gupta. (1973). The yogi claim of voluntary control over the heart beat: An unusual demonstration. *American Heart Journal* 86: 282–84.

Kramer, H., and J. Sprenger. (1948). *The Malleus Maleficarum*. New York: Dover.

Kripal, J. (1998). *Kali's Child: The Mystical and the Erotic in the Life and Teachings of Ramakrishna*. Chicago: University of Chicago Press.

———. (2001). *Roads of Excess, Palaces of Wisdom: Eroticism and Reflexivity in the Study of Mysticism*. Chicago: University of Chicago Press.

———. (2007). *Esalen: America and the Religion of No Religion*. Chicago: University of Chicago Press.

———. (2010). *Authors of the Impossible: The Paranormal and the Sacred*. Chicago: University of Chicago Press.

———. (2011). *Mutants and Mystics: Science Fiction, Superhero Comics, and the Paranormal*. Chicago: University of Chicago Press.

Krippner, S., ed. (1977). *: Advances in Parapsychological Research,* vol. 1, *Psychokinesis*. New York: Springer.

Lacarriere, J. (1963). *The God-Possessed*. London: George Allen & Unwin.

Laing, R. D. (1967). *The Politics of Experience*. New York: Ballantine Books.

Lambertini, P. (Benedict XIV) (1740–1758). *De Servorum Dei Beatificatione et Beatorum Canonizatione*. 4 vols. Bologna.

Lancaster, J. (2005). *In the Shadow of Vesuvius: A Cultural History of Naples*. London, New York: I. B. Taurus & Co.

Lang, A. (1897). *Modern Mythology*. London: Longmans, Green.

———. (1898). *The Making of Religion*. London: Longmans, Green.

Lanternari, V. (1963). *The Religions of the Oppressed*. New York: Alfred Knopf.

Larson, E. J., and L. Witham. (1997). Scientists are still keeping the faith. *Nature*. 386: 435–36.

Laski, M. 1961. *Ecstasy: In Secular and Religious Experience*. Los Angeles: Jeremy Tarcher.

Lee, R. (1968). The sociology of Kung Bushman trance performances, pp. 35–53. In R. Prince, *Trance and Possession States*. Montreal: R. M. Bucke Memorial Society.

Leibniz, G. W. (1843). *Gesammelte Werke*. Hrsg. Von G.H. Pertz: Hannoverae, IV, 1 Folge.

Levack, B. (2013). *The Devil Within: Possession and Exorcism in the Christian West*. New Haven and London: Yale University Press.

Locke, R. (1999). *The Gift of Proteus: Shamanism and the Transformation of Being*. Chapel Hill, NC: SCI Publication.

London, J. (1987). *The Star Rover*. Malibu: Valley of the Sun Publishing.

Luibheid, C. (1987). *Dionysius the Areopagite: The Complete Works*. New York: Paulist Press.

Luzzatto, S. (2007). *Padre Pio: Miracles and Politics in a Secular Age*. New York: Picador.

Maiorano, L. (2002). *San Giuseppe da Copertino*. Lecce: Manni.

Manning, M. (1975). *The Link*. New York: Holt, Rinehart and Winston.

Marshall, P. (1992). *The Living Mirror: Images of Reality in Science and Mysticism* London: Samphire Press.

———. (2005). *Mystical Encounters with the Natural World: Experiences and Explanations*. London: Oxford University Press.

Martin, M. (1976). *Hostage to the Devil*. New York: Reader's Digest Press.

Mason, A. A. (1952). A case of congenital ichthyosiform erythroderma of Brocq treated by hypnosis. *British Medical Journal* 2: 422–23.

Mathews, T. (1993). *The Clash of Gods: A Reinterpretation of Early Christian Art*. Princeton, NJ: Princeton University Press.

Mathieu, P. F. (2006). *Histoire Des Miracules e Des Convulsionnaires de Saint-Medard*. Paris: Elibron Classics.

Mattelini, G. C. (2003). *Giuseppe da Copertino: Uomo Santo*. Padua: Edizioni Messagero.

Mauskopf, S. H., and M. R. McVaugh. (1980). *The Elusive Science: Origins of Experimental Psychical Research*. Baltimore: The John Hopkins University Press.

Mavromatis, A. (1987). *Hypnagogia: The Unique State of Consciousness between Wakefulness and Sleep*. London: Thyrsos Press.

Maxwell-Stuart, P. G. (2006). *Ghosts: A History of Phantoms, Ghouls and Other Spirits of the Dead*. Stroud, Gloustershire: Tempus.

McDaniel, J. (1989). *The Madness of the Saints: Ecstatic Religion in Bengal.* Chicago: University of Chicago Press.
McGinn, B. (1981). *Meister Eckhart.* Mahwah, NJ: Paulist Press.
———. (1994). *The Foundations of Mysticism.* Vol. I. New York: Crossroad.
———. (1998). *The Flowering of Mysticism.* Vol. III. New York: Crossroad.
McIntyre, J. L. (1903). *Giordano Bruno.* London: Macmillan & Company.
McMoneagle, J. (1993). *Mind Trek: Exploring Consciousness, Time, and Space through Remote Viewing.* Charlottesville, VA: Hampton Roads.
Medhurst, R. G (1972). *Crookes and the Spirit World.* New York: Taplinger Publishing Company.
Medhurst, R. G., and K. M. Goldney. (1963). William Crookes and the physical phenomena of mediumship. *Proceedings of the Society for Psychical Research* 54:251–57. London.
Melchiori, G. (1960). *The Whole Mystery of Art: Pattern into Poetry in the Work of W. B. Yeats.* New York: The Macmillan Company.
Mendoza, R. G. (1995). *The Acentric Labyrinth: Giordano Bruno's Prelude to Contemporary Cosmology.* Rockport, MA: Element.
Merrill, J. (1986). *Recitative: Prose by James Merrill.* Edited by J. D. McCatchy. San Francisco: North Point Press.
———. (1993). *The Changing Light at Sandover.* New York: Alfred A. Knopf
Montmasson, J. M. (1932). *Invention and the Unconscious.* New York: Harcourt.
Moody, R. A. (1975). *Life After Life.* Covington, GA: Mockingbird Books.
Mooney, J. (1896–1965). *The Ghost Dance Religion and the Sioux Outbreak of 1890.* Chicago: University of Chicago Press.
Moore, T. (1996). *The Education of the Heart.* New York: HarperCollins.
Mottola, A., trans. (1964). *The Spiritual Exercises of St. Ignatius.* New York: Image Books.
Mueggler, E. (2001). *The Age of Wild Ghosts.* Berkeley: University of California Press.
Murphy, G., and R. O. Ballou, eds. (1960). *William James on Psychical Research.* London: Chatoo & Windus.
Murphy, M. (1992). *The Future of the Body: Explorations into the Further Evolution of Human Nature.* New York: Jeremy P. Tarcher.
Musa, M. (1973). *Dante's Vita Nuova.* Bloomington & London: Indiana University Press.
Myers, F. (1892). The subliminal consciousness. *Society for Psychical Research.* 436–535.
———. (1903). *Human Personality and Its Survival of Bodily Death* (2 vols.). London: Longmans, Green.
———. (1904). *Fragments of Prose and Poetry.* London: Longmans, Green.
Nagel, T. (2012). *Mind, Life, and Cosmos.* New York: Oxford University Press.
Nahm, M., and B. Greyson. (2009). Terminal lucidity in patients with chronic schizophrenia and dementia. *The Journal of Nervous and Mental Disease* 197: 12.
Nahm, M., and B. Greyson. (2011). Terminal lucidity: A review and case collection. *Archives of Gerontology and Geriatrics* 1–5.
Neihardt, J. G. (1972). *Black Elk Speaks.* New York: Pocket Books.

Nicholson, R.A. (1973). *Rumi: Divani Shamsi Tabriz*. San Francisco: The Rainbow Bridge.
Nietzsche, F. (1927). *The Philosophy of Nietzsche*. New York: Random House.
Noë, A. (2009). *Out of Our Heads: Why You Are Not Your Brain, and Other Lessons from the Biology of Consciousness*. New York: Hill and Wang.
Nuti, R. (1678). *Vita Del Servo di Dio Fra Giuseppe da Copertino*. Palermo, Italy: Ordine de'Minori Conventuali.
Otto, W. F. (1965). *Dionysus: Myth and Cult*. Bloomington: Indiana University Press:
Owen, I. M., and M. Sparrow. (1977). *Conjuring Up Philip: An Adventure in Psychokinesis*. New York: Pocket Books.
Owen, J. (1908/1970). *The Skeptics of the Italian Renaissance*. London: Kennikat Press.
Owen, R. D. (1871). *The Debatable Land*. New York: Carleton & Co.
———. (1899). *Footfalls on the Boundary of Another World*. London: Kegan Paul.
Palmer, J. (1978). Extrasensory perception: research findings. In S. Krippner, ed *Advances in Parapsychological Research: Extrasensory Perception*. New York: Plenum Press.
Parisciani, G. (1963). *San Giuseppe da Copertino: Alla Luce Dei Nuovi Documenti*. Osimo, Ancona: Pax et Bonum.
———. (1967/2003). *San Giuseppe da Copertino*. Padova: Messaggero di Sant'Antonio.
———. (1968). *The Flying Saint*. (Trans. Nevin Hammon) Osimo, Ancona: Pax et Bonum.
———. (1988). *San Giuseppe da Copertino e la Polonia*. Padova: Edizioni Messaggero.
———. (1996). *L'Inquisizione e Il Caso S. Giuseppe da Copertino*. Padova: Messaggero di S. Antonio.
Pastrovicchi, A. (1980). *Saint Joseph of Copertino*. Rockford, IL: Tan Books.
Peers, E. A. (1960). *The Autobiography of St. Teresa of Avila*. Garden City, NY: Image Books.
Penny, N. (1988). *Piranesi*. London: Bloomsbury Books.
Penrose, R. (1995). *The Large, the Small, and the Human Mind*. New York: Cambridge University Press.
Perlove, S. K. (1990). *Bernini and the Idealization of Death*. University Park and London: The Pennsylvania State University Press.
Petersen, M. (2008). *Our Daily Meds*. New York: Farrar, Strauss and Giroux.
Pieper, J. (1964). *Enthusiasm and Divine Madness: On the Platonic Dialogue Phaedrus*. New York: Harcourt, Brace & World.
Plato. (1966). Trans. Fowler. *Dialogues*. (*Phaedo*). Cambridge, MA: Harvard University Press.
Poole, W. (1987). *The Heart of Healing*. Atlanta, GA: Turner Publishing.
Popolizio, B. (1955). *Il Santo Che Volava*. Laterza: Bari.
Popov, A. A. (1996). How Sereptie Djaruskin of the Nganasans became a shaman. In Vilmos Dioszegi and Mihaly Hoppal, eds., *Folk Beliefs and Shamanistic Traditions in Siberia*. Budapest: Akademiai Kiado.

Popper, K., and J. C. Eccles. (1977). *The Self and Its Brain.* New York: Springer-Verlag.
Poulain, A. (1912). *The Graces of Interior Prayer: A Treatise on Mystical Prayer.* London: Kegan Paul.
Prabhavananda, S., and F. Manchester (1957). *The Upanishads.* New York: A Mentor Book.
Price, H. H. (1995). *Philosophical Interactions with Parapsychology.* Edited by Frank Dilley. New York: St. Martin's Press.
Prince, W. H. (1927/1964). *The Case of Patience Worth.* New Hyde Park, NY: University Books.
Radin, D. (1997). *The Conscious Universe: The Scientific Truth of Psychic Phenomena.* San Francisco: Harper*Edge*.
Redgrove, H. S. (1921). *Joseph Glanvill and Psychical Research in the Seventeenth Century.* London: William Rider.
Rees, M. (1998). *Before the Beginning: Our Universe and Others.* New York: Basic Books.
Richmond, Z. (1938). *Evidence of Purpose.* London: G. Bell & Sons.
Rimbaud, A. (1957). *Illuminations.* Translated by Louise Varese. New York: New Directions.
Robb, P. (1998). *M.* London: Bloomsbury.
Robinson, E. (1977). *The Original Vision: A Study of the Religious Experience of Childhood.* Manchester College: Oxford.
Rogo, D. S., and R. Bayless. (1980). *Phone Calls from the Dead.* London: New English Library.
Roll, W. (1972). *The Poltergeist.* New York: New American Library.
Roob, A. (1997). *Alchemy and Mysticism.* New York: Taschen.
Rorty, R., and G. Vattimo. (2005). *The Future of Religion.* New York: Columbia University Press.
Rosenblum, B., and F. Kuttner. (2006). *Quantum Enigma: Physics Encounters Consciousness.* New York: Oxford University Press.
Ruffin, B. (1982). *Padre Pio: The True Story.* Huntington, IN: Our Sunday Visitor.
Russolo, L. (1986). *The Art of Noises.* New York: Pendragon Press.
Said, E. (1979). *Orientalism.* New York: Vintage Books.
———. (1993). *Culture and Imperialism.* New York: Alfred A. Knopf.
Saltmarsh, H. F. (1938). *Evidence for Personal Survival from Cross-Correspondences.* London: Bell & Sons.
Sartre, J. P. (1958/1989). *Being and Nothingness: An Essay on Phenomenological Ontology.* London: Routledge.
Scheler, M. (1961). *Man's Place in Nature.* Boston: Beacon Press.
Schlitz, M., and W. Braud. (1997). Distant intenionality and healing: Assessing the evidence. *Alternative Therapies* 3(6): 62–73.
Schmeidler, G. (1977). Research findings in psychokinesis. In S. Krippner, ed., *Advances in Parapsychological Research: 1 Psychokinesis,* pp. 79–132. New York: Plenum Press.
Schmidt, H. (1974). Psychokinesis. In E. D. Mitchell, *Psychic Exploration: A Challenge for Science.* New York: G. P. Putnum's Sons.

Schrenck-Notzing, B. (1920). *Phenomena of Materialization*. London: Kegan Paul.
Schrödinger, I. (1969). *What Is Life? Mind and Matter*. New York: Cambridge University Press.
Schug, J. (1975). *Padre Pio: He Bore the Stigmata*. Huntington, IN: Our Sunday Visitor.
Sebasti, G. (2003). *Il Caso Giuseppe Da Copertino*. Milano: Sugarco.
Skeat, W. W. (1963). *A Concise Etymological Dictionary of the English Language*. New York: Capricorn Books.
Smith, F. (2006). *The Self Possessed: Deity and Spirit Possession in South Asian Literature and Civilization*. New York: Columbia University.
Somer, A. (2009). Tackling taboos: Albert von Schrenck-Notzing (1862–1929). *Journal of Scientific Exploration* 23(3).
Stace, W. (1960). *The Teachings of the Mystics*. New York: A Mentor Book.
Stannard, D. E. (1992). *American Holocaust: The Conquest of the New World*. New York: Oxford University Press.
Stapp, H. (2009). The Mind Is *Not* What the Brain Does. Saa49.ucsf.edu/psa/.
———. (2015). A quantum-mechanical theory of the mind-brain connection. In *Beyond Physicalism*, eds. E. Kelly, A. Crabtree, and P. Marshall. Lanham, MD: Rowman & Littlefield.
Stern, K. (1998). *Flight from Women*. New York: Paragon House.
Stevenson, I. (1974). *Twenty Cases Suggestive of Reincarnation*. Charlottesville: University of Virginia Press.
———. (1987). *Children Who Remember Previous Lives: A Question of Reincarnation*. Charlottesville: University of Virginia Press.
———. (1997a). Vol. 1. *Reincarnation and Biology*. Westport, CT: Praeger.
———. (1997b). *Where Reincarnation and Biology Intersect*. Westport, CT: Praeger.
Stoller, P., and C. Olkes. (1987). *In Sorcery's Shadow: A Memoir of Apprenticeship among the Songhay of Niger*. Chicago: University of Chicago Press.
Summers, M. (1950). *The Physical Phenomena of Mysticism*. London: Ryder & Company.
Symonds, J. A. (1886). *The Catholic Reaction, Part II*. New York: Henry Holt.
Taimni, I. K. (1961). *The Science of Yoga: A Commentary on the Yoga-Sutras of Patanjali in the Light of Modern Thought*. Wheaten, IL: A Quest Book.
Tannahill, R. (1982). *Sex in History*. New York: Stein and Day.
Tart, C. (2009). *The End of Materialism: How Evidence of the Paranormal Is Bringing Science and Spirit Together*. Oakland, CA: New Harbinger Publications.
Tart, C. T., ed. (1997). *Body Mind Spirit*. Charlottesville, VA: Hampton Roads.
Taylor, J. B. (2006). *My Stroke of Insight: A Brain Scientist's Personal Journey*. New York: Viking.
Thomas, K. (1971). *Religion and the Decline of Magic*. New York: Charles Scribner's Sons.
Thouless, R. H., and B. P. Wiesner. (1946). On the nature of psi phenomena. *Journal of Parapsychology* 10: 107–19.
Thurston, H. (1952). *The Physical Phenomena of Mysticism*. London: Burns Oates.
Thurston, H., and D. Attwater. (1980). *Butler's Lives of the Saints*, III, p. 588. Westminster, MD: Christian Classics, Inc.

Treece, P. (1989). *The Sanctified Body.* New York: Doubleday.
Trevor-Roper, H. R. (1968). *The European Witch-Craze.* New York: Harper Torchbacks.
Tsakiris, A. (2012). Neurosurgeon's near-death experience defies medical model of consciousness. *New Dawn.* Vol.6, no. 2. 17–26.
Tucker, J. (2005). *Life Before Life: A Scientific Investigation of Children's Memories of Previous Lives.* New York: St. Martin's Press.
———. (2013). *Return to Life: Extraordinary Cases of Children Who Remember Past Lives.* New York: St. Martin's Press.
Turner, E. (1994). A visible spirit form in Zambia. In D. E. Young and J. Goulet Eds. *Being Changed by Cross-Cultural Encounters: The Anthropology of Extraordinary Experience.* Ontario: Broadview Press.
Tyrrell, G. N. M. (1961). *Science and Psychical Phenomena.* : New Hyde Park, NY: University Books.
Underhill, E. (1919). *Jacapone da Todi: Poet and Mystic.* New York: E. P. Dutton.
———. (1956). *Mysticism.* New York: Meridian Books.
Vallee, J. (1975). *The Invisible College.* New York: E. P. Dutton.
Van de Castle, R. (1994). *Our Dreaming Mind.* New York: Ballantine Books.
Van Lommel, P. (2010). *Consciousness beyond Life: The Science of the Near-Death Experience.* New York: Harper Collins.
Van Lommel, P., and R. van Wees, V. Meyers, and I. Elfferich. (2001). Near-death experiences in survivors of cardiac arrest: A prospective study in the Netherlands. *Lancet* 358: 2039–45.
Von Franz, M. L. (1988). *Psyche and Matter.* Boston: Shambala Publications.
Von Hugel, F. (1961). *The Mystic Element of Religion.* (2 vols.) London: Dent & Sons.
Walker, B. (1970). *Sex and the Supernatural.* New York: Harrow Books.
Wallace, A. R. (1878/1955). *Miracles and Modern Spiritualism.* London: Spiritualist Press.
Wavell, S., A. Butt, and N. Epton. (1967). *Trances.* New York: Dutton.
Weber, M. (2009). *The Protestant Ethic and the Spirit of Capitalism.* New York: Norton Critical Edition.
Weinstein, D., and R. M. Bell. (1982). *Saints and Society: The Two Worlds of Western Christendom, 1000–1700.* Chicago: University of Chicago Press.
White, R., and M. Murphy. (1978). *The Psychic Side of Sports.* Reading, MA: Addison-Wesley Publishing Company.
Whitehead, A. N. (1926). *Religion in the Making.* New York: Macmillan.
———. (1938). *Modes of Thought.* New York: Putnam Capricorn.
Williams, W. E. (1992). *Unbounded Light: The Inward Journey.* York Beach, ME: Nicolas-Hays.
Wilson, I. (1989). *Stigmata.* New York: Harper & Row.
Wittkower, R. (1955). *Gian Lorenzo Bernini: The Sculptor of the Roman Baroque.* London: The Phaidon Press.
Woelfflin, H. (1932). *Principles of Art History.* New York: Dover Publications.

Wolman, B. B., ed. (1977). *Handbook of Parapsychology*. New York: Van Nostrand Reinhold Company.
Woodward, K. (1990). *Making Saints*. New York: Simon & Schuster.
———. (2000). *The Book of Miracles*. New York: Simon & Schuster.
Yogananda, P. (1975). *Autobiography of a Yogi*. Los Angeles: Self-Realization Fellowship.
Young, D. E., and J. G. Goulet. (1994). *Being Changed by Cross-Cultural Encounters: The Anthropology of Extraordinary Experience*. New York: Broadview Press.
Zaehner, R. C. (1978). *Mysticism: Sacred and Profane*. Oxford: Oxford University Press.

Index

acausal coincidences, 42, 185
Adams, Henry, 156
Adams, John, 47, 156
The Age of Wild Ghosts (Mueggler), 6
Albert, Leon Battista, 161
Albertus Magnus, 186
Albotto, Michael di Monte, 99
Alessandro VII, 31–32, 106
Alexander, Eben, 10
alms-gathering, 19
alternating personality, 196
Alvarez de Toledo, Don Pedro, 15
American Heart Journal, 51
Anandamayi Ma, 126
Angela of Foligno, 118
Angelucci, 92
animals, 114–15
Anthony of Padua, 21
Antonio of Mauro, 24, 28–29
apparitions, 108, 210–12
Aquinas, Thomas, 115
architecture, 158, 163–64
Ars Magna Luci et Umbrae (Kircher), 159
Ascension, 59, 72, 152
asceticism, 20, 24; extreme ascetic, 45, 124
The Assayer (Galileo), 175
Atmanspacher, Harald, 185

attainments (*siddhis*), 51, 64, 111
attraction, 23, 25
Augustine, 193
authenticity, 26, 113
automatic writing, 50, 56, 78
autosuggestion, 48
Avalon, Arthur, 137
Axial Age, 133

backward levitations, 73–76, 83, 166
Bacon, Francis, 193
Baggally, W. W., 173
ballet, 45–46
Baring-Gould, S., 87–88
Barker, David, 30, 51
Barker, J. C., 48
baroque art, 154–55, 161–63
Barrett, William, 49, 194
Baryshnikov, Mikhail, 45
Batcheldor, Kenneth, 57–58, 202, 204
Bauer, Hermann, 163
Bayle, Pierre, 193
beatification, 34, 80, 86–89, 101, 215
Beauregard, Mario, 10
belief, 43–44; in life after death, 206–12; in miracles, 212–15; performance artist and, 165; in power of belief, 201–3; in power of prayer, 203–6; in

spiritual world, 199–201.
  See also faith
Bender, Hans, 49
Benedict XIV, 34, 86, 101. *See also*
  Lambertini, Prosper
Bengali siddhas, 124–27
Beraud, Marthe, 54
Bergson, Henri, 11, 126, 133, 196
Bernini, Domenico: on caring
  custodian, 31; on childbirth, 107;
  on clothing, 77; on conversion,
  82–83; on demons, 105; on
  disruptions, 85; on ecstasies,
  70; on ecstatic history, 80;
  on foreknowledge, 97; on
  Immaculate Conception statue, 81;
  on infused wisdom, 99; on Maria of
  Savoy, 141–42; on meeting brothers,
  117; on mental excess, 154;
  on mind reading, 94;
  on miracles, 105–6; on odor of
  sanctity, 63, 92–93; on physical
  appearance, 147; on poverty, 123;
  on residence in heaven, 75; on self-
  laceration, 24; on temperament, 21;
  on temptations, 136; on three crosses
  vision, 78–79
Bernini, Gian Lorenzo, 118–19, 154,
  159, 162–64
Bhaduri, Nagendra, 59
bhava, 125–27
Big Bang, 183
big mind, 200
birth and childhood, 15–18
The Birth of Tragedy (Nietzsche), 157
Black Elk, 51
Blake, William, 64, 140, 201
Boccaccio, Giovanni, 144
bodily metamorphosis, 62–64
Boehme, Jacob, 159
Boethius, A. M., 121
Boff, Leonardo, 4, 122–23
Bonfini, Baccelliere, 134
Boniface, Ennemond, 9
Bozzano, Ernesto, 50, 210

brain, 10; consciousness and, 132, 134,
  175; mind-brain threshold, 134–35
Brain Wars (Beauregard), 10
Braud, William, 200
Braude, Anne, 198
Braude, Stephen, 37
British Society for Physical Research,
  182, 194, 196
Broad, C. D., 98–99, 184
Brown, Peter, 77–78
Browning, Elizabeth, 38
Browning, Robert, 38, 172
Bruno, Giordano, 155, 161
Bucke, Richard, 200
Buddha, 118, 192, 194
Buddhism, 137–38, 191–92
Bulkeley, Kelly, 41
bullying, 22
Butler, E. C., 114
Byrd, Randolph, 205

Calderon de la Barca, Pedro, 165
Cannon, W., 48
canonization, 34, 86–88, 101, 215
Capuchins, 77; censure and departure,
  19; as lay brother, 18–19
Caravaggio, 154, 155, 159–60, 165
Carosi, Giacinto, 84
Carr, Bernard, 182–84
Carrel, Alexis, 103–4
Carrington, Hereward, 173
Catherine of Genoa, 113, 117
Catherine of Siena, 28, 113;
  divine adventure and, 17;
  ring of espousal, 144
Catholic Church: beatification and
  canonization in, 34, 80, 86–89,
  101, 215; celestial harmonies
  and, 157; as cultural force, 154;
  displacements by, 85–87, 155;
  hiding mystic, 23–24;
  miracles and, 35;
  proof of sainthood, 33; as refuge, 18
celestial harmonies, 157
Cenneo, Domenica, 108

Chaffin, James, 211
chanting, 42, 59, 126
Chapple, Christopher, 191–92
charisms (gifts), 51, 62, 64; controversial, 111; relationship to God, 80; Thurston on saints', 69–70. *See also* talents
chastity, 124, 135, 137, 140, 166
chiaroscuro, 159–60
childbirth, 107
Christ, 194–95; Ascension, 59, 72, 152
Cimabue, 28, 75, 141, 158
City of God (Augustine), 193
clairvoyance, 153, 182
Clement XII, 101
Clement XIII, 34
clothing, 77–78
coincidences, 42–43
Comstack, Anthony, 138
consciousness: activists, 5–10; brain and, 132, 134, 175; creating reality, 174; emergence, 132, 175; endless, 148; mind and, 3, 177; mysteries of, 2; nature of, 6; near-death experience and, 6–7; nonemergence, 132–33; in revolt, 2–3; skeleton in physics closet, 176
constructivism, 112
Conventuals, 95, 134; ordination and priesthood, 20, 23; as tertiary, 19
conversion, 82–83
Copernicus, 195
Cossandri, Antonio, 72
Costanzo, Angelica di, 107
Council of Trent, 156–57
Counter-Reformation, 16, 19, 31, 64, 126; Devil during, 144; restrictions, 140
couplets, 100. *See also* strophes
Cox, Sergeant, 172
creative illness, 18, 154
Crookes, William, 37–38, 53, 56, 80, 88, 182; on human organization, 174; on levitation, 173; on psychic force, 172; Spiritualism investigation, 171–72
Culture and Imperialism (Said), 4
Curran, Pearl, 78, 98–99

Danielou, Alain, 137
dark, 159–61. *See also* light
Darrow, Clarence, 4
Darwin, Charles, 38
Darwinism, 194
da Silva, Jerome, 65
David-Neel, Alexandra, 60
death: apparitions after, 108; autopsy, 108; ecstasy at, 134; miracles after, 105–9; performance artist at, 167; post-mortem healing miracles, 34, 108–9; prediction of, 33; witness testimonials, 33–34
debased supernaturalism, 114
The Debatable Land (Owen), 198
de Herran, Carol, 62
Delumeau, Jean, 15, 70
demonology, 15–16
demons, 77–78, 91, 105, 196. *See also* Devil; exorcism; possession
depression, 27–28
Desa, Felix, 16–17
Desa, Frances, 16–17, 22–23, 29, 166
Desa, Francis, 18
Desa, Livia, 16–17, 22
De Vesme, Cesar, 197
Devil, 19, 27; during Counter-Reformation, 144; diabolic intensities, 143–46; fear of, 146
The Devil Within (Levack), 145
diabolic intensities, 143–46
Dingwall, Eric, 70
Dionysius the Areopagite, 111, 115
dissociative identity disorder, 48
divination rite, 8
divine adventure, 17

divine ardor, 63
Donatus, John, 19
Donne, John, 155–56, 165
Dossey, Larry, 203
Douglas, Norman, 86
Dowling, John, 104
Doyle, Arthur Conan, 198
dream spaces, 183–84
Duffin, Jacalyn, 102, 103
d'Youville, Marie-Marguerite, 102

Eagleton, Terry, 189
Eckhart, Meister, 111, 113, 118
ecstasies: Bernini, D., on, 70, 80; at death, 134; ecstatic dissociation, 2; ecstatic walking, 46; fear of, 116; foreshadowing raptures, 76; frequency, 32; Myers on, 195; NDE and, 146–50; Parisciani on, 71; prolonged, 127
ecstatic levitation, 20, 27, 41; sexual tension and, 135–40
ectoplasm, 54
Einstein, Albert, 182
Eisenbud, Jule, 53, 69
élan vital, 126
Elemental Mind (Herbert), 175
11-D space, 182
Ellacuria, Aloysius, 62
Ellenberger, Henri, 18
Emerson, Ralph Waldo, 133, 200
Emmerton, Bill, 46
endless consciousness, 148
endosomatic PK, 39–40, 48
enlightenment, 11, 191; collective, 113; European Enlightenment, 4, 6; nirvana, 191; obstruction to, 135; quest for, 146; spiritual, 138
Ennemoser, Joseph, 16, 197–98
epiphenomena, 3
ESP. *See* extrasensory perception
European Enlightenment, 4, 6
Evelyn, John, 26–27
event horizon, 183–84
exorcism, 24, 91, 99, 105, 145
exosomatic PK, 39

experimental philosophy, 193
experiment effect, 134–35
extrasensory perception (ESP), 45, 94, 97, 205
extrovertive mysticism, 113
Ezekiel, 58

faith, 34, 101, 211; driving force, 201; power of, 202; in supernatural, 104
fanaticism, 16, 35
Farewell to Reason (Feyerabend), 5
Farnell, L. R., 204
fasting, 17–18, 20, 124, 150. *See also* inedia
Fechner, Gustav, 133–34
Feilding, E., 173
Ferrand, Marie, 103–4
Feyerabend, Paul, 3, 5
Ficino, Marsilio, 93–94
5-D space, 182
Flight from Women (Stern), 140
flying dreams, 40–41
Fodor, Jerry, 132
Fodor, Nandor, 45
Footfalls on the Boundary of Another World (Owen), 198
foreknowledge, 94, 97
Forman, Robert, 112
Foster, Genevieve, 40
4-D space, 182–84
Fragments of Inner Life (Myers), 193–94
Franca, Martina, 124
Francis I, 123, 191
Francis of Assisi, 17, 28, 29, 72, 156; as model, 115; poverty and, 122–23; relics, 76, 139; voice heard by, 158
Frankfort School, 4
free will, 4, 177
From the Closed World to the Infinite Universe (Koyre), 161

Galgani, Gemma, 118
Galileo, 2, 174–75
Galton, Francis, 38, 205
Gapingmouth, 154

Geiger, John, 46
Gentileschi, Artemisia, 159
Geuss, Raymond, 4
ghosts, 5–6, 210–12. *See also*
  poltergeists
gifts. *See charisms* (gifts)
Glanvill, Joseph, 193
Gods of Love and Ecstasy
  (Danielou), 137
Gordon, Henry, 61
gorilla experiment, 88–89
Goulet, J., 8
El Grand Theatro del Mondo, 165
Gravini, Andriella, 95
gravity, 41, 182
greater mind, 200–201
El Greco, 159
Greyson, Bruce, 149
Grindal, Bruce, 8
Gurney, Edmund, 99, 208
Gustafsson, Mai Lan, 5–7, 211–12

Habermas, Jürgen, 4
hair shirt, 18
hallucinations, 37, 144–45, 196
haunting, 5–6
healing: ceremony, 8; Lambertini on,
  101, 106; mental, 102–3; miraculous,
  100–104; post-mortem, 34, 108–9;
  from prayer, 102, 104; self-healing,
  44; supernatural, 106; as talent,
  95–96, 100–105
Herbert, Nick, 175, 177, 180
heresy, 15, 144, 154
hermeneutics, 189
hex death, 48
Hildegard of Bingen, 203
Hodgson, Richard, 208
Home, D. D., 37–38, 88, 172–74, 182
Hufford, David, 40, 211
Huggins, William, 174
Hughes, Robert, 161, 162
humanism, 5
Human Oddities (Dingwall), 70
human organization, 174
Hume, David, 39, 197, 213–15

Huxley, Aldous, 200
hypnosis, 44–45
hysteria, 48, 87–88, 122

ideology, materialism as, 3–5
Ignatius of Loyola, 154
illusionism, 162–63
imaginal quasi-psychokinesis, 144
Immaculate Conception statue, 81–82
Indridason, Indridi, 55–56
inedia, 52–53, 64, 127
infinite universe, 161
infused wisdom, 98–100
Inge, W. R., 114
inner life, 17–18, 114–15;
  emotional, 118; Rosmi on, 192.
  See also spirituality
Innocent X, 29–30
Inquisition, 2, 15, 87, 155; fear of, 146;
  innocence determined, 27;
  levitation questioned, 25–26;
  orders to appear, 25; trial, 21
invisible force, 61, 82
isolation, 28, 31–32

James, William, 132–33, 177, 193, 208
Jani, Prahlad, 52–53
Jefferies, Richard, 113
Jefferson, Thomas, 47
Johnson, Don Hanlon, 138–39
John XXIII, 34–35
joint flights, 80–81
Jordan, Pascual, 176
Joseph of Copertino.
  See specific topics
Jung, C. G., 42–43, 73, 156;
  unus mundus of, 184–86

Kali, 139
Kaluza-Klein theory, 182
Kant, I., 133, 162
Karezza, 138
Karger, F., 50
karma, 210
Keener, Craig, 7, 104
Kelly, Ed, 147

Kelly, Emily, 46–47
Kelsey, Morton, 102
Kepler, Johannes, 195
Kircher, Athanasius, 159
Koyre, Alexandre, 161
Krebiozen, 43–44, 47, 204
Kripal, Jeffrey, 7, 138–39, 190
Kundalini Yoga, 118, 137
Kuttner, Fred, 9, 176–77
Kvaran, Einar, 55

Lambertini, Prosper, 34, 80, 86; on healing, 101, 106
The Lancet, 148
Lang, Andrew, 196–97
Lao-tzu, 194
Leibniz, G. W., 71, 84, 121
Leopardi, Giacamo, 193
Levack, Brian, 146
levitation, 2; beginnings, 23; Crookes on, 173; duration, 80; Inquisition questioning, 25–26; during Mass, 27, 33, 72, 74, 75, 87, 139; psychotherapeutic potential, 81; in public, 24–25; resistance to, 87–88; sexual tension and, 153; sleeping, 59; walking, 60; of yogis, 59. *See also* ecstatic levitation
levitation, case for: embarrassment of raptures, 71–74; eyewitness accounts, 69–71, 86, 88; during holidays and festivals, 72; Madonna and, 75–76, 180; multiple triggers, 74–85, 83, 166; as overpowering, 71; overview, 69–71; summary of evidence and objections, 85–89; suspending judgment, 69; wax doll and, 72–73
levitation, new force of: disturbing and negative effects, 46–48; flying dreams, 40–41; hypnosis interlude, 44–45; inedia, 52–53, 64; making PK happen, 50–52; materialization, 53–56; overview, 37–40; PK in controlled settings,
56–58; placebo effect and, 43–44; poltergeists, 49–50, 56; quasi-levitation experiment, 41–42; in religious history, 58–66; sport, ballet, PK, 45–46; synchronicities, 42–43; telekinetic enunciations of death, 50
levitation, physics of: higher dimensional space and, 181–84; mind and quantum mechanics, 174–79; neo-Platonism redux, 174; overview, 171; Schmidt machines and goal-oriented PK, 179–80; Schrödinger and, 180–81; unexplained force, 171–73; *unus mundus*, 184–86
Life after Life (Moody), 211
light, 159–61
Lodovico, 24, 29, 163–64
Lourdes, France, 103
love: for Madonna, 140–41; virtue of mystic, 120–21
Luzzato, Sergio, 9, 34

Madonna: case for levitation and, 75–76, 180; love for, 140–41; performance artist and, 167; veil of, 76
Madonna of Grotella, 20, 28, 72, 74; first flight and, 158; pull toward, 120–21
magic, 197, 204
magicians, 22, 50, 103
magnetism, 197–98
The Making of Religion (Lang), 196
Manning, Matthew, 50
Maria of Savoy, 29–30, 71, 136–37, 141–43
Marshall, Paul, 113, 121
Martin, Malachi, 60–61
Mason, A. A., 44
Mass: levitation during, 27, 33, 72, 74, 75, 87, 139; meaning of, 156–57; Parisciani on, 74; performance artist and, 165–66; as ritual transformation of consciousness, 73

materialism, 194–96; as ideology, 3–5; metaphysics of, 3–4; promissory, 150; rebirth of, 2–3; reductive, 8–10
materialization, 53–56
maternal impressions, 47
Mather, Cotton, 61
Mattei, Victor, 101
Mattellini, G. C., 16, 18
Mauskopf, Seymour, 199
McDaniel, June, 125
McDougall, William, 199
McGinn, Bernard, 127
McMoneagle, Joseph, 147–48
McVaugh, Michel, 199
meditation, 20, 42, 117, 150
mediums, 37, 54, 98–99, 199; Myers study, 208–9; séances, 55, 202, 208
mental excess, 118, 154
mental healing, 102–3
mental space, 182
metaphysics: dark side, 5; of materialism, 3–4
Milarepa, 59–60
mind: alternative model, 131–35; big, 200; consciousness and, 177; expanding, 150; greater, 200–201; mind-body connection, 1; mind-body effects, 47; mind-body interactions, 85; mind-brain threshold, 134–35; mindlike qualities, 175–76; mind reading, 94; one mind, 180–81; quantum mechanics and, 174–79; Universal Mind, 184
Mind and Matter (Schrödinger), 181
minimalism, 177, 201
miracles, 2; belief in, 212–15; Bernini, D., on, 105–6; Catholic Church and, 35; cultural imperialism and, 7; after death, 105–9; healing, 100–104; politics of, 9; post-mortem healing, 34; skepticism, 26, 34. *See also* canonization
mobile psychophysical threshold, 133–34
Mohammed, 194

monitio (warning), 27–28
Moody, Raymond, 6, 211
moti (movements), 26, 72–73
M-theory, 182
Mueggler, Eric, 6
multiple triggers: backward levitations and, 73–74, 83, 166; in case for levitation, 74–85; confession, 75; esthetic sensations, 79; experience of sky, 79; illness, 84; Immaculate Conception statue, 81–82; joint flights and, 80–81; Madonna and, 75–76; relics and, 76
multiplicity, 48
multiplying food, 54
Mumler, William H., 53
Murphy, Michael, 45–46
Myers, Frederic, 48, 50, 99, 133, 189, 198; on ecstasies, 195; materialism and, 194–96; medium study, 208–9; world-soul, 200
mystic: Bengali siddhas compared to, 124–27; high-strung spirituality, 114–20; mystical experience, 112–14; mystical rapture, 69–70; overview, 111; simultaneity experience, 121; virtues, 120–24
mysticism, 2, 45, 50; effects, 58; experimentation, 32; extrovertive, 113; flowering of new, 127; hot and cool, 118

Nardo, Dianora di, 97
Nati, Marino, 94
near-death experience (NDE), 6–7, 10; affective branch of, 149; cognitive branch of, 149; ecstasy and, 146–50; endless consciousness in, 148; paranormal branch of, 149; transcendental branch of, 149–50; yogis and, 148–49
Neihardt, John, 51
neo-Platonism, 174
Neri, Filippo, 76
Neumann, Erich, 185

neurochemistry, 3
Newton, Isaac, 182, 195
Nietzsche, Friedrich, 157
nihilism, 194
Nijinsky, Romola, 45
Nijinsky, Vaslav, 45–46
nirvana, 118
Noë, Alvin, 132
Noyes, John Humphrey, 138
Nuti, Roberto, 34, 94, 114, 116

OBE. *See* out-of-body experience
obedience, 19–20, 150; as virtue of mystic, 123–24
Oddgeirsson, Thordur, 56
odor of sanctity, 63, 178; Bernini, D., on, 92–93; Padre Pio, 92; producing joyous emotion, 93–94; as talent, 91–94
One Mind (Dossey), 203
one world (*unus mundus*), 184–86
Orientalism (Said), 4
The Original Vision (Robinson), 112
out-of-body experience (OBE), 207–8
Owen, Robert Dale, 198
ownership inhibition, 57

Padre Pio, 9, 34–35; odor of sanctity, 92; stigmata, 158–59
Paine, Thomas, 4
Palamolla, Joseph, 25–26, 38
Palestrina, 157, 203
Palladino, Eusapia, 173
Palmer, John, 202
paranormal psychology, 2, 33, 198
parapsychology of religion, 189; belief in life after death, 206–12; belief in miracles, 212–15; belief in power of belief, 201–3; belief in power of prayer, 203–6; belief in spiritual world, 199–201; hidden history, 192–99; new science of spirit, 192; overview, 191–92
Parisciani, Gustavo, 21, 70; on autopsy, 108; on ecstasies, 71; on experimentation, 32; on eye witnesses, 86; on Mass, 74; on tragedy, 26
Passitea, 65
past lives, 7
Patanjali's yoga sutras, 51, 111, 193
"Patience Worth," 78, 98
Pauli, Wolfgang, 42, 184–85
Pecorella, Antonio, 96
Penrose, Roger, 174
Perennial Philosophy (Huxley), 200
performance artist: belief and, 165; at death, 167; light and dark and, 159–61; Madonna and, 167; Mass and, 165–66; overview, 153–54; playing to audience, 167; psychic intensity of age and, 154–58; sacred illusionism and, 162–64; sense and psychophysics and, 158–59; singing and dancing rhyming strophes, 32, 111, 156, 165, 180; space and, 161–62; summary of, 165–67
Perlove, Karen, 164
Peter, 58–59
Phaedo (Plato), 148, 160
Phaedrus (Plato), 135
physics: classical, 175–76; consciousness as skeleton closet, 176; new physics, 1, 3, 175, 181; psychophysics, 158–59; quantum mechanics, 3, 10, 174–79; skeleton in closet of, 9. *See also* levitation, physics of
Pierpaoli, Francesco, 33
Piper, Leonora, 208
Piranesi, Giovanni Battista, 158
PK. *See* psychokinesis
placebo effect, 43–44, 204–5
Plato, 133, 135–36, 148, 160, 194, 195; neo-Platonism, 174
Plotinus, 118, 133
A Pluralistic Universe (James), 193
Podmore, Frank, 37
poltergeists, 49–50, 56

Popper, Karl, 150
possession, 5–7, 60–62; high point of, 15; symptoms, 145
poverty, 17, 21, 38; Bernini, D., on, 123; esoteric sense, 121–22; Francis of Assisi and, 122–23; as virtue of mystic, 121–23; vow of, 23
Pozzo, Andrea, 163
Prater, Andreas, 163
prayer, 19, 20, 150; belief in power of, 203–6; healing from, 102, 104
precognition, 91, 97
Price, H. H., 184, 205
priesthood, 17–18, 20, 23, 156, 166
Prince, Morton, 98
prolonged ecstasy, 127
promissory materialism, 150
prophetic powers, 21–22, 29
pseudocyesis, 46–47
psi-missing, 203, 205
psychic force, 88, 172–73
psychic photography, 53–54
psychic sport, 45, 60
The Psychic Side of Sports (White and Murphy), 45
psychokinesis (PK), 39–40, 178; in controlled settings, 56–58; dice-throwing experiments, 57; endosomatic PK, 39–40, 48; evidence for, 196; goal-oriented, 179–80; in group settings, 57; making happen, 50–52; sport and ballet and, 45–46
psychomotor skills, 18
psychospiritual reality, 46
psychosynthesis, 117

quantum animism, 175, 180
quantum mechanics, 3, 10, 174–79
quantum Zeno effect, 177–80

Radin, Dean, 57, 215
Ramakrishna, 139–40
raptures, 127; ecstasies foreshadowing, 76; embarrassment of, 71–74; mystical rapture, 69–70; preceded by scream, 77, 81; Teresa of Avila on, 119–20
reason, 4–5, 123, 133, 201
Rechung, 59
reductive materialism, 8–10
reincarnation, 209–10
relics, 76, 139
religion: new force of levitation in history of, 58–66; reductionist assumptions, 7; science debate, 1–2; transcendent side of, 2, 7, 11. *See also* parapsychology of religion
Rembrandt, 159, 160, 165
Rhine, J. B., 57, 199
Rhine, Louisa, 199
Riberas, Jusepe de, 159–60
Richet, Charles, 54
ring of espousal, 144, 153
Rinzing, Gunsang, 51
Robb, Peter, 155
Robinson, E., 17, 112
Romero, Oscar, 34
Roncagli, Giacomo, 100
Rorty, Richard, 2, 215
Rosenberg, Robert, 195
Rosenblum, Bruce, 9, 176–77
Rosmi, Arcangelo, 34, 71, 73, 114; on fall of Adam, 74; on interior life, 192; on invisible force, 82
Royal Society, 37, 172, 193
Rule, Margaret, 61–62
Rumi, 124

Saccalossi, Cornelio, 107
sacred illusionism, 162–64
Said, Edward, 4
Saint Francis (Boff), 4
saints: absence of rigidity at death, 63–64; *charisms* of, 69–70. *See also specific saints*
Saluzzo, Horatio, 97
Samkhya yoga, 113, 121, 191–92
Sartre, Jean-Paul, 132
Scared to Death (Barker, J. C.), 48

Schlitz, Marilyn, 200
Schmeidler, Gertrude, 201–2
Schmidt, Helmut, 57, 204–5; machines, 179–80
Schopenhauer, Arthur, 133
Schrödinger, Irwin, 180–81
Schrödinger's equations, 177
science: different kind of, 10–11; Newtonian physics, 3; religion debate, 1–2; scientific revolution, 2. *See also* levitation, physics of; physics; technology
séances, 55, 202, 208
secret thoughts and futures, 94–98
self-centered cosmology, 155
self-destruction, 48
self-laceration, 24
Serios, Ted, 53–54
sexual tension: diabolic temptation and, 137; ecstatic levitation and, 135–40; levitation and, 153
Shah, Sudhir, 52
Shaivism, 118, 137
Shakespeare, William, 165
shamans, 41, 45, 50; effects produced by, 58
sheep-goat effect, 202
siddhis (attainments), 51, 64, 111. *See also* Bengali siddhas
Sidgwick, Henry, 99, 194, 208
Sin and Fear: The Emergence of Western Guilt Culture (Delumeau), 15
Smith, Frederick, 7
Society of Jesus, 15, 154
Socrates, 148
solitude, 20, 23
Somer, Andreas, 54
sorcery, 8
soul, 3, 196; as endangered, 5; world-soul, 200
space: 2-D space, 184; 3-D space, 182; 4-D, 182–84; 5-D space, 182; 11-D space, 182; dream, 183–84; higher dimensional, 181–84; mental space, 182; performance artist and, 161–62; uber-space, 182; waking, 184
spirit, 3, 192
Spiritualism, 171–72, 198–99
spirituality: fiery side, 118; high-strung of mystic, 114–20; spiritual world, 199–201
sport, 45–46
Stace, Walter, 113–14
Stapp, Henry, 10, 175, 177–80
Stein, Edith, 34
Stern, Karl, 140
Stevenson, Ian, 7, 47, 209
stigmata, 9, 34, 63, 153; of Padre Pio, 158–59
St. Jerome in a Dark Chamber, 160
Stockham, Alice Bunker, 138
Stoller, Paul, 8
strophes, 32, 111, 156, 165, 180
Student at Table by Candlelight, 160
Sufism, 118
Suger, 160
supernatural, 7–9; communing with, 165–66; debased supernaturalism, 114; faith in, 104; happenings, 70, 91; healing, 106; life, 20; light, 159; power, 85, 158
superstring theory, 182
symbolic thinking, 100
synchronicities, 42–43, 185–86

table-tilting experiment, 55
talents: exorcism, 105; healing, 95–96, 100–105; infused wisdom, 98–100; miracles after death, 105–9; odor of sanctity, 63, 91–94; overview, 91; penetrating secret thoughts and futures, 94–98
Taylor, Jill, 10
technology, 2, 10, 122, 146, 176
telekinesis, 63, 178, 210
telekinetic enunciations of death, 50
telepathy, 94, 97, 182, 189
temperament, 21, 126, 157, 172
temptations, 136–38, 140, 143–44

tenebrism, 154, 159–60
Teresa of Avila, 17, 65–66, 111; on rapture, 119–20; as reformer, 118; sculpture, 118–19
terminal lucidity, 211
The Terror That comes in the Night (Hufford), 211
thinking entity, 179
Thirty Years War, 154
Thomas, Keith, 144
Thorlaksson, Brynjolfur, 56
thought-transference, 196
3-D space, 182
Thurston, Herbert, 54, 173; on bodily metamorphosis, 62–64; on *charisms* of saints, 69–70
Tibetan Book of the Dead, 198
Todi, Jacopone da, 121–22
transcendence, 1; architecture and, 158; side of religion, 2, 7, 11; unity, 185
Trevor-Roper, H. R., 15–16
trickery, 87
Tucker, Jim, 7
tummo techniques, 60, 153
Turner, Edith, 8
2-D space, 184

uber-space, 182
Ugolini, Francesco, 144
Universal Mind, 184
unus mundus (one world), 184–86
Upanishads, 181
Urban VIII, 28, 29, 94

Van de Castle, Robert, 40
Van Lommel, Pim, 148, 150
The Varieties of Religious Experience (James), 193
Vattimo, Gianni, 2, 215
Veronese, Paolo, 156
virtues of mystic: chastity, 124, 135, 137, 140, 166; fasting, 17–18, 20, 124, 150; love, 120–21; obedience, 123–24; poverty, 121–23
visions, 18, 127;
  angels at Osimo, 32; three crosses, 78–79
Von Franz, Marie-Louise, 186
Von Hugel, Friedrich, 113, 117
Von Neumann, John, 177–79
von Schrenck-Notzing, Albert, 54
voodoo death, 48

waking space, 184
Wallace, Alfred Russell, 38, 198
warning (*monitio*), 27–28
Waza, John Casimir, 71
weather control, 30
West, Philip, 43
White, Rhea, 45–46
Whitehead, Alfred North, 1, 2, 11, 131
Whitman, Richard, 113
Wilson, Ian, 64, 154
witchcraft, 16
witch doctors, 8
Woelfflin, Heinrich, 161–62
women: close encounters with, 142; flight from, 140; gifts from, 142–43; love for Madonna, 140–41; sending away, 141–42.
  See also Maria of Savoy
Woodward, Kenneth, 9, 34

Yogananda, P., 45, 59
Yogesvari, 125
yogis, 45, 50; effects produced by, 58; experiments, 51–52; levitation, 59; NDE and, 148–49
Young, D. E., 8

Zaehner, R. C., 113–14
Zicha, G., 50
Zizek, Slavoj, 191

About the Author

Michael Grosso studied classics at Columbia University where he also got his Ph.D. in philosophy. An independent scholar, until recently he taught humanities and philosophy at Marymount Manhattan College, City University of New York, and City University of New Jersey. His most recent books include *Experiencing the Next World Now*, *The Millennium Myth*, and *Soulmaking*. Recent co-authored books with Ed Kelly and others include *Irreducible Mind* and *Beyond Physicalism*. The author's central interest revolves around consciousness studies and the theory of religion. Michael is a painter and lives in Charlottesville, Virginia.

Lightning Source UK Ltd.
Milton Keynes UK
UKHW011121181220
375442UK00001B/32